THE ULTIMATE HISTORY OF

fast cars

Jonathan Wood

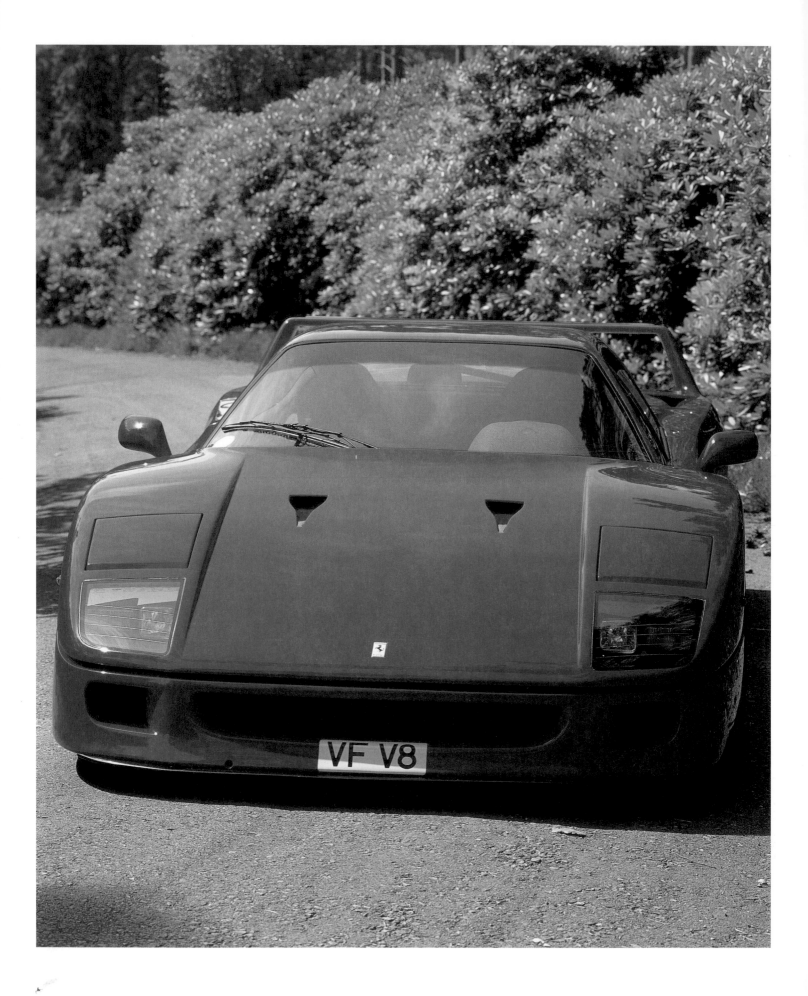

THE ULTIMATE HISTORY OF

fast cars

Jonathan Wood

p

This is a Parragon Publishing Book
This edition published in 2003

Parragon Publishing
Queen Street House
4 Queen Street
Bath BA1 1HE, UK

Copyright © Parragon 2002

Designed, produced, and packaged by
Stonecastle Graphics Limited

Text by Jonathan Wood
Edited by Philip de Ste. Croix
Designed by Paul Turner and Sue Pressley

ISBN 1-40541-593-2

Printed in China

Please note: Unless
otherwise stated, the
performance figures
of the cars featured
in this book refer to
the speeds recorded
at the time of the
model's introduction.

The dollar prices
quoted in this book
are converted from
British sterling
values and do not
necessarily reflect
U.S. list prices.

Photographic credits.

The GP Library: Page 22; page 23 *top*; page 23
below.
Andrew Morland: Page 42; page 43 *all three*; page
49 *center*; pages 182-3 *all four*.

Other pictures © Neill Bruce's Automobile
Photolibrary by:

Ian Dawson: page 186 *below*; page 187 *below*.

Geoffrey Goddard: Page 12 *below*; page 14; page
46 *both*; page 73 *top*; pages 100-1 *all five*; pages
152-3 *all four*; page 168 *both*; page 178 *center*.

Christian Gonzenbach: pages 290-1 *all four*; page
306 *both*; page 307.

Christian Hatton: Page 157 *center*.

Stefan Lüscher: Page 110 *below right*; page 111
top; page 190 *below*; page 202 *both*; pages 218-9
all four; page 231 *top right and center*; pages 232-3
all five; page 280 *below*; page 281 *both*; pages 300-
1 *all three*.

Richard Meinert: Page 150 *both*; page 274 *all
three*; page 275 *center right and below*; page 276;
page 277 *center and below*.

F Naef: pages 252-3 *all four*.

All other photographs © Neill Bruce's Automobile
Photolibrary, with the exception of the following,
which are manufacturer's press pictures supplied
from The Peter Roberts Collection c/o Neill Bruce:

Page 1; page 3; page 6; page 7 *both*; page 23
center; page 131 *top*; page 171 *center*; pages 176-7
all four; page 179 *center right*; page 188 *top*; page
195 *top*; page 197 *below*; pages 198-9 *all four*;
page 211 *center*; page 213 *both*; page 215 *top and
center left*; pages 216-7 *all three*; page 227; page
229 *both*; 231 *top left*; page 245 *both*; page 249
top; pages 254-5 *all four*; pages 256-7 *all three*;
page 259 *both*; 260-1 *all three*; pages 262-3 *all
five*; page 264 *center right*; pages 266-7 *all three*;
pages 268-9 *all three*; pages 270-1 *all four*; pages
272-3 *all five*; page 275 *top*; page 278 *both*; page
279 *top*; pages 282-3 *all four*; pages 284-5 *all five*;
pages 286-7 *all four*; pages 288-9 *all four*; pages
292-3 *all three*; pages 294-5 *all four*; pages 296-7
all four; pages 298-9; pages 302-5 *all eight*; pages
308-9 *all four*; page 310; pages 312-3 *all four*;
pages 314-17 *all seven*.

All picture research by Neill Bruce, who gives
special thanks to Bonhams Auctioneers Ltd., Nigel
Dawes Ltd. and Duncan Hamilton Ltd. for making
so many superb cars available.

Contents

Introduction

Below: A McLaren F1, currently the fastest road car in the world. In 1994 Autocar magazine attained a speed of 231mph (372km/h), but in 1998 Andy Wallace unofficially achieved 240mph (386km/h) on Volkswagen's Ehra-Lessien proving ground. But now the F1 is being challenged by the impending Bugatti Veyron with a claimed top speed of 252mph (405km/h)...

Speed! The very word sends a tingle down the spine, particularly when it refers to a motor car that has been specifically designed for out and out performance *and* driver enjoyment. Such models have evolved over the years, originating with the birth of the sports car in the pre-1914 era and developing through the aerodynamically refined grand tourers of the post-war era to today's supercars which are the latest manifestation of the breed.

All are (or were in their day) fast cars. But how fast is fast? Today there are a handful of models which can attain 200mph (321km/h) while the makers of the projected Bugatti Veyron claim that it will be able to exceed 250mph (402km/h). However, to the pioneers of the automobile in the 1880s even 60mph (96km/h) must have appeared unattainable. Yet such was the growth of the industry and pace of technical development that, by 1902, this speed was perfectly achievable.

In 1901 Daimler had introduced its superlative 35hp Mercedes racer for the road, the model which gave its name to the marque, and its 60hp derivative could reliably and rapidly reach that speed. But it was to be a further 46 years before a production sports car was consistently capable of attaining twice that figure, namely 120mph (193km/h). When Jaguar launched its XK120 sports car in 1948, so-called because it could achieve precisely that speed, the general motoring public could scarcely believe that such performance was possible. Although this stunning open two-seater was powered by an engine with race-proven twin overhead camshafts, this configuration had not hitherto been associated with reliability…

1948 also saw the launch of the first production Ferrari – the company's berlinettas (coupés) initially shared their V12 engines with the firm's grand prix cars. Produced in tiny numbers and enhanced with magnificently styled bodywork by some of Italy's finest *carrozzerias* (coachbuilders), these blood-red beauties from Modena were the fastest cars of the 1950s, being capable of 160mph (257km/h) and beyond.

Jaguar E-Type

Jaguar contributed another landmark model in 1961 with the launch of the delectable E-Type. Although slower than some Ferraris, it was mass-produced, even if the 150mph (241km/h) achieved on test by members of the motoring press was not carried over to the production cars!

Then came the supercar, perhaps typified by the Miura of 1966 that was produced by the new Lamborghini marque. It not only looked sensational, it was good for over 170mph (274km/h).

The recession that engulfed the world in the 1970s was swept aside during the 1980s – this was the decade of the Ferrari F40 which was capable of 201mph (323km/h). And there was no doubting the phenomenal achievement of the McLaren F1 of 1993 when it was timed at 240mph (386km/h). This figure still stands as the speed record for a production car. But for how long…

Above: The Bugatti Veyron, which is scheduled to enter production late in 2003, looks likely to become the fastest car on Earth. Volkswagen, custodian of the marque since 1998, claims a 0-60mph (96km/h) figure of just 3 seconds but with 987bhp on tap from the mid-located 8 liter W16 engine, anything is possible!

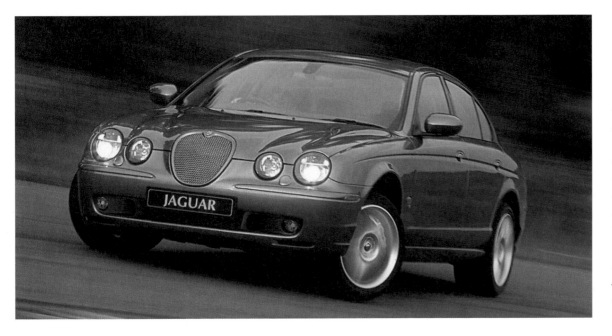

Left: Just as Jaguar set the performance pace in the 1960s with the E-Type, it does today with its XK8 sports cars and with this supercharged 4.2 liter R model of the S-Type, which, with 400bhp on tap, makes it the company's most powerful sedan ever. New for 2002, it has a claimed governed top speed of 155mph (249km/h).

1886–1940
Birth of the Sports Car

Performance motoring has now been with us for over 100 years. The arrival in 1901 of the assured, innovative Mercedes, a car that was specifically designed with speed in mind, marks the birth of the sports car.

Initially such vehicles were expensive and thus exclusive, as the Bentley, Bugatti, and Alfa Romeo marques of the inter-war years proved. But the appearance in the 1930s of the lower cost, visually attractive MG brought the sports car within the reach of a far wider public and created a buoyant market that continues to this day.

Birth of the Sports Car

In the years prior to the outbreak of World War II fast cars were predominantly the preserve of an exclusive club of wealthy, young enthusiasts. They owned sports cars to capture the sheer delight and exhilaration of speed and to enjoy the sensation of rapid acceleration, the rip-roaring rasp of straight-cut gears or the scream from a supercharger that came in its wake.

And it was essentially an European passion. For the world's fastest road cars emanated principally from Germany, Italy, France, and, to a lesser extent, Great Britain.

When Karl Benz and Gottlieb Daimler, each working independently of the other, first created motor cars in Germany in 1886, the 'horseless

carriages' they produced were capable of only around 10mph (16km/h). Both were powered by rear-mounted single-cylinder engines. It was only when, in 1891, French engineer Emile Levassor transferred the power unit to the front of the car, from where it drove the rear wheels via a clutch and in-line gearbox, that a configuration was born that was capable of almost infinite development.

Just 15 years after the German duo's pioneering efforts, the vehicle that should be accorded pole position on the historic starting grid of fast cars first saw the light of day. The 35hp Mercedes of 1901 was the work of Daimler's company, but it was designed after its founder's death by his able assistant, Wilhelm Maybach. Named after Mercedes Jellinek, the 10-year-old daughter of a

Below: A sports car in everything but name, this 60hp Mercedes dates from 1903 and in that year it won two major races. The absence of windshield and doors was clearly no deterrent to the indefatigable motorists of the day.

valued Daimler customer, the designation was adopted to allay anti-Germanic feeling then prevalent in the all-important French market.

Featuring a low-slung pressed steel chassis and a fan-cooled honeycomb radiator, the Mercedes' engine used a throttle in the modern sense and employed soon to be universal mechanical inlet valves, rather than the atmospheric type then commonly in use. This potent car, capable of 60mph (96km/h) in its best known 60hp guise, was thus a design of great technical competence and it laid the foundations of a corporate high-performance image that endures to this day. (The merger with Benz to create the Mercedes-Benz marque did not occur until 1926.)

Mercedes was also in the forefront of motor racing although the grand prix, as such, did not exist until the first running of the French event in 1906. From then on racing cars would be in the vanguard of technological innovation that would then be passed down to the benefit of their roadgoing first cousins.

The French Peugeot company was responsible for the introduction in 1912 of the high efficiency twin-overhead-camshaft engine; this racing initiative was soon extended to sports cars which still use 'twin-cam' power units to this day. Prior to Peugeot's initiative most sporting models were powered by relatively simple side-valve engines. This certainly applied to Marc Birkigt's exquisite race-bred Alfonso Hispano-Suiza of 1911 which used a 3.6 liter 'four' that featured a dated T-head design. It was capable of a sparkling, safe, and reliable 70 to 75mph (113-121km/h).

Later in the same year came Laurence Pomeroy's magnificent Prince Henry Vauxhall powered by a high revving 3 liter side-valve engine. It is often acclaimed as the world's first true sports car. This in turn gave birth to the equally impressive 4.5 liter 30/98 Vauxhall of 1913 which set the standard for British sports models of the 1920s. Able to attain over 80mph (129km/h) on the road, examples prepared for the racetrack could hit the magic 100mph (161km/h).

Above: Laurence Pomeroy's landmark Prince Henry Vauxhall, so named because two examples entered the 1910 Prince Henry Trials enjoying a trouble-free run and proving themselves capable of 72mph (116km/h), a respectable speed from a 3 liter engine. The road cars were sold with a guaranteed speed of 65mph (105km/h). The company described them as 'light carriages suitable for travelling or speed work.'

Above: A 3 liter Bentley of this type won the second Le Mans race of 1924 at 53.78mph (86.55km/h).

Below: A continental sports coupé: the 1938 Touring-bodied Alfa Romeo 8C2900B which ran at Le Mans in 1938.

The newly minted Bentley was Vauxhall's great rival of the 1920s and the 3 liter of 1921, the first of the line, could be pressed to exceed 90mph (145km/h). Powered by a single-overhead-camshaft engine, this configuration had been a significant feature of aero engine design during the war. W.O. Bentley went on to produce further variations on the same theme and his final 8 liter model could top the 100mph (161km) mark. With engine reliability a key tenet of Bentley's design philosophy, the big green cars from London's

Cricklewood dominated the Le Mans 24 hour race, the first of which was held in 1923, and they won the event on no less than five occasions between 1924 and 1930.

If Britain was a force to be reckoned with in sports car racing, the same could not be said of grand prix events which were dominated during the interwar years by the car makers of Continental Europe. The Italian Fiats and Alfa Romeos, the Bugattis from France, and, later, the might of the German Mercedes-Benz and Auto Union teams continued to push forward the frontiers of competition-charged technology.

The fevered and highly competitive atmosphere of the circuits stimulated the science of aerodynamics with racing car bodywork being tailored to the reduce wind resistance and thus improve a vehicle's performance. By the 1930s this principle was being extended to road cars and the trend was give extra impetus by the arrival of straight, purpose-built, dual-carriage motorways. The Italian *autostradas* date from 1924 and Germany's first *autobahn* was opened in 1933.

While Britain remained faithful to the traditional open two-seater sports car, Europeans recognized that closed bodywork was more aerodynamically efficient. That is why both Porsche and Ferrari, two new makes which appeared in the early post-war years, featured predominantly coupé coachwork. This concept was to give birth to the grand tourer that became better known by its GT initials.

Invention of the 'blower'

The most significant mechanical innovation, the supercharger – in effect an engine-driven pump that forces air into the cylinders to improve the volumetric efficiency of the power unit – was born on the motor racing circuits of Europe. Introduced in 1923 on the Fiat 805, the 'blower' continued to be an obligatory fitment on racing cars until the early 1950s.

Most of the manufacturers that participated in grand prix racing also produced supercharged sports cars. For instance, there was Vittorio Jano's visually stunning Alfa Romeo 8C of 1931 which sold for $2400 and which could attain 115mph (185km/h). And the delectable Type 55 Bugatti, similarly only one notch removed from a grand prix winner, could be wound up on a good day to exceed 110mph (177km/h).

In Germany Mercedes-Benz offered its SSK powered by a massive 7.1 liter supercharged engine which could easily hit 110mph (177km/h). Germany was also the home of a relative latecomer to motor manufacture, namely the Bavarian Motor Works (Bayerische Motoren Werke) which marketed its products under the BMW badge. It had built aero engines and motorcycles before initiating car production in 1929, and it soon introduced a performance ingredient to its increasingly sophisticated products.

Below: Bugatti, like Alfa Romeo, produced costly and exclusive supercharged sports cars that were closely related to their grand prix cars. This 1932 Type 55 is powered by a 2.3 liter twin-overhead-camshaft straight eight engine that was based on the Type 51 racer. Its price new was $1700.

Above: State of the art: a 1938 BMW 328 sold in Britain by Frazer Nash and thus right-hand-drive. Recessed, rather than free-standing, headlamps were just one of its advanced features.

Opposite above: Railton Eight – the concept of a cheap, powerful American engine mounted in a European chassis was pioneered in Britain by Reid Railton.

Opposite below: For many the quintessential pre-war sports car, an MG J2 of 1932 vintage. Its memorable lines were to survive, in essence, until 1955.

The BMW 328 sports car of 1936 made practically all of its competitors look dated overnight. With aerodynamically efficient open two-seater bodywork and integral headlights, an ingenious cross pushrod 2 liter engine, rack-and-pinion steering and hydraulic brakes, the 328 could attain 95mph (153km/h) while competition versions topped 110mph (177km/h).

This BMW was light years away from its British equivalent. The 2 liter Aston Martin was beautifully built, exclusive, expensive but with its engineering firmly rooted in the 1920s. It was, accordingly, some 768lb (348kg) heavier than the German car and only able to attain 82 mph (132km/h). In the event the Aston Martin company ceased production in 1938 to re-think its design strategy. However, the market for the lower-powered sports car for the man and women in the street was buoyant, thanks to the efforts of Cecil Kimber, creator of the MG marque (it stands for Morris Garages).

His delightful boat-tailed Morris Minor-based M-type Midget of 1928, powered by a 847cc single-overhead-camshaft engine, might only be capable of 65mph (105km/h) but it cost an affordable £175 in the UK and, with 3235 produced in four years, this MG was to become by far and away the world's most popular sports car.

Setting the pace

Kimber, a stylist of formidable talent, was to go on to greater things and his J2 of 1932 was destined to set the visual pace for traditional sports car design for the next 30 or so years. This version of the Midget with its humped scuttles, cutaway doors, bolster fuel tank and flowing fenders was to delight a new generation of European enthusiasts and, after the World War II, American ones too.

MG's great rival of the 1930s was the SS marque, a company headed by young William Lyons, who, like Kimber, was responsible for styling his own products. With a top speed of 95mph (153km/h), his 2.5 liter SS Jaguar 100 of 1936 looked as well as it performed, yet it cost British drivers only £395. With the arrival of a 3.5 liter version in 1938, the 100 could attain 104mph

(167km/h), a remarkable figure for an unsupercharged sports car. Lyons' company was renamed Jaguar after the war and it would establish itself as one of the world's great sporting marques.

Chasing a similar market to SS was the Railton. An accomplished engineer, Reid Railton's formula differed radically from that of Lyons. His Eight of 1933 was powered by a large capacity but cheap 4 liter straight eight engine, courtesy of the American Hudson Motor Car Company. Despite the side valves and primitive splash lubrication to the big ends, the Railton tourer was an impressive performer. Able to sprint to 60mph (96km/h) in less than 13 seconds, even the sedan version could exceed 90mph (145km/h). And all for under $700. It was a formula that was to be widely copied in the years that followed the outbreak of World War II in 1939.

1945–1950
Enter Ferrari and Porsche

With the ending of the war in 1945, most fast car makers dusted off their 1939 models which were quickly snapped up by a car-hungry public. While Britain remained faithful to its open two-seaters, which attracted American buyers in the wake of a UK government-directed exported drive, Continental Europe saw the birth of two new marques that would spawn some of the greatest performance cars of the post-war years – usually built in coupé form.

In 1948 Enzo Ferrari in Italy began the production of his 166 model and in the same year Porsche built the 356, the first of a legendary line. In this new world order times were certainly a-changing.

HRG 1500

**Top speed
85mph**
137km/h

*Right: The 1.5 liter engine
of the 1949 car opposite.
Smoother in operation than
the Meadows unit it
replaced, the twin SU
carburetors and four-
branch exhaust were
peculiar to HRG.*

*Below: The Aerodynamic
HRG was introduced in
1946 although this prototype
dates from 1940. The bodies
were produced by Fox and
Nicholl but, sadly, build
quality was poor and very
few survive.*

An unashamedly pre-war design, it is not
surprising to find that although the HRG
dated from 1935, it was spiritually rooted
in the 1920s. Yet these light, chunky, no-nonsense,
open two-seaters were no sluggards and in 1.5 liter
form were able to nudge 85mph (137km/h).

The HRG took its name from its trio of
creators. Ted Halford had created the Vale Special
of 1933/36 vintage, while Guy Robins was a design
engineer for Trojan. The last of the three, Ron
Godfrey, had been one of the originators of the GN
cyclecar, precursor of the Frazer Nash. The HRG
similarly featured distinctive and unyielding front
quarter-elliptic springs.

Built at a small factory in Tolworth, Surrey, the
HRG was powered by the proven 1.5 liter
Meadows 4ED engine. The open alloy two-seater
body was both functional and traditional in look,
and was designed to appeal to those customers who
had previously bought chain-driven Frazer Nashes,
the production of which had all but ceased by 1935.
However, the Hurg, as it was affectionately known,
used conventional shaft-drive to its live rear axle.

Ideal for competition

A versatile competition car, used in cross-country
rallies and trials and in sports-car racing, it was
able to exceed 90mph (145km/h). Unfortunately the
Meadows pushrod engine became unavailable after
1938, so from 1939 a choice of Singer overhead
camshaft units were offered. The 1074cc four was
courtesy of Singer's Bantam sedan but
ministrations at Tolworth produced 44bhp and the

HRG 1100 was capable of over 75mph (121km/h). The faster 1500 used a 1435cc engine – its stroke was reduced to bring it within the 1.5 liter class, while the post-war cars employed a 1496cc unit.

In 1945, and in striking contrast to the 1939 models which were still offered, the company produced the supplementary Aerodynamic 1500 with full-width bodywork in the continental manner. But only 31 had been built by the time that its production ceased in 1947.

The marque did well in sports-car races in Europe in the early post-war years with class wins at Spa in Belgium in 1949 and, creditably, at Le Mans where a Hurg was not only placed eighth but also won its class.

The end of an era

These car-hungry years guaranteed the survival of the delightfully anachronistic HRG in the short term, but it was only a matter of time before it succumbed. The 1100cc went first and ceased production in 1950 after 49 cars had been completed. However, the 1500, with 138 built, survived until 1955, latterly in 1496cc form. HRG continued as an engineering business until 1966 when it succumbed to voluntary liquidation.

Below: The ultra traditional Hurg. This is a lightened Le Mans 1500, expensive in 1949 at $1775. Note the front quarter-elliptic springs and cable brakes.

Bottom left: The dashboard of a 1500, well equipped with the rev counter placed in front of the driver. The hand brake is of the fly-off type.

Specification	HRG 1500
Engine location	Front, in-line
Configuration	Four-cylinder
Bore and stroke	68 x 103mm
Capacity	1496cc
Valve operation	Single overhead camshaft
Horsepower	65bhp @ 4800rpm
Transmission	Manual four-speed
Drive	Rear
Chassis	Channel section
Suspension – front	Quarter-elliptic spring
Suspension – rear	Half-elliptic spring
Brakes	Mechanical drum
Top speed	85mph (137km/h)
Acceleration	0-60mph (0-96km/h): 18.2 seconds

MG TC

**Top speed
75mph**
121km/h

Right: The dashboard of a sensitively restored 1947 TC. The steering wheel was telescopically adjustable and the seat back could also be altered.

Below: Essentially carried over from the pre-war TB, the TC's distinctive lines still delight enthusiasts today. The exposed horn and the spotlight were standard fitments.

Like the HRG, the TC's design dated from the 1930s. However, here the similarities end because the MG became the world's most popular sports cars of the early post-war years. With the British government encouraging its car makers to export their products to gain valuable foreign currency, the stylish, practical two-seater, that was good for a top speed of 75mph (121km/h), brought MG a global audience, first in Australia and then, even more significantly, in America.

MG stands for Morris Garages and the company was the creation of its general manager, Cecil Kimber, who possessed a formidable flair for style and form. The TC's visual origins are to be found in the J2 Midget of 1932. This open two-seater with its wire spoked wheels, double humped scuttle, cutaways doors and bolster gas tank, with all enveloping fenders following in 1933, fathered an impressive stylistic line that was destined to survive until 1955.

The J2 was succeeded by the P-type Midget of 1934, but the TC's mechanical forebear was the larger Wolseley-engined 1.3 liter TA of 1936. This was replaced by the outwardly similar but Morris-powered 1.2 liter TB of 1939. The war interrupted production and when the MG factory at Abingdon, Berkshire restarted motor manufacture in 1945, the TB was dusted off, mildly updated and renamed the TC. Initially it was only available in black.

Although by then an archaic design which lacked independent front suspension and sporting a body that did not possess a whiff of aerodynamic refinement, the public nevertheless responded to its undoubted charm. A car-hungry marketplace that was singularly bereft of open two-seaters, and a selling price of a little over $700 did the rest.

Wind through the hair

When the TC's hinged windshield was in the fold-flat position with the wind blowing through the driver's hair, it felt as though this harshly sprung little car was doing 90mph (145km/h), rather than the 75mph (121km/h) of which it was capable.

By the time production ceased in 1950, an unprecedented 10,000 of these MGs had been sold, of which 65 per cent were dispatched overseas. It was, to coin the company's corporate advertising slogan, 'the sports car America loved first,' and the TC paved the way for the outwardly similar TD. This was enhanced with independent front suspension. A total of 30,000 were produced, of which some 80 per cent found American customers. This was in its turn replaced by the TF of 1953, the last of the line, which survived until 1955.

But MG's transatlantic successes had not been wasted on its competitors at home and abroad. The race for the American sports car market was on!

Specification	MG TC
Engine location	Front, in-line
Configuration	Four-cylinder
Bore and stroke	66 x 90mm
Capacity	1250cc
Valve operation	Pushrod
Horsepower	54bhp @ 5200rpm
Transmission	Manual four-speed
Drive	Rear
Chassis	Channel section
Suspension – front	Half-elliptic spring
Suspension – rear	Half-elliptic spring
Brakes	Hydraulic drum
Top speed	75mph (121km/h)
Acceleration	0-60mph (0-96km/h): 22.8 seconds

Left: The TC was powered by Morris's durable EXPAG unit, that was shared with in-house Wolseley. The twin SU carburetors were an Abingdon refinement.

Below: The 1947 TC showing its cutaway doors and elegantly shaped rear fenders which combined to convey a sense of speed.

Cisitalia 202 Gran Sport

**Top speed
99mph**
159km/h

*Below: Although the
Cisitalia was principally
produced in coupé form,
there was also an open
version of which about 20
examples were built in
1947/48. With bodies by
Garella and Stabilimenti
Farina and originally
called the Spyder Sport
Special, it was soon re-
named the Spyder Nuvolari
as the great Tazio Nuvolari
drove one to second place
in the 1947 Mille Miglia.*

Although the little Cisitalia coupé of 1947 was only powered by an 1100cc engine, which was significantly smaller than the HRG and MG power units, it was capable of close on 100mph (161km/h).

No model more expresses the potential of Italy's post-war motor industry than the newly-minted Cisitalia make, created by Turin industrialist Piero Dusio. It had an impressive pedigree, having been designed by Dante Giacosa, the distinguished Fiat engineer who was responsible for the Fiat 500 *Topolino* of 1936, one of the most significant European small cars of the interwar years.

Giacosa undertook his Cisitalia work on a freelance basis. In the first instance he designed, in 1946, a single-seater racer with tubular space-frame chassis and transverse leaf independent front suspension, powered by an 1100cc Fiat engine. It was intended as a curtain-raiser at grand prix events but Dusio also wanted a roadgoing version for which Giacosa was also to be responsible.

However, Fiat was soon demanding all his time and attention and his place was taken by a colleague, Giovanni Savonuzzi, who joined Dusio's company. He, like Giacosa, designed a coupé, rather than a convertible body in the British tradition, because a closed car is aerodynamically more efficient, and thus potentially faster, than an open one.

His first wind tunnel-refined design, which featured two large stabilizing fins, was capable of 122mph (196km/h) but it did not lend itself to production. At Dusio's behest Savonuzzi tried again and created an exquisitely proportioned coupé that was shorn of any unnecessary decoration. Its construction was entrusted to Pinin Farina.

Excellent aerodynamics

Powered by a 55bhp engine, the Cisitalia 202 Gran Sport was launched at the 1947 Paris Motor Show. Production began in the following year but its size proved to be deceptive; it was found to be faster than many larger-engined vehicles because of its excellent aerodynamics and low weight of 1713lb (777kg). When enhanced with an optional 60bhp engine, top speed was pushed to beyond the 105mph (169km/h) mark.

Then the car's styling attained international recognition when in 1951 it was lauded, along with seven others, by the New York Museum of Modern Art. The display enhanced Pinin Farina's coachbuilding reputation, although the Cisitalia's body was by then being built by Stablimenti Farina and Vignale.

Unfortunately Piero Dusio became distracted by a costly and complicated four-wheel-drive grand prix car and lost interest in his road model which ceased production in 1952. By then only 170 or so lucky customers had been able to sample the results of his inspired creation.

Above: A Cisitalia of a type which Taruffi ran in the 1948 Mille Miglia in 1200cc form before succumbing to piston failure.

Left: The definitive Cisitalia coupé of 1948 with a body by Pinin Farina that secured the stylist's international reputation.

Below left: Extraordinarily modern for 1947, like many other prestigious Italian marques of the day, it is right-hand drive.

Specification	Cisitalia 202 Gran Sport
Engine location	Front, in-line
Configuration	Four-cylinder
Bore and stroke	68 x 75 mm
Capacity	1089cc
Valve operation	Pushrod
Horsepower	55bhp @ 5500rpm
Transmission	Manual four-speed
Drive	Rear
Chassis	Unitary
Suspension – front	Transverse leaf spring and wishbones
Suspension – rear	Half-elliptic spring
Brakes	Drum
Top speed	99mph (159km/h)
Acceleration	0-60mph (0-96km/h): N/A

Jaguar XK120

**Top speed
120mph**
193km/h

Below: This 1949 XK120 is a rare aluminum-bodied example. Most of these are identifiable by the curved windshield pillars and accompanying large rubber grommets; the rest of the outward features are shared with the steel-bodied cars. Although this is a right-hand-drive version, the vast majority of 120s were left hookers destined for the American market.

 The first of Jaguar's fabled XK sports car line, the 120 was so named because it could attain 120mph (193km/h), an unprecedented speed for a production model of its day. Announced at the 1948 London Motor Show, the line was destined to survive until 1961 when the XK150 made way for the sensational E-Type.

The 120's powerful performance came courtesy of a 3.4 liter, twin-overhead-camshaft, six-cylinder engine, the legendary XK unit, that had been conceived during the war to power the company's new 100mph (161km/h) Mark VII sedan. This, paradoxically, appeared in 1950, *after* the open two-seater sports car.

Manufactured for export

William Lyons, Jaguar's accomplished chairman who also styled his company's products, ensured that his new model had the looks to match its performance. It was conceived at a time when the British government was directing the country's

motor manufacturers to export their products overseas and the overwhelming majority of the Coventry-built XK120s were produced in left-hand-drive form for the American market.

Based on the chassis of the simultaneously announced Mark V sedan, the public was astounded by the new Jaguar's much publicized top speed. Lyons confounded his critics by carefully preparing a mildly streamlined test car which, in 1949, attained 132mph (212km/h) on the Jabbeke motorway in Belgium.

Demand for the 120 was intense. After the first 240 cars, which used aluminum bodywork, had been completed, steel panels replaced the aluminum – a change that modestly increased the model's weight.

The new XK engine undeniably proved its worth. While the twin-cam concept had a pre-war reputation for unreliability, the new Jaguar unit was durable and dependable, to the extent that it remained in production until 1992.

ESJ 563

Left: How it achieved 120mph (193km/h): the 120's legendary twin-overhead-camshaft XK engine. The absence of studs on the front of the cam covers indicates an early car.

Left below: Most 120s had a black steering wheel, but white was occasionally offered during the XK150 production run. The roof was stored behind the seats when not in use.

Below: This fine XK120 fixed-head coupé in rallying guise has optional wire wheels in place of the usual discs and hood straps. Unlike the roadster, this possessed a walnut dash and door cappings, courtesy of Jaguar's sedan line.

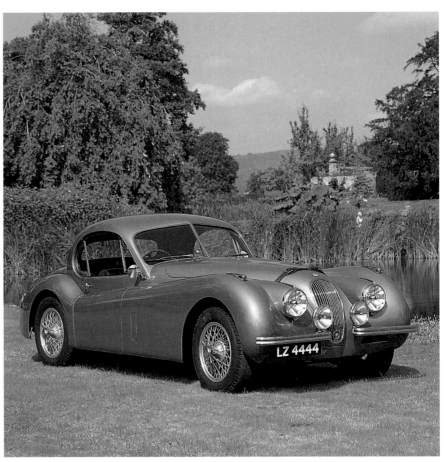

Enter the drophead coupé

In 1951 the XK120 roadster was joined by a drophead coupé version. This was not only stylistically successful but it also had an enhanced interior with walnut veneer replacing the open car's leathercloth-covered instrument panel.

A Special Equipment package was offered for both versions from 1952 and this included high lift camshafts, a lightened flywheel, twin exhaust pipes and handsome center-lock wire wheels which replaced the original discs. These ministrations added 20bhp to the 160bhp the XK unit developed in 1948.

The final variation on the XK120 theme was a drophead coupé which appeared in 1953. This combined the comfort of the fixed head coupé with the fresh air of an open car. Mechanically there was little to choose between all three models although the later versions used a quieter Salisbury rear axle.

XK 120 production ceased in the fall of 1954. By then, Jaguar had established itself as one of the world's leading sports car manufacturers.

Specification	Jaguar XK120
Engine location	Front, in-line
Configuration	Six-cylinder
Bore and stroke	83 x 106mm
Capacity	3442cc
Valve operation	Twin overhead camshafts
Horsepower	160bhp @ 5000rpm
Transmission	Manual four-speed
Drive	Rear
Chassis	Box section
Suspension – front	Wishbone and torsion bar
Suspension – rear	Half-elliptic spring
Brakes	Drum
Top speed	120mph (193km/h)
Acceleration	0-60mph (96km/h): 12 seconds

Above: The XK140 effectively perpetuated the acclaimed lines of its 120 predecessor. It also featured a detachable windshield which permitted owners to race their cars if they wished to do so. This is an American specification 1956 example, identifiable by its left-hand steering and large flashing turn signals let into the front fenders.

Right: The cockpit of a 1960 XK150 drophead coupé. The instrument panel differed from the one used on the 140. The padded leather dashboard roll was making its first appearance on any production Jaguar, with the material extended to the entire dash with a contrasting color being used for the center panel.

The theme was perpetuated for the 1955 season by the outwardly similar XK140 which was available with the same range of body styles. However, the drophead coupé version was offered with a pair of occasional seats into which protesting children could, if necessary, be squeezed. Unlike its famous predecessor, the 140 tag did not indicate top speed; in fact the 140 was capable of about the same 120mph (193km/h). But acceleration was improved because engine output was boosted to 190bhp. The Special Equipment option was continued; this gave 210bhp and the car came complete with wire wheels.

Outwardly the 140 was identifiable by its narrower radiator grille with fewer slats and a medallion on the trunk lid which proclaimed Jaguar's Le Mans wins. Below the surface there was more positive rack and pinion steering which replaced the original recirculating ball unit.

The XK150, the last of the line, followed in the spring of 1957. First offered in fixed and drophead coupé forms, it was identifiable by a wider but thinner-slatted radiator grille and higher fender line. XK150s were invariably shod with wire wheels and fitted with race-proven all-round disc brakes. There was similarly an S, for Special Equipment, version.

Inside there were significant differences because the 140's handsome walnut-faced dashboard and door fillets were discontinued and replaced with leather trim, while the instrument panel was finished in a lighter contrasting hide.

Strictly a two-seater

The open two-seater, the last of the XK150 line, did not appear until March 1958. It differed from both the 120 and 140 roadsters by having wind-up windows, rather than traditional side screens. But unlike the earlier versions, this was strictly a two-seater, although rear luggage space behind the seats was increased. It also came in an S version which used a new cylinder head with 'straight through' ports and three rather than the usual twin SU carburetors. In this form the model could attain 135mph (217km/h).

The open two-seater was destined to be the rarest of the 150 family – only 2265 examples were produced and of these a mere 92 were sold on the home market. The overwhelming majority of those cars exported were destined for America.

The XK150 was further developed with the arrival of a 3.8 liter engine for 1960. It was available with a choice of heads with the option of twin carburetors (260bhp) or a top-of-the-range 265bhp three-carb layout. Top speed remained about the same, although acceleration was improved. The XK150 was discontinued in 1961 so leaving the way clear for the sensational E-Type that was powered by the triple-carb 3.8 liter S engine. After 13 years the famous XK line was no more.

Below: Another US-spec car, a 150S. The S engine was fitted with a race-proven straight port cylinder head.

Bottom left: The 150S roadster's engine, the Special Equipment unit with triple carburetors.

Specification	Jaguar XK150 (3.8 liters)
Engine location	Front, in-line
Configuration	Six-cylinder
Bore and stroke	87 x 106mm
Capacity	3781cc
Valve operation	Twin overhead camshafts
Horsepower	220bhp @ 5500rpm
Transmission	Manual four-speed
Drive	Rear
Chassis	Box section
Suspension – front	Wishbones and torsion bar
Suspension – rear	Half-elliptic spring
Brakes	Disc
Top speed	135mph (217km/h)
Acceleration	0-60mph (0-96km/h): 7.7 seconds

Ferrari 166 Inter

**Top speed
100mph**
161km/h

The 166 has the distinction of being Enzo Ferrari's first road car, but it was not his first model, that accolade being accorded to the competition-honed Type 125 of 1947. Unusually for the day Ferrari opted for a V12 engine and the 2 liter, 60 degree unit which had a single overhead camshaft per bank was designed for him by Gioacchino Colombo, creator of Alfa Romeo's famous Alfetta racing car of 1938.

The 166's engine was mounted in an oval tubular chassis enhanced by transverse leaf front suspension although the live axle was sprung with conventional half-elliptic rear springs. A five-speed gearbox with synchromesh on third and top gears was employed.

Enzo Ferrari

Enzo Ferrari had managed Alfa Romeo's racing team in the 1930s, and so (not surprisingly) he adopted a similar approach to competition when he established a marque under his own name. During 1947 and 1948 all the cars produced at the Maranello works were either campaigned by the factory or by their prosperous owners.

Introduced in competition-proven 166 Sport form in 1947, the 166 Inter was a touring Ferrari, if that is not a contradiction in terms. Announced at the 1948 Turin Motor Show, the first two examples were fitted with coupé bodies by the respected Carrozzeria Touring concern and built to its superleggera (super light) principles featuring a sub-structure of small diameter tubes.

The closed car conjured up echoes of the body that Touring had already produced for Alfa Romeo; the finely proportioned, austere open version with its distinctive sculptured front was named the barchetta (little boat) and it was widely imitated.

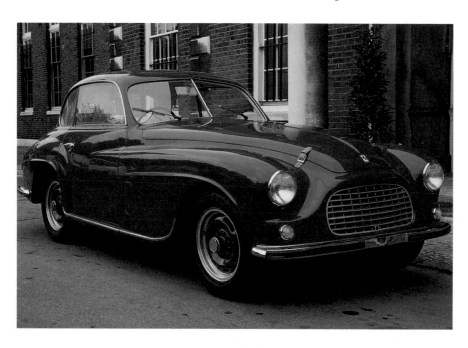

Above: One of a handful of pillarless coupés that Touring built on the 166 chassis, each differing slightly from one another. Even though produced in Italy, these early Ferraris are right-hand-drive cars.

Right: A Spyder Corsa competition version of the 166 with an open two-seater body for sports racing events, but with the minimum of weather equipment. Note the length of the hood which concealed a V12 engine, a feature of the marque that still endures.

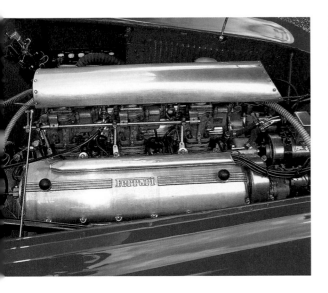

Specification	Ferrari 166 Inter
Engine location	Front, in-line
Configuration	V12
Bore and stroke	60 x 58mm
Capacity	1995cc
Valve operation	Single overhead camshaft per bank
Horsepower	110/115bhp @ 6000rpm
Transmission	Manual five-speed
Drive	Rear
Chassis	Oval tubular
Suspension – front	Wishbones and transverse leaf spring
Suspension – rear	Half-elliptic spring
Brakes	Drum
Top speed	100mph (161km/h)
Acceleration	N/A

Above left: Although Ferrari maintained that he chose a V12 engine because of its use by Packard in 1915, it was a configuration employed in Mercedes-Benz and Alfa Romeo racing cars in the immediate pre-war years.

Left: The no-frills barchetta two-seater created for the 166MM chassis by Touring. The company's famous Superleggera badge can be seen on the front right-hand side of the hood with the nearby cold air intake serving the engine's carburetors.

At that time Ferrari only sold his cars in chassis form – they were then bodied in response to a specific customer or dealer order. This is why no two 166s are exactly alike! In all Touring created the bodies for some five cars, but other examples were the work of a variety of talented Italian coachbuilders, namely Stablimenti Farina, Vignale, Bertone, Allemano, and Ghia.

Three prestigious road race wins

Capable of a reliable and sustainable 100mph (161km/h), in 1949 Ferrari 166s won the world's three most prestigious road races, namely the Mille Miglia, the Targa Florio and Le Mans. The 24 hour race in 1949 was the first to be held since the end of World War II, and Chinetti and Selsdon averaged 82.27mph (132.4km/h). Ferrari would go on to take the checkered flag at the Sarthe circuit on no less than nine occasions.

Below left: The barchetta's cockpit with the distinctive leather beading around its edge readily apparent, as is Ferrari's prancing horse motif on the steering wheel boss. Unusually for the day, the 166 was fitted with a five-speed gearbox.

In two years about 39 examples of the 166 were produced, three Sports and 36 Inters. Although the 166 was listed into 1953, it had been replaced the previous year by the 2.5 liter 212. Ferrari was on his way!

Frazer Nash Le Mans Replica

**Top speed
130mph**
209km/h

*Below: This 1950 Le Mans
Replica has a colorful
history. It was displayed in
chassis form at the 1950
Turin Motor Show, being
acquired by Italian racing
driver/collector Count
'Johnny' Lurani, who had a
coupé body built by Motto.
It later returned to Britain
where the Italian coachwork
was removed and restorer
Dick Crossthwaite produced
this copy of a Le Mans
Replica body*

Capable of speeds approaching 130mph
(209km/h), Frazer Nash's Le Mans
Replica was a well-engineered, expensive
sports racer in the continental manner, being a
derivative of BMW's fabled 328 sports car of 1936.
Its origins are, however, somewhat convoluted!
From 1935 until the outbreak of war in 1939,
Frazer Nash had marketed the German make in
Britain under the Frazer Nash-BMW name.

With the coming of peace in 1945, 'Nash's H.J.
Aldington formed an association with the Bristol
Aeroplane Company, which wanted to join the
ranks of motor manufacturers. It was decided that
as well as making the Filton-built Bristol, the firms
would jointly create a new generation of Frazer
Nashes that would continue to be assembled at
Isleworth, Middlesex.

BMW designs and personnel were accordingly
'liberated' from Germany and the Bristol 400
coupé, a selective cocktail of proven BMW
concepts, entered production in 1947. In that year

the association between the two business was
unscrambled and Frazer Nash car production,
similarly BMW-based, began in 1948. There were
two models, a Fast Tourer with full-width two-
seater coachwork, and the more powerful, stark,
and purposeful High Speed.

The work of former BMW engineer Fritz
Fiedler, both shared the same 328-derived twin
tubular chassis, while the 2 liter, six-cylinder, high
efficiency pushrod engine sprang from the same
source and was already being used in the Bristol.

Streamlined two-seater

Developing 120bhp when fitted in the High Speed
'Nash, 40hp more than the Fast Tourer, it was clad
in a functional, streamlined, open two-seater body,
complete with cycle fenders, for which Fiedler was
also responsible. But at $4300 it was expensive and
would have bought no less than six MG TCs!

It was clearly geared for the competition owner-
driver. One such was Norman Culpan who entered

his car for the first post-war Le Mans race held in 1949. With Aldington as co-driver, the duo averaged 78.53mph (126.38km/h) for the 24 hours and attained a creditable third placing. As a result the High Speed name was discontinued, and the Le Mans Replica was born for the 1950 season. It remained in production until 1953 – a revised simpler chassis having arrived in 1952. A total of 34 were completed.

The touring car had passed through Fast Tourer, Roadster, and Millie Miglia guises, and in 1952 it was again updated and became the Targa Florio. The Fixed Head Coupé was created for the 1953 Le Mans event where it won the 2 liter class but the racing Sebring roadster of 1954 was the last of the line and only three were built. The final cars were assembled in 1956 and that, effectively, was the end, after 32 years, of the Frazer Nash.

Left: Instrumentation was impressive and dominated by a 5in (127mm) diameter 120mph (or 200km/h) speedometer and 6000rpm revolution counter. Other dials included water and oil temperature gauges. The driver could also activate a foot-operated pump for a 'one-shot' chassis lubrication system.

Below left: The view other drivers experienced as a Le Mans Replica overtook them. The hinged tail was a feature of the later cars, it was originally made in one piece. An aluminum 24-gallon (91lit) gas tank was fitted. The external exhaust system is an original feature and the small muffler at its end is another authentic touch.

Bottom left: The Frazer Nash's Bristol engine of BMW ancestry. The triple Solex carburetors are mounted on the top of the alloy cylinder head, rather than on its side, a layout necessitated by the ingenious cross pushrod design.

Specification	Frazer Nash Le Mans Replica
Engine location	Front, in-line
Configuration	Six-cylinder
Bore and stroke	66 x 96mm
Capacity	1971cc
Valve operation	Pushrod
Horsepower	120bhp @ 5200rpm
Transmission	Manual four-speed
Drive	Rear
Chassis	Twin tube
Suspension – front	Transverse leaf spring and wishbones
Suspension – rear	Torsion bar
Brakes	Drum
Top speed	130mph (209km/h)
Acceleration	0-60mph (0-96km/h): 7.5 seconds

Allard J2

**Top speed
130mph**
209km/h

*Below: Stripped for action:
a J2X destined for the
American market and fitted
with aero screens rather
than the usual full-width
windshield. The longer
nose concealed the coil
springs that had been
exposed on the J2.*

Sydney Allard had campaigned Ford V8-based specials in pre-war days and in 1938 he began limited production of such cars at his garage in the south London suburb of Clapham. Work stopped during World War II but manufacture resumed in 1946. Allard offered the chunky no-frills K1 open two-seater with its distinctive waterfall-style cowled radiator.

The accent was on simplicity and a good power-to-weight ratio. Allard used a straightforward chassis and a simple but effective divided independent front suspension axle although he retained Ford's crude Model T-inspired transverse leaf springing. The three-speed gearboxes came from the same source.

Monte Carlo Rally

The robust 3.6 liter side-valve V8 engine provided both reliability and acceleration and the K1 was joined by L and M1 four-seaters, while Sydney Allard himself won the 1952 Monte Carlo Rally in the P1 sedan version.

But the sports-racing J2 of 1949 saw a return to first principles. The open two-seater body did away with doors and was removable; it was even starker than its predecessors and came complete with cycle fenders. It was ideal transport for the enthusiast who wanted to drive to the racetrack and then compete there. The J2's mechanicals differed from the earlier models with the use of a de Dion rear axle and all-round coil springs.

Even when Ford V8-powered, with a 4.4 liter Mercury ohv conversion, the J2 was capable of over 100mph (161km/h), but when one of the new generation of American V8s was installed, then the Allard really went motoring. These engines, it should be said, were usually fitted in those cars sold on the US market, because import restrictions prevented the Allard company from spending precious dollars on the purchase of new units.

However, the firm was able to acquire a few engines for experimental purpose and the prototype 331cid (5.4 liter) Cadillac-engined J2 with 160bhp on tap was capable of a spirited 130mph (209km/h), no less than 100mph (161km/h) in second gear and 80mph (129km/h) in first cog!

Specification	Allard J2 (Cadillac engine)
Engine location	Front, in-line
Configuration	V8
Bore and stroke	3.81 x 3.63in (97 x 92mm)
Capacity	331cid (5.4 liters)
Valve operation	Pushrod
Horsepower	160bhp @ 4000rpm
Transmission	Manual three-speed
Drive	Rear
Chassis	Box section
Suspension – front	Divided beam and coil spring
Suspension – rear	De Dion axle and coil spring
Brakes	Drum
Top speed	130mph (209km/h)
Acceleration	0-60mph (96km/h): 7 seconds

With such acceleration it could pull away from a Jaguar XK120. American enthusiasts also delighted in fitting alternative Oldsmobile or Chrysler V8s. This latter unit, also of 331cid, was a feature of the revised J2X for the 1952 season. This outwardly resembled its predecessor although it had a longer nose section because the engine was mounted 7in (178mm) further forward to allow more room for the occupants.

Built until 1952, the X was succeeded by the Cadillac-engined JR of 1953, the last of the line. Its aerodynamic body was in stark contrast to the functional appeal of its predecessor. In all 187 J Series cars were built, 99 J2s, 83 J2Xs and just five JRs. By 1960 the Allard was no more.

Above: A J2 showing its original windshield and distinctive triangulated side pieces in place. The spare wheel could be fitted on either side of the body.

Left: A J2 fitted with a 3.6 liter British-built Ford V8. Although a side-valve unit, aluminum cylinder heads were added to extract 90bhp rather than the usual 85.

Healey Silverstone

**Top speed
105mph**
169km/h

*Opposite top: The
Silverstone's cockpit. This
1950 car is an example of
the E-type model with a
bench-type front seat in
place of the original two
buckets. It is also slightly
wider than the original
version and a telescopic
steering column adds a
further refinement.*

*Opposite below: The E-type
Silverstone is instantly
identifiable by the air scoop
on the top of the hood. The
fenders were easily
detachable for racing and
the headlamps, concealed
for aerodynamic
considerations behind the
radiator grille, are a
notable feature. Note the
alloy trailing arm
independent front
suspension, a costly
refinement!*

*Right: The Silverstone's tail
contained a 20-gallon
(77lit) gas tank while the
protruding segment of the
spare wheel did double duty
as a rear bumper, one not
being fitted for cost
considerations. It was held
in place by a fixing, access
to which was obtained
through a small panel
located directly above the
license plate.*

Rally driver Donald Healey began
manufacturing cars under his own name
in 1946. In the next eight years he
produced no less than eight mostly Riley-engined
models from a small factory at Warwick. Of these
the best known is the 105mph (169km/h)
Silverstone of 1949/50.

The first Healeys, the Westland Roadster and
Elliott sedan, were some of the fastest cars of their
day – an example of the latter model was timed at
104.7mph (168.5km/h) on an Italian *autostrada*.
This was because Healey had adopted Riley's
potent and efficient 104bhp 2.5 liter engine. These
were expensive cars, the sedan cost $2240, and, as
a small, newly established manufacturer, Donald
Healey recognized his vulnerability when in 1948
the British government doubled the rate of purchase
tax, from $33\frac{1}{3}$ to $66\frac{2}{3}$ per cent, on all cars that
sold for over £1000 ($1400).

The result was the cost-conscious two-seater
Silverstone of 1949, named after Britain's newly
opened motor-racing circuit. Aimed at the club
racing fraternity in Britain and America, it sold for
$1365 and was thus liable for the lower $33\frac{1}{3}$ per
cent rate of duty. Based on the standard Healey 100
chassis, the engine and gearbox were moved 8in
(203mm) back in the frame and its rear was
modified to accommodate an enlarged 19.2 gallon
(73lit) gas tank.

Streamlined headlamps

As the emphasis was placed on simplicity and low
cost, the bodywork was of straightforward
construction. Designed by Len Hedges of the
Birmingham-based Panelcraft concern, in the
interests of aerodynamics the headlamps were
contained within the cowled radiator grille in the
manner of pre-war streamlined Peugeots.

The windshield was a novel feature as it could
be lowered into the bodywork for racing. To keep
costs down there was no rear bumper; instead the
horizontally mounted spare wheel, which resided in
a sort of letterbox-like slot, performed that function
too. Weighing some 448lb (203kg) less than the
earlier Healeys, the Silverstone could easily exceed
100mph (161km/h) and was able to hit 80mph
(128km/h) in third gear.

In 1949 an example won the manufacturers
team prize in the British Racing Drivers' Club
Production Car Race, appropriately held at
Silverstone. No less than eight participated in the
following year's event and Duncan Hamilton won
his class at 79mph (127km/h).

By the time that production ceased in
September 1950 a total of 105 Silverstones had
been completed. But Healey was beginning to
recognize that his cars were too big, heavy, and
expensive. The result was the Healey 100 which
appeared in 1952.

Specification	**Healey** Silverstone
Engine location	Front, in-line
Configuration	Four-cylinder
Bore and stroke	80 x 120mm
Capacity	2443cc
Valve operation	Pushrod
Horsepower	104bhp at 4500rpm
Transmission	Manual four-speed
Drive	Rear
Chassis	Box section
Suspension – front	Trailing link and coil spring
Suspension – rear	Torque tube and coil spring
Brakes	Drum
Top speed	105mph (169km/h)
Acceleration	0-60mph (0-96km/h): 11 seconds

Porsche 356

**Top speed
101mph**
163km/h

*Below: Early days: the
Porsche marque had only
been in existence for three
years when this 356 coupé
was completed in 1951.
This example was owned
for many years by arch-
enthusiast Betty Haig. The
smooth body contours
reflect a shape that was the
product of scrupulous
aerodynamic refinement.
The divided windshield was
replaced by a single curved
unit for 1952.*

Porsche is one of the great German
sporting marques of the post-war years.
However, the 356, the first of the line,
actually began life in Austria. In the fall of 1944
Dr Ferdinand Porsche's engineering consultancy
business, that was principally located in Stuttgart,
had also established a base at a former sawmill
which the family owned at Gmund, high in the
Austrian mountains. It was thus out of reach of
allied bombing raids.

In 1948 Porsche's son Ferry, inspired by the
Fiat-powered Italian Cisitalia, decided to produce a
sports car using Volkswagen mechanicals, Dr
Porsche having been responsible for the design of
the famous Beetle in 1933-38. The first
experimental 356 coupé was completed in June
1948 and, although VW-based, it had its own
distinctive aerodynamically refined body. However,
beneath the louvered engine cover sat the Beetle's
rear-mounted, air-cooled, 1131cc flat four engine
with twin carburetors which produced 40 rather
than 25bhp. By contrast, most production Porsches
used a 1086cc version to bring the model within the
1100cc sports racing class.

Capable of 85mph (137km/h), this
unconventional sports car was also produced in
open (cabriolet) forms, and it continued to be built
in Austria until 1951. But in the previous year
assembly had been transferred to Stuttgart and that
was when 356 development began in earnest.

In 1951 a supplementary 1286cc engine was
introduced, and this was followed for 1952 by a 1.5
liter version available in 54bhp and Super 69bhp
states of tune. The latter designation was to remain
a 356 feature from then on.

Another leap in engine size occurred in 1955,
this time to 1582cc for the 356A. This capacity,
invariably referred to as a 1600, was perpetuated
until the 356 line ceased production. The 75bhp
Super version was capable of over 100mph
(161km/h), but the 356A was also available with
the existing 1.3 and 1.5 liter units. The top-of-the-
range Carrera is considered separately on page 60.

The stark Speedster 1600, a convertible in the
spirit of the Ferrari barchetta, was produced for the
increasingly important American market. It gained
unfortunate immortality when 1950s film star
James Dean died at the wheel of his.

Increased power

With the arrival of the 1.6 liter 356B for 1960 the basic version developed 60bhp while the Super 90 was now capable of 110mph (177km/h). The 356C, the last of the line, introduced for the 1964 model year had all-round disc brakes – the first Porsche road car to be so equipped. Horsepower was up again, with 75bhp now available for the basic version and 95 on the Super. The C survived until 1965, by which time the six-cylinder 911 – the 356's replacement – was moving center stage. From then on the 911 would dominate an ever-expanding Porsche model line.

Above: This 1955 Speedster was also owned by Betty Haig. This no-frills model was supplied with a roof which looked unsightly when raised and also leaked in the rain!

Left: It could be no other car. The rear-located engine of this 356A is revealed by the presence of an air intake grille.

Below left: The 1582cc engine of the 356A, still displaying its flat four Volkswagen Beetle ancestry and its twin carburetors readily apparent.

Specification	Porsche 356A
Engine location	Rear, in-line
Configuration	Horizontally opposed four-cylinder
Bore and stroke	82 x 74mm
Capacity	1582cc
Valve operation	Pushrod
Horsepower	70bhp @ 4500rpm
Transmission	Manual four-speed
Drive	Rear
Chassis	Platform
Suspension – front	Trailing arm and torsion bar
Suspension – rear	Swing axle and torsion bar
Brakes	Drum
Top speed	101mph (163km/h)
Acceleration	0-60mph (0-96km/h): 15.4 seconds

Aston Martin DB2

**Top speed
118mph**
190km/h

*Right: Unusually, the entire
front end of the DB2 hinged
forward to permit access to
the Bentley-designed twin-
overhead-camshaft engine
and independent front
suspension.*

*Below: The DB2 in its
original form with body
lines inspired by the Italian
berlinettas of the day. At this
stage only two occupants
could be accommodated.*

 The famous Aston Martin marque was
effectively reborn with the appearance, in
April 1950, of the DB2. Named after
David Brown, the company's owner since 1947, the
model was destined to survive until 1959.

It represented the union of Aston Martin with
the Lagonda make that Brown had acquired in
1947. The chassis, of square section tubes, came
courtesy of a 1939 Aston Martin prototype sedan
named the Atom, while the 2.6 liter, 100bhp, twin-
overhead-camshaft, six-cylinder engine was the
work of W.O. Bentley, no less. It had been designed
to power the post-war Lagonda sedan car line
which Brown also perpetuated.

However, his first Aston Martin was the 2 liter
Super Sports of 1948, retrospectively dubbed the
DB1. This, like the pre-war cars, was an open
model and used the Atom's chassis and ohv engine.
But it was an expensive concept and only 15 were
sold. Production ceased in 1950.

It was replaced in that year by the DB2 which
boasted closed coachwork in the manner of the
latest sporting *gran turismos* from Italy. The work
of talented Lagonda stylist, Frank Feeley, it was
every inch a thoroughbred and performed as well as
it looked. Top speed was in the region of 110mph
(177km/h), but later in 1950 a more powerful
116bhp Vantage version appeared and a drophead
coupé body was also introduced.

Arrival of the new DB2/4

The 1954 season saw the arrival of the DB2/4 which turned the mainstream coupé into an occasional four-seater which had a rear-opening door, an innovation at that time. A curved windshield replaced the original divided one. The extra weight meant that the Vantage engine was fitted as standard but it was soon replaced, from April 1954, by an enlarged, race-proven, 3 liter unit. Top speed rose to 118mph (190km/h).

A Mark II version followed for 1956 which was outwardly similar but identifiable by its more angular rear fenders. Although the drophead option continued, there was also a notchback version which lacked the rear door.

The final version, the DB Mark III, was launched at the 1957 Geneva Motor Show. This differed visually by having a new front end with a curved radiator grille and lower hood line. It concealed a revised 162bhp engine and the company's competition experience was reflected in the optional fitment of front Girling disc brakes that had been developed on the company's DB3S sports racer. Originally only available for export, American influence was reflected when an automatic gearbox became available for 1959. Production ceased that year as the III made way for the DB4, a total of 1724 examples of the line having been built since 1950.

Above: A DB2/4 with a one-piece windshield rather than the divided one of its predecessor and two small seats introduced in the rear.

Left: The DB2's interior. The rubber heel pad on the driver's side is an original fitting, as is the grab handle on the passenger's.

Specification	Aston Martin DB Mark III
Engine location	Front, in-line
Configuration	Six-cylinder
Bore and stroke	83 x 90mm
Capacity	2992cc
Valve operation	Twin overhead camshafts
Horsepower	162bhp @ 5500rpm
Transmission	Manual four-speed
Drive	Rear
Chassis	Tubular square section
Suspension – front	Trailing arms and coil spring
Suspension – rear	Radius arm and coil spring
Brakes	Front disc, rear drum
Top speed	118mph (190km/h)
Acceleration	0-60mph (0-96km/h): 9.4 seconds

1951–1960
The Sports Car Boom

With the American economy booming in the 1950s, Britain became the world's largest provider of fast cars with Jaguar and MG roadsters joined by the newly minted Austin-Healey and a revived Triumph marque.

In Europe the grand touring theme was given expression in the delectable gullwing-doored Mercedes-Benz 300SL coupé, a reminder that Germany was, once again, a force to be reckoned with.

France produced the Facel-Vega that used a powerful but low-cost American engine, while the ubiquitous V8 was also to be found under the hood of the United States' own Chevrolet Corvette. After years of mass producing family sedans, the Americans were now building a fast car of their own.

Triumph TR2

**Top speed
103mph**
169km/h

*Below: Although created
with the American market
in mind, a fair proportion,
some 30 per cent, of TR2
production was sold in the
home market. This was a
much higher figure than
Triumph's Jaguar and MG
rivals, so right-hand-drive
Triumph roadsters are
nothing like as rare. Its
functional lines reflect a
very cost-conscious product.
This example is fitted with
optional wire wheels.*

Triumph's famous family of TR sports cars first took the stage in 1953 with the appearance of the TR2. It was destined to endure until the TR7, the last of the line, ceased production in 1981.

In 1944 the moribund Triumph company had been acquired by Standard's Sir John Black with the intention of challenging the growing stature of Jaguar. Its superlative XK120 had been created at governmental behest for the American public, a market which had been first exploited by MG's TC Midget. The TR line (standing for Triumph Roadster) was intended to occupy the territory between these two models.

Triumph's tentative design appeared at the 1952 London Motor Show. Retrospectively designated the TR1, this used a pre-war Standard Flying 9 chassis enhanced by a chunky, open two-seater body essayed by Standard's Walter Belgrove and powered by a 1991cc version of the engine used in the new Vanguard sedan.

In truth, these unrelated components required 'sorting out' and the task was successfully accomplished by Standard's Harry Webster and ex-BRM driver Ken Richardson. The most significant modification was the introduction of a stronger purpose-designed chassis. Their ministrations resulted in the definitive TR2 which entered production in August 1953.

Rally success

With engine output boosted from 75 to 90bhp and capable of exceeding the magic 100mph (161km/h), Triumph's new sports car got off to a flying start when it won the 1954 RAC Rally. This was to prove to be the first of many successes in such events. But in sales terms the TR2's achievement was more modest and by the time that production ceased in the fall of 1955, a total of 8628 had been completed. Of these about 70 per cent had found American owners.

Its TR3 replacement for 1956 was outwardly

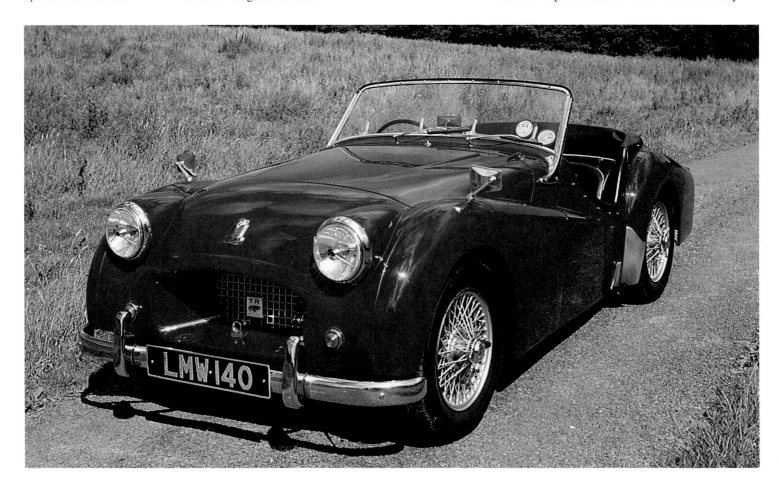

similar, although it was identifiable by its egg-crate radiator grille in the Ferrari idiom. Front disc brakes arrived for the 1957 season and were a notable first for a British car. This model lasted until mid-1957 when the TR3A was announced. Sharing the same body style, it was fitted with a full-width radiator grille while under the hood the engine was boosted to 100bhp. The A was initially sold exclusively on the American market.

The four-cylinder TR line came of age with this model and between the fall of 1957 and October 1962 some 61,000 examples were produced – of these an overwhelming 98 per cent were exported, mostly to the United States.

Throughout, TR performance had remained at about the same level with the accent on continual refinement. These first models of the line were noted for their mechanical simplicity and, in consequence, for reliability. These were sound foundations on which the company built when it planned its next generation of TR sports cars for the 1960s.

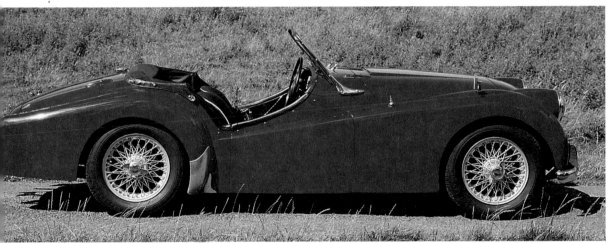

Above: The TR2 line would not acquire a forward-mounted radiator grille until the TR3's arrival.

Left: This is a 1954 car, for 1955 the doors were decreased in depth and sills were added.

Below left: The TR2's engine was shared with the in-house Standard Vanguard and Ferguson tractor.

Specification	Triumph TR2
Engine location	Front, in-line
Configuration	Four-cylinder
Bore and stroke	83 x 92mm
Capacity	1991cc
Valve operation	Pushrod
Horsepower	90bhp @ 4800rpm
Transmission	Manual four-speed
Drive	Rear
Chassis	Box section
Suspension – front	Wishbones and coil spring
Suspension – rear	Half-elliptic spring
Brakes	Drum
Top speed	103mph (169km/h)
Acceleration	0-60mph (0-96km/h): 11.9 seconds

Bentley Continental

**Top speed
115mph**
185km/h

*Right: The Continental's
driving compartment with
the polished walnut
dashboard almost wholly
occupied by instruments.
The right-hand gear change
is clearly visible.*

*Below: This is the prototype
Continental of 1951,
affectionately known as
'Olga' on account of its
distinctive license plate,
which happily escaped from
the factory. Its roof is 1in
(25mm) higher than the
production versions.*

 With a top speed of 115mph (185km/h), and clothed in a handsome and distinctive fastback body by H.J. Mulliner, the Bentley Continental of 1952 was, in its day, the fastest production four-seater car in the world.

Destined for a seven-year manufacturing life, the Continental was a spiritual successor of the Bentley Corniche, an experimental aerodynamic sedan of 1939 that did not enter production because of the outbreak of war. As such, it was a model that carried on the traditions of the well-appointed intercontinental grand tourers that were popular in the 1930s.

In 1946 Rolls-Royce introduced its Silver Wraith and related Bentley Mark VI lines. While the former was only available with bespoke coachwork, over 80 per cent of the Bentleys were fitted with a standardized four-door sedan body by Pressed Steel.

Corniche II

Based on the R-Type chassis that was to replace the Mark VI frame in 1952, Rolls-Royce had begun work on what had been internally coded 'Corniche

II' in 1950. The emphasis was placed firmly on aerodynamic refinement and weight-saving and the memorable body was styled by RR's Ivan Evernden. However, the sedan's 4.6 liter, overhead inlet/side exhaust engine had its compression ratio raised from 6.4 to 7.3:1 and a new exhaust system was fitted.

The prototype, completed in August 1951, was taken to the Montlhéry racing circuit near Paris where it proceeded to average 118.75mph (191.1km/h) over five laps.

Invoice 57501 - D - SOS
Thursday October 2020 1 33 PM

LIBERTY NICKELS
[SVC]
LIBERTY NICKELS
[SVC]   6.50   20 %   5.20
BOOK
A4   2.00

Merchandise Subtotal
State Tax
Items Total

Paid by Cash
Tendered   20.00
Change Due   0.34

CASH SALES

All Sales Are Final
Thank you!
Please come again

Announced in February 1952, the Continental was priced at $9700, which made it one of the most expensive cars on the market. Initially it was only available for export but a right-hand-drive version appeared for the 1953 season.

In the event the overwhelming majority of the 208 R-Type Continentals built were sold in Britain, which accounted for 108 of them. France was in second place with 33, followed by America's 28, and Switzerland's 24. Belgium, Canada and Portugal each took two cars apiece.

Engine capacity increased

After two years in production, in July 1954 the capacity of the Continental's engine was increased to 4.9 liters and four-speed automatic transmission became an option.

In 1955 came the S-Series sedan, the Bentley version of the Rolls-Royce Silver Cloud, both of which used Pressed Steel bodywork. However, the bespoke Continental option was perpetuated although the resulting car was slightly longer than its predecessor because of a new lengthened chassis. The model remained in production until 1959. Its demise spelt the end, for the time being at least, of a Bentley with a purpose-designed body. However, the concept was later revived with the Continental R of 1991.

Specification	**Bentley** Continental (R-Type)
Engine location	Front, in-line
Configuration	Six-cylinder
Bore and stroke	92 x 114mm
Capacity	4566cc
Valve operation	Overhead inlet/side exhaust
Horsepower	Not disclosed
Transmission	Manual four-speed
Drive	Rear
Chassis	Channel section
Suspension – front	Wishbones and coil spring
Suspension – rear	Half-elliptic spring
Brakes	Drum with mechanical servo
Top speed	115mph (185km/h)
Acceleration	0-60mph (0-96km/h): 13.5 seconds

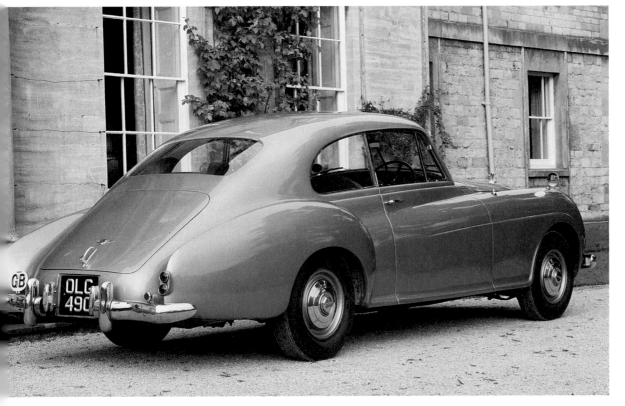

Above: The view that most other drivers experienced when a Bentley Continental overtook them! To help keep weight down, the bumpers were made of heavy-gauge light alloy. The trunk was commodious and the tools and jack were carried in a separate compartment.

Left: Originally the rear wheels were covered with spats in the interests of aerodynamic efficiency. The stop lights mounted on each fender doubled as flashing indicators at a time when semaphore units were the norm. There were also twin reversing lights positioned alongside the license plate.

Pegaso Z102

**Top speed
125mph**
201km/h

*Right: The Pegaso seats
are unusual with a one-
piece shaped aluminum
backrest to which leather
upholstery was clipped.*

*Below: One of the 19
coupés Touring built for
Pegaso in 1954. Produced
in Milan on the Z102B
chassis to its superleggera
principles, this featured a
sub-structure of strong
load-bearing tubes.*

 Cars built regardless of cost were not
uncommon in the interwar years but they
did not feature much in the harsher
realities of the early post-war era. However, the
Spanish Pegaso was precisely that. Capable of
125mph (201km/h), it was looked upon by its
makers as a publicity vehicle to draw attention to
its truck, bus, and coach lines.

The business in question was the nationalized
ENASA, the acronym for *Empresa Nacional de
Autocamiones SA*, which was established in
Barcelona in 1946. Its products were named
Pegaso, after Pegasus, the winged horse of Greek
mythology, and this name was extended to the car
that was unveiled at the 1951 Paris Motor Show.

It was the work of Spanish engineer Wilfredo
Ricart, who in the 1920s had been responsible for
the Ricart Espania car and who subsequently
became technical director of Alfa Romeo. Hand-
built in the Barcelona factory which had previously
produced the costly and prestigious Hispano-Suiza,

the Z102 Pegaso was a car in very much the same
idiom. All its mechanical components, with the
exception of the Bosch electrics, were produced in
the Calle de Segrera works while the bodies were
respectively by two of the world's finest
coachbuilders, Touring in Milan and the Paris-
based Saoutchik concern.

Chain drive replacement

The engine was a fearsome, light, alloy 2.5 liter V8
with twin overhead camshafts per cylinder bank.
Although initially chain driven, they were soon
replaced by more efficient but costly and noisy
gears. A single twin-choke Weber carburetor was
specified although a more potent version was listed
with no less than four. The five-speed gearbox was
mounted in unit with the De Dion rear axle.

The steering gear was a study in its own right
and passed through the dashboard rather than the
floor. Its subsequent contortions made it probably
the most complex such system ever fitted to a
production car. And, unusually for any car, the
interior controls were set out on the dash rather like
a row of piano keys!

But such ambitious specifications were
expensive and the Z102 cost $4200. Customers
were initially offered an alternative 2.8 liter engine,
then a supercharged 2.5. Handling, brakes, and
steering were, not surprisingly perhaps, in the Alfa
Romeo league and the Pegaso could attain 100mph
(161km/h) in fourth gear.

Later, in 1954, came yet another engine
variation in the shape of a 3.2 liter V8 with twin
Roots superchargers and magneto ignition. A
perhaps optimistic 185mph (298km/h) was quoted
as its top speed. Finally in 1956 came the Z103
with a new pushrod V8 and, again, varying
capacities of 4 or 4.7 liters. Just four were
completed, making a total of 84 Pegasos built by
1958 which was when ENASA ceased car-making
to concentrate on its more popular commercial
vehicle lines, an activity that continues to this day.

Specification	Pegaso Z102 (2.5 liter)
Engine location	Front, in-line
Configuration	V8
Bore and stroke	75 x 70mm
Capacity	2474cc
Valve operation	Twin overhead camshafts
Horsepower	165bhp @ 6500rpm
Transmission	Manual five-speed
Drive	Rear
Chassis	Unitary
Suspension – front	Wishbones and torsion bar
Suspension – rear	De Dion axle and torsion bar
Brakes	Drum
Top speed	125mph (201km/h)
Acceleration	0-60mph (0-96km/h): 10.3 seconds

Fiat 8V

Top speed 120mph
193km/h

Below: Although the majority of 8Vs were bodied by the factory, some chassis were enhanced by specialist Italian carrozzerias, namely Ghia, Bertone, Zagato, and Vignale. This 1953 example, arguably more attractive than the standard car, is the work of Bertone. This coachbuilder's associations with Fiat stretched back to a time soon after Giovanni Bertone established his business in Turin in 1912.

Fiat is best known for providing small, distinctive cars for the ordinary 'Italian in the street.' But in 1952 it introduced what can be regarded as a 'poor man's Ferrari' in the shape of the 8V, a hand-built coupé for the discriminating few that was capable of 120mph (193km/h) and proved its worth in GT class races.

This was Fiat's first sports cars since the Ballila of 1934. The 8V, *Otto Vu* in its native land and so called because Ford owned the rights to the V8 name, was launched at the 1952 Geneva Motor Show. Work on the project had begun in 1950 under the direction of chief engineer Dante Giacosa. The compact 2 liter alloy V8 engine was initially designed for use in a prestigious Pinin Farina-styled version of Fiat's impending 1900 sedan, but this never actually got into production.

It was used in the 8V in no less than three states of tune: the standard model was powered by a 105bhp unit, but there were alternative versions, with higher compression ratios and different camshafts, which variously produced 115 and 127bhp. So there was plenty of choice!

The bodies, the styling was by Rapi, were produced by Fiat in its experimental workshops. However, the cars were assembled by SIATA, the Turin-based tuning business that specialized in Fiats, and this company developed a five-speed gearbox for the 8V. The model also had the distinction of being the first Fiat to employ all-independent suspension.

The body panels were built around a tubular framework and were invariably finished in metallic cellulose. Later versions featured twin vertical headlamps, a styling feature that was rediscovered by the Americans in the early 1960s. The bumpers and body moldings were made of stainless steel, a nice touch.

Competition successes

Strictly a two-seater with the spare wheel occupying the space behind, the 8V was able to attain a noisy 89mph (143km/h) in third gear and 120mph (193km/h) in top. It enjoyed some competition successes, notably taking the Italian 2 liter GT Championship in 1954. However, a works

Above left: This body on an 8V chassis is by Alfredo Vignale, who established his own carrozzeria in Turin in 1948, having been foreman at Stabilimenti Farina.

Above: An 8V by Zagato of Milan. Its owner, Elio Zagato, son of the founder, ran such an 8V himself in which he achieved many sporting successes.

Left: Not a production 8V but an experimental gas-turbine-powered version completed in 1954, hence the excess of dashboard instrumentation!

sortie to Le Mans in the previous year had been less successful when an example fitted with an experimental SIATA five-speed gearbox proved to be quicker in fourth gear than in top!

In addition to the usual factory coachwork, there were versions by Ghia and Zagato. The factory also exhibited an emerald green glass-fiber-bodied example at the 1954 Geneva show but the idea was not taken any further. An experimental gas turbine version produced in the same year suffered a similar fate.

A lack of demand resulted in production ceasing at the end of 1954 after a mere 114 examples of this all too exclusive Fiat had been completed but its memory lingers on.

Specification	Fiat 8V
Engine location	Front, in-line
Configuration	V8
Bore and stroke	72 x 61mm
Capacity	1996cc
Valve operation	Pushrod
Horsepower	105bhp @ 6000rpm
Transmission	Manual four-speed
Drive	Rear
Chassis	Unitary
Suspension – front	Wishbone and coil spring
Suspension – rear	Wishbone and coil spring
Brakes	Drum
Top speed	120mph (193km/h)
Acceleration	0-60mph (0-96km/h): 12.3 seconds

Chevrolet Corvette

**Top speed
105mph**
169km/h

The first of a legendary line, the Corvette was created by America's General Motors Corporation in response to the British open two-seaters that were increasingly appearing, albeit in modest numbers, on American roads during the early 1950s.

The result was distinctly transatlantic in flavor with, to European eyes, a garish open two-seater body created by GM's styling supremo, Harley Earl. Because of the low production volumes envisaged, it was made of glass fiber. This was mounted on a bespoke chassis and under the hood was a 235cid (3.8 liter) six-cylinder engine; two-speed automatic transmission, with a floor gear change, was fitted.

In truth this first Corvette of 1953 was a bit of a horror but then America's last true sports car had been the Mercer Raceabout of 1911! Only available in that first year in polo white with a red interior, GM's first performance model was marred by indifferent handling, a worrying characteristic when the top speed was an alarming 105mph (169km/h).

Against a background of poor sales, the Corporation contemplated scrapping the 'Vette but wisely, in 1955, replaced the six with a 265cid (4.3 liter) V8. A three-speed manual gearbox arrived for the 1956 season. Performance perked up and the car was now capable of speeds nudging the 120mph (193km/h) mark.

All-new design

The body was rethought for 1956 with the unveiling of an all-new design – the hitherto rather bland profile was enhanced by the introduction of sculptured side panels which were sometimes finished in a contrasting color. A detachable hardtop was an option and quadruple headlights followed in 1958.

Right: A 1955 Corvette's dashboard with centrally positioned rev counter. This is one of a few cars built in that model year to be fitted with a manual gearbox.

Right: Exterior of the same 1955 car with smoother body panels than previously – teething production bugs of the two previous years had been ironed out.

Opposite below: This is one of only a handful or so '55 Corvettes to be six-cylinder-powered. Most used the V8 engine, a configuration which would apply to every 'Vette from then on.

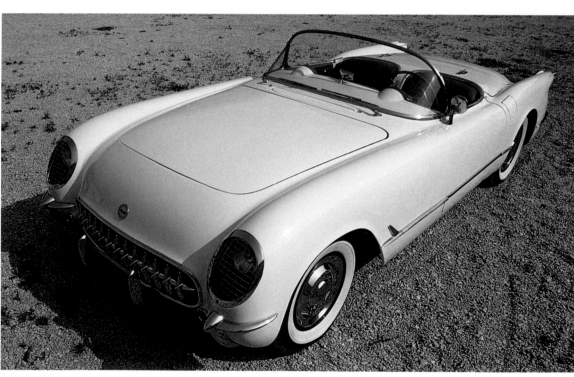

Millionaire racer

The engine's capacity had been upped to 283cid (4.6 liters) for the 1957 season and, interestingly, fuel injection was available as an option although initially it proved to be unreliable. More significantly, in 1960 American millionaire Briggs Cunningham entered a team of three Corvettes in that year's Le Mans race. Although he crashed in the third hour, one car was placed a creditable eighth and the other also finished.

More changes were in store: in 1961 further body refinements included a neatly sculptured tail, which was the work of William Mitchell who had replaced Earl in 1958. Performance was now top of the agenda and in 1962 the engine was again enlarged, this time to 327cid (5.3 liters).

With the Corvette now capable of 150mph (241km/h), Mitchell opted for a complete facelift. The result for the 1963 season was the Sting Ray, arguably the most memorable Corvette of all.

Below: A 1955 Corvette, the first year in which the model was powered by a V8. A 265cid unit was fitted, the CheVrolet script on the side of the front fender being so embellished.

Specification	Chevrolet Corvette (1953)
Engine location	Front, in-line
Configuration	Six-cylinder
Bore and stroke	3.56 x 3.93in (90 x 100mm)
Capacity	235cid (3.8 liters)
Valve operation	Pushrod
Horsepower	150bhp @ 4200rpm
Transmission	Automatic two-speed
Drive	Rear
Chassis	Box section
Suspension – front	Wishbones and coil spring
Suspension – rear	Half-elliptic spring
Brakes	Drum
Top speed	105mph (169km/h)
Acceleration	0-60 mph (96km/h): 11.2 seconds

AC Ace

**Top speed
118mph**
190km/h

*Right: The 2 liter Bristol
engine, as fitted to the Ace
from 1956. At $1875 it cost
a significant $335 more
than the AC-powered
version.*

*Below: A 1955 AC-engined
Ace. It was owned for some
years by photographer Neill
Bruce, whose work appears
in this and many other
motoring books.*

 The handsome, sure-footed, open two-seater Ace, a car capable of over 115mph (185km/h) in its most potent form, enjoyed a respectable ten-year production life. More significantly it is best remembered for having formed the basis of the legendary Cobra.

Paradoxically, the Ace did not begin life at AC's Thames Ditton, Surrey factory but at the Hertfordshire premises of engineer John Tojiero who designed, for the club racing fraternity, a tubular chassis fitted with all-independent transverse leaf suspension. Cliff Davis was one such competitor and in 1952 he acquired a Tojiero frame in which he fitted a Bristol engine. The mechanicals were then enclosed by an open two-seater body inspired by the Ferrari 166 Barchetta that had won the 1949 Mille Milgia race.

Following a successful 1953 racing season, by chance AC's Charles Hurlock heard of this car and decided to acquire it. There followed a rapid transformation which turned it into the Ace which the company then displayed at the 1953 London Motor Show. The only principal difference was the removal of the Bristol engine and its replacement by AC's long-running, 2 liter, overhead-camshaft, six-cylinder alloy unit. However, while this was extraordinarily advanced when it was unveiled in 1919, 34 years on it was nearing the end of its life.

Choice of engines

Nevertheless, it was destined to remain available in triple carburetored 85bhp form throughout the Ace's production span; so powered, this lively open two-seater was able comfortably to exceed 100mph (161km/h). Early in 1956 the Ace was also offered with a choice of 105 and 120bhp Bristol engines which transformed its performance. So equipped, the Ace could now exceed 115mph (185km/h).

By this time the model had spawned a derivative in the shape of the Aceca coupé of 1955 that was also available in Bristol-powered form. Yet a further variant was the longer-wheelbase Greyhound coupé of 1960 with coil spring and wishbone independent front suspension.

Unfortunately in its latter years the Ace was threatened with a loss of engines. AC's six was nearing the end of its development, while Bristol was making the switch to a Chrysler V8 and so its potent and versatile six was destined for extinction. As a result in mid-1961 the Ace was offered with a 2.6 liter Ford Zephyr engine in varying states of tune. Perhaps surprisingly, the Ford-powered open two-seater could exceed 110mph (177km/h).

The model ceased production in 1963. But this was far from being the end of the story because American racing driver Carroll Shelby proposed that it should form the basis of the Cobra (see page 94). So the Ace survived, in essence, for a further six years.

Specification	AC Ace (Bristol 100D engine)
Engine location	Front, in-line
Configuration	Six-cylinder
Bore and stroke	66 x 96mm
Capacity	1971cc
Valve operation	Pushrod
Horsepower	120bhp @ 6000rpm
Transmission	Manual four-speed
Drive	Rear
Chassis	Twin tubular
Suspension – front	Transverse leaf and wishbone
Suspension – rear	Transverse leaf and wishbone
Brakes	Drum
Top speed	118mph (190km/h)
Acceleration	0-60mph (0-96km/h): 9.2 seconds

Left: Cockpit of the 1955 Ace, the 50th built. Owners occasionally specified that the handbrake should be moved from the transmission tunnel to the right of the driver's seat.

Below: The earlier cars had circular rear lights while later versions had a shorter trunk lid to improve aerodynamics when the roof was raised.

Mercedes-Benz 300SL

**Top speed
140mph**
225km/h

One of the truly delectable dream cars, the 300SL coupé is forever remembered for its upward-opening gullwing doors to the extent that its 140mph (225km/h) top speed, fast now but truly sensational in 1954, is often overlooked. It was an instant thoroughbred.

The 300SL, signifying 3 liter super light, was competition bred, its sports-racing predecessor having appeared in 1952. It was powered by a six-cylinder overhead camshaft engine, courtesy of the 300S road car, but this and other production components imposed a weight penalty. The Stuttgart engineers strove to save precious kilograms by the use of a light, strong, but complex tubular space-frame chassis. This demanded that the tubes should be continued as high as possible along the sides of the driving compartment which, in turn, ruled out the use of conventional doors. The answer was the imaginative and ingenious gullwing units that opened vertically and were hinged along the coupé's roof line.

These cars had dominated the 1952 racing season but they were not campaigned in the following year because corporate resources were dedicated to the successful launch and running of the W196 Formula 1 car.

However, in New York, Max Hoffman, a car dealer *par excellence* who specialized in the import of European sports models, convinced Mercedes-

Right: The steering wheel hinged along its center to allow the driver to get in. Only left-hand-drive cars were built.

Below: The gullwing 300SL in all its glory. The grille in the front fender was intended to permit hot air to escape from the engine compartment.

Left: The 300SL's 3 liter, six-cylinder, single-overhead-camshaft engine inclined 50 degrees from the vertical to permit a low hood line. Fitted with Bosch fuel injection, it was the first production car to be so equipped. A dry sump unit, it was a modified version of that used in the company's 300 model which appeared in 1951.

Benz of the viability of a roadgoing version of the gorgeous gullwing coupé and promptly ordered 1000. The resulting model was the star of the 1954 New York sports car show.

Racing pedigree

Under the hood the 3 liter, six-cylinder, Bosch fuel-injected engine, the first to be fitted in a production car, was inclined to the left to permit a low body line, although this ruled out a right-hand-drive version. The use of dry sump lubrication was a further reminder of the model's racing pedigree while an all-synchromesh gearbox with a floor change, rather than Mercedes' usual column system, was employed.

With room for only two occupants, the steering wheel hinged forward at its lower edge to permit the driver to get in. There was some space behind the seats for luggage but, although the trunk outwardly appeared reasonably large, most of the space was occupied by the spare wheel and the large gas tank.

The coupé's acceleration was phenomenal: it could reach 70mph (113km/h) in second gear and 98mph (158km/h) in third. But handling was tricky and maintenance costs formidable. Nonetheless exactly 1400 examples had been completed when production ceased in 1957. Of these, 29 were lightened cars. These desirable models had all-alloy bodywork and enhanced engines, and were capable of 155mph (249km/h).

Left: One of the famous gullwing doors in the open position. They do take a little time to open and Mercedes-Benz experimented with a variety of handles before finalizing the design. Luggage was stored behind the front seats, the manufacturer offering bespoke suitcases that were held in place with straps to fit into the space.

Specification	Mercedes-Benz 300SL
Engine location	Front, in-line
Configuration	Six-cylinder
Bore and stroke	85 x 88mm
Capacity	2996cc
Valve operation	Single overhead camshaft
Horsepower	190bhp @ 6100rpm
Transmission	Manual four-speed
Drive	Rear
Chassis	Tubular steel space-frame
Suspension – front	Wishbones and coil spring
Suspension – rear	Swing axle and coil spring
Brakes	Drum
Top speed	140mph (225km/h)
Acceleration	0-60mph (0-96km/h): 8.9 seconds

But this was not quite the end of the 300SL story because a roadster version, which replaced the coupé, was unveiled at the 1957 Geneva Motor Show. This featured substantially the same styling and included the distinctive vented hot air outlets in the fenders. The fact that it was an open car did, of course, preclude the fitment of gullwing doors, but the space-frame chassis was retained and modified to accommodate conventionally hung ones.

Unpredictable handling

While the 3 liter fuel-injected engine was retained, changes were made to the rear swing axle. The coupé's unpredictable handling was put down to shortcomings in its design and a third horizontal compensator spring was introduced to reduce rear-end roll stiffness and so aid roadholding.

However, this was no sports car in the sense of the traditional British open two-seater – the folding roof was contained out of sight beneath a cover when not in use, and the windows were of the wind-up variety with not a side screen to be seen! There was also a smart and substantial factory hardtop available.

It was offered with a choice of no less than five different rear axle ratios which meant that top speeds varied between 129mph (208km/h) and what the factory optimistically claimed as a flat-out speed of 155mph (249km/h).

In fact the open car was rather slower than the coupé because of its inferior aerodynamics and the fact that the roadster was also heavier by some 2000lb (907kg). It could, nevertheless, exceed 135mph (217km/h). From 1961 this impressive performance was kept in check by all-round disc brakes; previously all-round discs had sufficed.

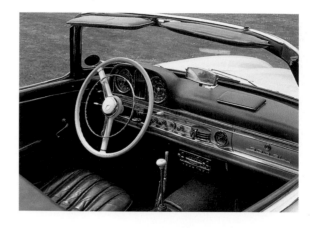

The 300SL roadster was destined to remain in production until 1963 during which time 1858 examples were sold, making it rather more popular than the coupé that inspired its creation.

The last member of this fabulous family was the sports racing 300SLR of 1954. This was, in truth, mechanically related to the W196 Formula 1 car mentioned earlier. It was also a roadster with a space-frame chassis although the engine was a 3 liter, fuel-injected, straight eight, 282bhp roller bearing unit with high efficiency desmodromic valve gear. This meant that the valves were closed mechanically rather than being operated by the usual springs.

Racing manager Rudolph Uhlenhaut ran a coupé version, which outwardly resembled a conventional 300SL coupé, apart from the twin exhaust pipes that wickedly emerged on the passenger's side of the car. Performance was shattering – it was capable of 136mph (219km/h) in fourth gear and 180mph (290km/h) in top. Needless to say it was never officially offered by Mercedes-Benz and just two were completed.

Above: *A legendary duo reunited at the 1995 Goodwood Festival of Speed. Stirling Moss at the wheel of a 1957 300SLR with Denis Jenkinson, Motor Sport magazine's famous correspondent, who had both won the 1955 Mille Miglia in such a car.*

Left: *The sports racing 300SL coupé of 1952 from which the roadgoing 300SL sprang. A trio of cars were entered in that year's Carrera-Pan American race and one car won at an incredible 102.35mph (164.71km/h) with another example in second place.*

Facel Vega HK500

**Top speed
147mph**
237km/h

*Below: Unmistakable and
rapid, the Franco/American
Facel Vega HK500 of 1959,
by which time right-hand-
drive was available. The
sills were protected by
stainless steel pressings
which also made a visual
contribution to the design.
The deep windshield and
low hood resulted in good
visibility for the driver.*

Take a powerful American V8 engine and
install it in a distinctive coupé body,
complete with aircraft-style controls, and
you have the essentials of the Facel Vega, a French
make that only survived a mere ten years.

Launched at the 1954 Paris Salon, the model
was the brainchild of Jean Daninos, whose
business, *Forges et Ateliers de Construction d'Eure
et Loire* (hence Facel), produced specialist car
bodies for the likes of Panhard, Simca and Ford
France. However, as the mass-produced sedan
moved center stage, this aspect of Daninos'
business began to decline, so he decided to produce
his own cars. The two-door Facel Vega FVS was
the result. The car's appearance was chunky, the
twin vertically mounted headlamps distinctive and
the well appointed interior was awash with
aeronautical themes.

Luxury seating

The instruments extended into a console located
between the front seats, establishing a trend in car
design that continues to this day. Occupants
luxuriously reclined in 'roly-poly' seats.
Refinements included such transatlantic influences
as electric windows and the twin radio aerials that
sprouted from the rear fins. In fact only one of
them was operative!

The engine compartment was pure Detroit.
Initially Daninos chose a 4.5 liter 'hemi' Chrysler
V8 which had been used in its De Soto make.
There was, inevitably, Powerflite two-speed
automatic transmission although a manual gearbox
was available at extra cost. Even in this form the
FVS was capable of some 130mph (209km/h) in
the manner of the pre-war *grand routiers* which
mopped up the kilometers with such ease.

Specification	**Facel Vega** HK500
Engine location	Front, in-line
Configuration	V8
Bore and stroke	104 x 85mm
Capacity	5910cc
Valve operation	Pushrod
Horsepower	360bhp @ 5200rpm
Transmission	Manual four-speed
Drive	Rear
Chassis	Unitary
Suspension – front	Wishbones and coil spring
Suspension – rear	Half-elliptic spring
Brakes	Disc
Top speed	147mph (237km/h)
Acceleration	0-60mph (0-96km/h: 8.5 seconds

Nevertheless, it was not long before Daninos began to opt for larger engines, their capacity first being increased to 4.8, then 5.4 and, ultimately, 5.8 liters. The less popular and unwieldy four-door Excellence followed in 1958.

The HK500, the definitive Facel, appeared in 1959. It was essentially an uprated FVS although it was by then packing a 5.9 liter V8 and 360bhp under its hood. Power steering was then well established and the 500 was a 147mph (237km/h) car, even if disc brakes did not arrive until 1960.

The end of the line

The 6.3 liter Facel II, the last of the line, appeared in 1962. It was outwardly more attractive, being lower and more angular, although this was to the detriment of the driving position. There was even more power with a 390bhp option but the model only survived for two years.

Sadly, Daninos' business foundered in 1964, partly because of his decision to introduce the smaller and cheaper Facellia with its own purpose-designed engine.

Above left: The Facel Vega's unusual deeply dished steering wheel. Note the quantity of instrumentation and that the minor controls are located within the innovative central console. The leather-trimmed seats were particularly comfortable, and the cockpit was roomy when judged by the standards of the day.

Left: The twin vertically mounted headlamps dated from the marque's origins in 1954 and were later adopted by the American motor industry in the early 1960s. The steering was moderately low-geared. By this time all-round Dunlop disc brakes had been fitted. In truth, the expensive, well-equipped HK500 had no direct rivals.

Porsche 356 Carrera

**Top speed
125mph**
201km/h

*Right: The presence of the
legendary Carrera name on
the rear engine cover
informed other motorists
that this was a rather
special 356.*

*Below: The well-appointed
356 GS Carrera cabriolet
of 1959 fitted with a rare
original factory hardtop.
Note the gold scripted model
name on the front fender.*

 The 356, the first model in the fabled
Porsche line, appeared in 1948. The
Carrera version, named in celebration of
Porsche's successes in the 1952/54 Carrera
Panamerica Mexico races, was a potent, noisy, yet
highly desirable derivative.

The Stuttgart-based Porsche design bureau was
responsible for the creation of the Volkswagen
Beetle, destined to be the world's best-selling car.
So when Dr Ferdinand's Porsche's son, Ferry,
decided to produce a sports cars, it was inevitably
based on VW mechanicals that were cloaked in an
aerodynamically refined body produced in mainly
coupé and also cabriolet (open) forms.

It was unsurprisingly powered by a rear-
mounted, air-cooled, 1.1 liter, horizontally opposed,
four-cylinder engine, boosted from 25 to 40bhp,
although purpose-designed components were
progressively introduced. The all-independent
torsion bar suspension also came from VW.

Top-of-the-range

For 1956 Porsche introduced the revised 1.6 liter
356A with the Carrera being the top-of-the-range
car. Its 100bhp, 1.5 liter engine (courtesy of the
company's 550 Spyder 1955 sports racer) was
detuned for road use. Instead of employing the
usual pushrods, a train of gears actuated inclined

Left: The driving compartment of the 1959 GS Carrera with its de luxe leather trim showing to advantage. The gear lever operated a four-speed gearbox, a great virtue of which was that unbeatable synchromesh was fitted to all gears. This was Porsche's own patented balk ring system.

Below: The 1963 Carrera 2, introduced in the previous year, was the fastest Porsche of its day, even if the company still claimed a top speed of 125mph (201km/h)! The enlarged 2 liter engine developed 130bhp; the model remained in limited production until 1965.

valves in hemispherical cylinder heads. There was a built-up roller bearing Hirth crankshaft with roller conrods and dual ignition which serviced two spark plugs per cylinder.

This raucous power unit endowed the Carrera with a top speed nudging the 125mph (201km/h) mark and made it the fastest 1.5 liter car of its day. Available in coupé, cabriolet, hardtop and no-frills two-seater Speedster forms, the only outwardly visible indication of its power was a gold-finished *Carrera* badge on the engine cover.

From 1958 engine capacity was increased to 1.6 liters. In a bid to quieten the beast, the original crankshaft was replaced by a conventional plain bearing unit.

The mainstream 356B line arrived for 1960 and the Carrera 2 version followed in 1962. This was powered by a 2 liter, 130bhp engine which produced about the same top speed as the original, although acceleration was improved. It also had the virtue of being the first Porsche road car to be fitted with all-round disc brakes.

Extensively raced and rallied, the Carrera was discontinued in 1965 as the company's purpose-designed sports racers moved center stage. However, the name has remained as an intrinsic and respected part of the Porsche model range ever since.

Specification	Porsche Carrera (1.5 liter)
Engine location	Rear, in-line
Configuration	Horizontally opposed four-cylinder
Bore and stroke	85 x 66mm
Capacity	1498cc
Valve operation	Twin overhead camshafts per bank
Horsepower	115bhp @ 6200rpm
Transmission	Manual four-speed
Drive	Rear
Chassis	Platform
Suspension – front	Trailing arms and torsion bar
Suspension – rear	Swing axle and torsion bar
Brakes	Drum
Top speed	125mph (201km/h)
Acceleration	0-60mph (0-96km/h): 11.3 seconds

Alfa Romeo Giulietta SS

**Top speed
124mph**
199km/h

 An inspired union of Alfa Romeo's sophisticated mechanicals and Bertone's extravagant styling resulted in the Giulietta SS coupé, a car that was able to exceed 120mph (193km/h) when it appeared in 1957. It is considered by many enthusiasts to be one of the most beautiful Alfa Romeos of the post-war years.

Its origins are to be found in the Giulietta Sprint of 1955, a Bertone-styled coupé capable of attaining 110mph (177km/h). This, perversely, appeared before the four-door sedan on which it was based! In both instances power came from a 1.3 liter, twin-overhead-camshaft engine which developed 55bhp in its most basic form. The Sprint, by contrast, had an 80bhp unit which was also available in 90bhp Sprint Veloce guise.

Styling by Bertone

Then, at the 1957 Geneva Motor Show, the SS was unveiled. The initials stood for Sprint Speciale. This creation had a daring and extravagantly styled Bertone body that revealed the influence of a series of experimental aerodynamically related BAT (*Berlina Aerodinamica Tecnica*) cars produced between 1953 and 1955.

Unlike the Sprint which was built by Alfa Romeo, Bertone had responsibility for the SS's production. The aim was to produce a lighter, more aerodynamically efficient coupé, and although aluminum was originally used for its construction, from 1959 this was changed to steel. The model was based on shortened version of the Sprint's sub-structure with a 7ft 5in (2260mm) wheelbase; this was 4in (101mm) less than its predecessor. There was only room for two people, and understandably not much space for their luggage. However, the SS was cheaper than the more spacious Sprint.

Ministrations to the SS's 100bhp engine included the fitment of twin Weber carburetors and a higher 9.7:1 compression ratio. A five-speed gearbox was employed. There was also a version

Above: The Bertone-bodied Giulietta Sprint Veloce, this version boasting 90bhp rather than the customary 80. In consequence it could attain 110mph (177km/h), rather than the usual 100mph (161km/h) plus. Handling was excellent.

Right: A 1961 Guilietta SZ. Zagato arrived at this shape without the aid of a wind tunnel but rather by trial and error on the autostrada. Unveiled at the 1960 Turin Motor Show, it featured a light steel frame clad with alloy panels.

Specification	Alfa Romeo Giulietta SS
Engine location	Front, in-line
Configuration	Four-cylinder
Bore and stroke	74 x 75mm
Capacity	1290cc
Valve operation	Twin overhead camshaft
Horsepower	100bhp @ 6500rpm
Transmission	Manual five-speed
Drive	Rear
Chassis	Unitary
Suspension – front	Wishbones and coil spring
Suspension – rear	Live axle, coil spring
Brakes	Drum
Top speed	124mph (199km/h)
Acceleration	0-60mph (96km/h): 11.3 seconds

with a chunky Zagato body called the SZ; 200 of these were built. This was lighter than the Bertone-built car as Zagato dispensed with much of the original underframe. Designed for racing, its top speed remained about the same although it accelerated harder than its stablemate.

Of the two, the SS was the more practical and thus the more popular car, and 1366 examples were completed by the time that the Giulietta, on which it was based, ceased production in 1962. Its replacement that year was the Giulia sedan. The SS remained in production and was accorded the new name. A further 1400 were duly completed with the last of the line being built in 1965, the final 30 examples being fitted with all-round disc brakes, a somewhat belated refinement.

Above: A 1963 Giulietta Sprint Speciale, the most beautiful of the post-war Alfa Romeos.

Above left: The Sprint Speciale's dials were readily visible to the driver.

MGA Twin Cam

**Top speed
113mph**
182km/h

*Below: The standard
pushrod-engined MGA
roadster of 1959, then the
most popular sports car in
the world. This 1.6 liter
version was enhanced by
front disc brakes and wire
wheels were available at
extra cost. Most were
exported to the USA.
However, side screens were
still fitted; winding windows
would have to wait until
the MGB.*

The long awaited replacement for the T-Series family, the MGA of 1955 was destined to become the world's most popular sports car. Over 100,000 had been completed by the time that production ceased in 1962 with about 80 per cent of this output having been sold in America.

If MG had been left to its own devices, the A could have entered production in 1952. That was when the Abingdon factory produced a prototype, designated EX 175, which closely resembled the finished product, but in the same year Morris Motors, of which MG was a part, had merged with Austin to form the British Motor Corporation. And the chairman, Leonard Lord, chose the Healey 100 (see page 82) as BMC's corporate sports car.

The MGA eventually reached public view three years later, but because the model had not yet been officially announced, a trio of cars were run at the 1955 Le Mans race under the EX 182 name. Two were placed 12th and 17th while the third one crashed in the fifth hour.

Open two-seater

Designed by MG's chief engineer, Syd Enever, the MGA was officially launched at the 1955 London Motor Show as a well proportioned, full-width, open two-seater. As befitted the merged businesses, the 1.5 liter pushrod engine was of Austin origin, and was known as the B- Series in corporate parlance. It endowed the A with a top speed of over 95mph (153km/h).

The 1957 season saw the roadster joined by a coupé version. The engine was enlarged to 1588cc in 1959 although top speed remained about the same. A Mark II version of the design followed in 1961 with the engine's capacity again being increased, this time to 1622cc; the revised cars were outwardly identifiable by a recessed radiator grille. The A was replaced in 1962 by the even more successful MGB.

In a meantime a more potent version of the MGA had entered production in 1958. This was the Twin Cam that was somewhat faster than the original, being able to exceed 110mph (177km/h).

Available in both roadster and coupé forms, it outwardly resembled the originals, with the exception of handsome center-lock Dunlop disc wheels. All-round disc brakes were a further departure from the original specification. Under the hood was a 1588cc, B-Series-based, 108bhp, twin-overhead-camshaft engine.

Twin Cams were briefly raced by MG in 1958, before a corporate ban on competition put a stop to such activities. However, the road cars, unusually for an Abingdon product, suffered from niggling faults. These were progressively resolved but they had damaged the model's sales prospects and production ceased in 1960 after just 2111 Twin Cams had been completed. They are, consequently, much sought after today by collectors.

Above: One of the few giveaways of what lurked beneath the hood, these badges adorned the top of each front fender.

Left: A Twin Cam roadster shod with the distinctive center-lock Dunlop wheels. Disc brakes were fitted all round. It was also available in coupé form.

Below left: The BMC-based twin-overhead-camshaft engine, which developed some 30bhp more than the pushrod version. Reliable – if sensitively maintained!

Specification	MGA Twin Cam
Engine location	Front, in-line
Configuration	Four-cylinder
Bore and stroke	75 x 89mm
Capacity	1588cc
Valve operation	Twin overhead camshaft
Horsepower	108bhp @ 6700rpm
Transmission	Manual four-speed
Drive	Rear
Chassis	Box section
Suspension – front	Wishbones and coil spring
Suspension – rear	Half-elliptic spring
Brakes	Disc
Top speed	113mph (182km/h)
Acceleration	0-60mph (0-96km/h): 13.3 seconds

Ferrari 410 Superamerica

**Top speed
165mph**
266km/h

Below: Rare and rapid, this style of Pinin Farina body was only applied in 1959 to 10 or 12 Superamericas. About half had cowled headlights while the final four or five, of which this car is one, featured exposed units. These so-called Series 3 cars were produced in 1958 and 1959 and their 4.9 liter V12 engines developed an impressive 400bhp.

 It did not take Enzo Ferrari long to recognize the potential of the transatlantic market. In 1951 he launched his potent, costly and exclusive America models, a line which led to the 410 Superamerica of 1955.

In those early years there was a close relationship between Ferrari's racing and road cars and this particularly applied to the America series. Formula 1 regulations of the 1946-1951 era specified that race cars should either have 1.5 liter supercharged engines or 4.5 liter uncharged ones. Prior to 1950, Ferrari, like most manufacturers, opted for the latter configuration. However, in that year his chief engineer Aurelio Lampredi created the Type 375 Formula 1 car which was powered by the larger V12 and the success it enjoyed effectively spelt the end of the supercharger in grand prix racing.

The first example of the line, the 340 America, was unveiled at the 1950 Paris Motor Show with a 4.1 liter V12 'Lampredi' engine mated to a five-speed all synchromesh gearbox. The cars which followed were variously bodied by Vignale and, in particular, Ghia. Most were sports racers – of the 22 completed, only about eight were road cars.

For 1953 came the 342 America, a more civilized road car, mostly bodied by Pininfarina. Only six were built. Its 375 America successor was produced in rather larger numbers. It had a 4.5 liter engine and the 350bhp it developed meant a top speed of some 130mph (209km/h).

Faster replacement

Its 410 Superamerica replacement for the 1956 season had a 340bhp 5 liter engine. It was even faster, being capable of between 137mph and 162mph (220km/h and 260km/h), depending on the rear axle ratio chosen by the owner. Again production was limited, only 15 were completed, and most were Pinin Farina coupés.

In 1957 the 410 received the longer 8ft 6in (2600mm) chassis of its Superfast stablemate; these were designated the Series 2 cars but only about seven were completed. However, the Series 3 of 1958-59 was, by contrast, almost mass produced because 15 were built. While this retained its predecessor's 4.1 liter V12 engine, changes to the cylinder head design saw its output soar to 400bhp.

As befitted their name, most of these cars were sold in America; tellingly the US *Road & Track* magazine recorded a top speed of 165mph (266km/h) in a three-year-old example with a slipping clutch!

For the record, the 410 Superamerica of 1960 was the last of the line and one of the fastest road cars in the world being able to hit the 180mph (290km/h) mark. It was a car with few rivals, with the possible exception of the Maserati 5000 GT.

Left: The vented side panels adjoining the rear windows of these Series 3 cars revived a feature that had appeared on Ferrari's 4.9 Superfast of 1957 and replaced the glass of the earlier cars. Note the Pinin Farina badge mounted on the door panel which has moved from its customary location on the fender because of the presence of hot air outlets.

Left: The Superamerica's dashboard is unusual because, instead of being covered in the customary leather, Ferrari instead opted for a black crackle paint finish that had previously been reserved for its sports-racing cars. Practically every example was left-hand drive.

Specification	Ferrari 410 Superamerica Series 3
Engine location	Front, in-line
Configuration	V12
Bore and stroke	88 x 68mm
Capacity	4962cc
Valve operation	Single overhead camshaft per cylinder bank
Horsepower	340bhp @ 6000rpm
Transmission	Manual four-speed
Drive	Rear
Chassis	Oval tubular
Suspension – front	Wishbones and coil spring
Suspension – rear	Half-elliptic spring
Brakes	Drum
Top speed	165mph (266km/h); see text
Acceleration	0-60mph (0-96km/h): N/A

BMW 507

**Top speed
125mph**
201km/h

*Right: The 507's engine
was not only Germany's
first V8 but also, in 1954,
the first in the world to be
mass-produced in alloy.
The twin carburetors are
Zenith units.*

*Below: A modern classic, a
507 with the hardtop in
place. Although it is
detachable, it looks an
integral part of the body.
Paradoxically, sales were
slow although today it is a
much sought-after car.*

 Capable of nearly 125mph (201km/h),
BMW's graceful but expensive 507 did
not, alas, attract customers in great
numbers; only 250 examples were produced
between 1956 and 1959. BMW cars had been built
before World War II at Eisenach in what
subsequently became East Germany. Production of
a 2 liter 501 sedan, based on the pre-war 326, did
not restart at the company's former aero-engine
factory in Munich until 1951.

The 507's origins can be traced to this model. It
was much improved by the fitting, in 1954, of a
new 2.5 liter aluminum V8 engine. This was a first
in Germany – the car was designated the 502. It
was designed by Fritz Fiedler, who had returned to
BMW after a spell in England, where he had been
responsible for the design of Frazer Nash's High
Speed model (page 30).

With its engine enlarged to 3168cc in 1955, the
502 was renamed the 3.2 and survived in this form
until 1961. At that year's Frankfurt Motor Show
BMW introduced the 503 which was based on the
3.2 chassis. This was endowed with a new coupé
body by the German-born freelance stylist Count

Albert Goertz, who had opened a design studio in
New York in 1951. He had been encouraged to bid
for the BMW assignment by importer Max
Hoffman, who specialized in the sale of European
cars and who had played a catalytic part in the
creation of the race-bred and fabulous Mercedes-
Benz 300SL gullwing coupé.

The 507, a short wheelbase derivative which
had 16in (400mm) taken out of its chassis, was
even more attractive. Goertz's flawless roadster
body is rightly regarded today as styling of the

Specification	BMW 507
Engine location	Front, in-line
Configuration	V8
Bore and stroke	82 x 75mm
Capacity	3168cc
Valve operation	Pushrod
Horsepower	150bhp @ 5000rpm
Transmission	Manual four-speed
Drive	Rear
Chassis	Box section and tubular
Suspension – front	Wishbone and torsion bar
Suspension – rear	Torsion bar with live axle
Brakes	Drum
Top speed	125mph (201km/h)
Acceleration	0-60mph (0-96km/h): 8.8 seconds

highest order. However, it differed from its predecessors by being the first BMW not to feature the marque's famous and distinctive kidney-shaped vertical twin radiator grilles. Instead he opted for a horizontal rendering of the familiar theme.

Inside, the car was compact – only two people could be accommodated. An optional substantial hardtop transformed the 507 into a coupé. The result was a very real rival to Mercedes-Benz's 300SL coupé, but without the latter's mechanical complexity and its challenging accommodation.

Sensational appearance

The engine was a 150bhp version of the V8 and performance matched the sensational looks. But the 507 was expensive. It was only available in left-hand-drive form and its price in Britain was £5251, a sum which would have bought two and a half Jaguar XK150s.

Sadly production only built up very slowly and America, which should have proved a strong

market for the model, did not receive its first 507 until two years after the 1955 Frankfurt launch. In consequence production only ran from November 1956 until May 1959. But the 507 concept survives, in spirit, in the form of BMW's current Z8 sports car of 2000 (see page 280).

Above left: The four-speed gearbox was an all-synchromesh unit and, unusually, was separate from the engine, being located under the front seat.

Above: Looking just as good without the hardtop, the 507 in more sporting mode. Echoes of its hot air outlet are to be found in BMW's current Z8.

Left: Nice lines, the 507's styling shown to good effect. For aerodynamic reasons an undershield was fitted, a feature that also applied to some Ferraris.

Jaguar XK SS

**Top speed
145mph +
233km/h**

Right: Essentially a D-Type but with revised dashboard and lacking the sports racers' central rib and cowl. The doors are small and hinge downward; the windshield is high enough to provide ample protection from the weather.

Below: The presence of a full-width windshield, bumpers, shielded muffler system, and luggage rack identifies the XK SS. The side windows do not wind. This car, chassis no 757, was dispatched in July 1957 and exported to Hong Kong.

A sports racer for the road, the XK SS was a mildly detuned version of Jaguar's Le Mans-winning D-Type. Able to attain over 145mph (233km/h), this rare and now highly collectible model was both expensive, at $5430, and impractical. As a consequence, only 16 examples were completed.

The Coventry company's first purpose-designed sports racer was the C-Type of 1951. Following a win that year at Le Mans and again in 1953, chief engineer William Heynes recognized that a new car would be necessary if Jaguar was to maintain its pre-eminent position.

The result in 1954 was the legendary D-Type, the most famous Jaguar sports racer of all time. Heynes' intention had been to reduce weight, improve aerodynamics, and increase the power of the 3.4 liter engine. To these ends the C-Type's tubular chassis was replaced by a monocoque tub with the engine and front suspension mounted on an extended framework of square section magnesium tubing. This was cloaked in a beautifully styled open two-seater body, with a distinctive fin behind the driver. This was the work of the company's aerodynamicist Malcolm Sayer.

Victory at Le Mans

Although the cars failed to win Le Mans in 1954, they proved victorious in 1955 and 1956, at which point Jaguar announced its withdrawal from racing. However, a D-Type entered by the Scottish Ecurie Ecosse racing stable was victorious in 1957.

Having withdrawn from racing, the firm retained a number of unsold D-Types and it decided to convert these to road use and market them as the XK SS. The lines remained essentially the same, but the fin was dispensed with. There was a rudimentary top and a full-width windshield. A passenger's seat and door were introduced while the exhaust, which emitted much heat and noise, emerged directly below it!

There was no room for a trunk. The space where one should have been was occupied by the spare wheel and twin flexible aircraft-style 43-gallon (164lit) gas tanks. So a luggage rack was attached to the tail to which could be secured a solitary suitcase.

Ravaged by fire

The 250bhp, dry sump, triple-Weber-carburetored, XK twin-cam engine was essentially the same as that fitted to the racers. However, sales, unlike acceleration, were sluggish. Then the production line was damaged by a fire that ravaged Jaguar's Browns Lane factory in February 1956.

Production restarted in March, but then stopped entirely in November. Of the 16 examples completed, a total of 12 were exported across the Atlantic, the car being eligible for Sports Car Club of America events. Despite its poor sales record, the seeds had been sown for the greatest of all Jaguar sports cars. The D-inspired E-Type appeared in 1961. This proved, unlike the XK SS, to be a stunning sales success.

Above: With its D-Type ancestry clearly apparent, in 1957 the Jaguar XK SS was one of the fastest cars on the road.

Left: With a forward-hingeing hood inherited by its legendary successor, the XK SS's engine is readily accessible.

Specification	Jaguar XK SS
Engine location	Front, in-line
Configuration	Six-cylinder
Bore and stroke	83 x 106mm
Capacity	3442cc
Valve operation	Twin overhead camshaft
Horsepower	250bhp @ 6000rpm
Transmission	Manual four-speed
Drive	Rear
Chassis	Monocoque/squared tubular front sub-frame
Suspension – front	Wishbones and torsion bar
Suspension – rear	Trailing arms and torsion bar
Brakes	Disc
Top speed	Over 145mph (233km/h)
Acceleration	0-60mph (0-96km/h): 5.2 seconds

Lotus Elite

**Top speed
115mph**
185km/h

*Right: A Stage II version of
the Coventry Climax FWE
engine with twin SUs, high-
lift cam and four-branch
exhaust.*

*Below: The Elite, still
looking good, was a
triumph for its amateur
stylist, accountant Peter
Kirwan-Taylor. This is a
1962 example.*

Lotus's first significant road car, the
visually stunning 115mph (185km/h) Elite
coupé of 1958, also had the distinction of
being the world's first glass-fiber monocoque. It
was undeniably noisy but it was light and it offered
its owners, in the best traditions of the marque,
outstanding handling.

Colin Chapman's North London-based Lotus
concern had produced its first kit car in 1953 and
initially offered club racers multi-tubular chassis
which were then powered by a variety engines,
mostly side-valve Ford units. The Elite, coded
Lotus 14 in the corporate design register, made its
appearance at the 1957 London Motor Show.
Endowed with a magnificent coupé body, the work
of Chapman's accountant friend Peter Kirwan-
Taylor, it was powered by a 1.2 liter, 75bhp, FWE
single-overhead-camshaft, Coventry Climax engine
derived from a fire pump unit!

Chapman strut

Suspension was all-independent with coil springs and wishbones at the front and a so-called Chapman strut, named after Lotus's founder, at the rear. Because of the pioneering construction, the Elite lacked a conventional chassis and accordingly weighed just 1484lb (673kg). Acceleration was impressive for a 1.2 liter car, 60mph (0-96km/h) arriving in a little over 12 seconds. A downside of the monocoque concept was that noise levels were unacceptably high, although this did not appear to adversely affect sales, initially at least.

The Elite was strictly a two-seater and the spare wheel lived on a shelf behind the occupants. There were roomy storage bins in the doors – these were for the windows which did not wind down, but which could be removed and stored in pockets behind the seats. This was regarded as a disadvantage by some potential buyers.

Production did not begin until December 1958, when the first customer was band leader, Chris Barber. In June 1959 Lotus moved from its cramped North London premises to a new, larger factory at Cheshunt, Hertfordshire. The overwhelming majority of cars were produced there although the bodies were made by Bristol.

Improvements were incorporated into the Series 2 Elite that arrived for the 1961 season – the principal alterations were suspension changes and the fitment of a ZF five-speed gearbox. In its original form the Elite had been fitted with a single carburetor, but the Special Equipment model, that also arrived for the 1961 model year, had a 83bhp engine fitted with twin SUs and a four branch tuned exhaust system.

Specification	Lotus Elite
Engine location	Front, in-line
Configuration	Four-cylinder
Bore and stroke	76 x 66mm
Capacity	1220cc
Valve operation	Single overhead camshaft
Horsepower	75bhp @ 6100rpm
Transmission	Manual four-speed
Drive	Rear
Chassis	Unitary
Suspension – front	Coil springs
Suspension – rear	Strut, coil spring, and radius arm
Brakes	Disc
Top speed	115mph (185km/h)
Acceleration	0-60mph (0-96km/h): 12.2 seconds

In 1962 the Elite became available in kit form. By the time that production ceased in 1963 about 1000 examples had been completed. However, Colin Chapman did not persist with the innovative construction – the new offering, called the Elan, had a separate chassis and was an open car, something the Elite, because of its ingenious design, could never have been.

Below: The Elite name was revived by Lotus in 1974 for this four-seater sports hatchback with the glass-fiber bodywork the only common denominator. This latter-day Elite survived until 1983.

Left: Access to the Elite's interior was reasonably good, thanks to the fact that the window opening extended into the roof structure. The wood-rimmed steering wheel was considered to be large in its day, being over 16in (406mm) in diameter. It was later reduced in size. Ingeniously the contours of the metal instrument panel echo the car's profile.

Aston Martin DB4, DB5, DB6

**Top speed
140mph**
225km/h

 The fastest British GT of its day, the magnificently Italian-styled DB4 of 1958 could attain 140mph (225km/h). It was the first model of a line that endured until 1971.

There were no legacies from the previous DB2 generation of road cars. Chief engineer Harold Beech was made responsible for the mechanicals while the 240bhp, 3.6 liter, twin-overhead-camshaft, alloy engine was the work of the company's Tadek Marek. However, there the home-grown influence ended. General manager John Wyer was determined that the body should be designed in Italy rather than being entrusted to a British stylist. The resulting coupé was the work of the famous Milan-based Carrozzeria Touring. Built to its superleggera principles, which featured a sub-structure of small diameter load-bearing tubes, the bodies were made under licence at Aston Martin's Newport Pagnell factory.

Announced at the 1958 Paris Motor Show, the DB4 was destined to survive until 1963. However, in truth, it entered production too soon and early examples were plagued with engine and gearbox

Below: The sought-after GT version of the DB4. Identifiable by its shorter wheelbase, enlarged hood scoop, lightweight Borrani wheels, and aerodynamically cowled headlamps, just 75 examples were completed between 1959 and 1963. The more potent engine differed from the standard DB4 in being fitted with twin sparking plugs and developed 272bhp, even if Aston Martin claimed 302!

problems. These shortcomings had been largely resolved by the time that the 260bhp Vantage engine arrived in 1962. When production ceased in the following year, a total of 1110 examples had been completed. This made the DB4 the best-selling model to date in Aston Martin's history.

The DB5 of 1964 was its much improved successor. Outwardly identifiable by its cowled headlamps that had featured on the last of the DB4s, the engine's capacity was increased to 4 liters and a ZF gearbox replaced the original four-speed unit. Once again there was a Vantage option which developed 314bhp.

Film star looks

The model was destined to gain immortality when James Bond drove an imaginatively enhanced example in the 1964 film *Goldfinger*. World demand for the model was instantaneous but, tantalizingly, the small factory could not cope with the demand.

Only destined for a two-year production life, the DB5 was replaced for the 1966 season by the

DB6. Instantly identifiable by its distinctive right angular Kamm tail and with its wheelbase lengthened by 3.75in (95mm), it was destined to survive until 1969. A Mark II version with flared wheel arches followed and this was built until 1971. By then the top-of-the-range Vantage version could attain 148mph (238km/h).

An open model had always been a feature of the Aston Martin line and accordingly the DB4 drophead coupé appeared in 1961. The concept was perpetuated with the DB5, and the open DB6 of 1967 was dubbed the Volante. This name has been applied ever since to all its open successors. The DB6 was destined to be the last six-cylinder Aston Martin. Therafter, until 1999, all its cars would be V8 powered.

Above: The drophead coupé version of the DB5 looked just as good as the coupé; it is considerably rarer.

Left: The longer wheelbase DB6, immediately identifiable by its truncated Kamm tail. Unlike its predecessors, most DB6s were not built to Touring's superleggera principles.

Below left: One of three DB5s built to James Bond's demanding requirements for the film Goldfinger *with overriders extended and machine guns armed!*

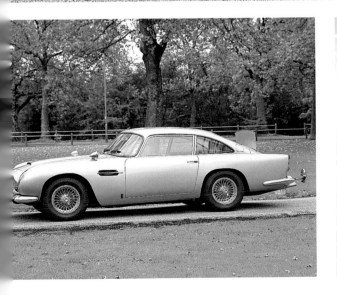

Specification	Aston Martin DB4
Engine location	Front, in-line
Configuration	Six-cylinder
Bore and stroke	92 x 92mm
Capacity	3670cc
Valve operation	Twin overhead camshafts
Horsepower	240bhp @ 5500rpm
Transmission	Manual four-speed
Drive	Rear
Chassis	Platform
Suspension – front	Wishbones and coil spring
Suspension – rear	Trailing link/Watts linkage coil spring
Brakes	Disc
Top speed	140mph (225km/h)
Acceleration	0-60mph (0-96km/h): 9.3 seconds

Maserati 5000 GT

**Top speed
170mph**
274km/h

Right: Allemano was responsible for bodying most 5000 GTs, with 20 examples to his credit. Its distinctive badge proudly proclaims the coachwork's design and construction.

Below: Costly coupé, a 'stock' 5000 GT. Allemano bodied his first example in 1961, introducing rectangular headlamps to the body which thereafter featured on all his work for Maserati. This is a 1964 car.

It was rare, raucous, and rapid. Maserati's 5000 GT was effectively a roadgoing version of its 350S sports racer of 1957. Little wonder that it was capable of 170mph (274km/h) even if refinement was another matter!

Maserati had withdrawn from its costly racing program in 1958 to concentrate on more lucrative road cars. However, the 5000 GT was never intended for series production. It seems more likely that its creation was prompted by the fact that the works had a number of racing V8 engines surplus to its requirements.

Introduced at the 1959 Turin Motor Show for the following year's season, under the hood of the Touring-bodied coupé was a 4935cc V8, courtesy of Maserati's competition car. Initially its four overhead camshafts were gear-driven although, happily, wiser counsels prevailed after the first three 5000 GTs had been completed, and they were replaced by quieter chains. Initially four Weber carburetors were fitted, although later examples used Lucas fuel injection.

The engine was installed in an appropriately modified tubular chassis, courtesy of the company's 3500 GT of 1958. A four-speed manual gearbox was an option, although most examples were fitted with five-cog ZF units. Like Ferrari, Maserati relied on a conventionally sprung live rear axle.

Production versions were fitted with handsome

and well appointed coupé bodies by Allemano, which was the only version to be cataloged by the factory, and it was responsible for bodying some 20 of them. Other versions were produced by Pinin Farina, Ghia, Frua, and Bertone, these variations no doubt being produced at the request of the model's very select clientele.

Affluent customers

These were expensive cars and Maserati ordered its retail outlets not accept an order for the 5000 GT without a significant deposit. It was acquired by some of the world's most affluent people, such as the Shah of Persia, the Aga Khan, and the head of Fiat, Giovanni Agnelli.

In 1962 the American *Sports Car Graphic* magazine published a road test on a 5000 GT which had attained a top speed of 152mph (245km/h). However, motoring journalist Hans Tanner had enjoyed trips on the Italian *autostradas* with Maserati's chief test driver when he had personally observed a top speed in excess of 170mph (274km/h).

Although only produced in small numbers, this exclusive Maserati's specifications were updated in 1961 when the engine was modestly enlarged to 4941cc and disc brakes were extended to the rear wheels. By the time that the last example had been completed in October 1964, total production amounted to just 34 cars.

Above: The Maserati's cockpit with handsome Nardi wood-rimmed steering wheel and featuring a clock located between the speedometer and rev counter.

Specification	Maserati 5000 GT
Engine location	Front, in-line
Configuration	V8
Bore and stroke	98 x 81mm
Capacity	4935cc
Valve operation	Twin overhead camshafts per cylinder bank
Horsepower	340bhp @ 6000rpm
Transmission	Manual four-speed
Drive	Rear
Chassis	Twin tubular
Suspension – front	Wishbones and coil spring
Suspension – rear	Half-elliptic spring
Brakes	Front disc, rear drum
Top speed	170mph (274km/h)
Acceleration	0-60mph (0-96km/h): N/A

Jaguar Mark II

**Top speed
125mph**
201km/h

*Right: Walnut veneer and
leather upholstery in the
British coachbuilding
tradition survived in the
mass-produced Mark II.*

*Below: A 1963 top-of-the-
range 3.8 liter version with
optional wire wheels. A
great visual improvement
on its 2.4 liter predecessor,
it could not be mistaken for
anything other than a
Jaguar.*

Jaguar's best-selling car of the 1960s, this
stylish and distinctive sedan was
comfortable, well equipped, and, in its 3.8
liter form, a fast and competitively priced model.

The Mark II sprang from the 2.4 liter Mark I
sedan of 1956 which was Jaguar's first unitary
construction car. As its name suggested, it was
powered by a new 2483cc version of the XK
engine, which was the first variation on the 3.4 liter
theme. Capable of speeds approaching 120mph
(193km/h), a supplementary 3.4 liter version
became available in 1957.

The model attained a new lease of life for the
1960 season with the arrival of the much improved
Mark II version. Chairman and stylist in chief, Sir
William Lyons, (knighted 1956), slimmed down the
window and door pillars which increased the glass
area. Rear vision was also improved by the fitment
of a wraparound rear window. All these changes
combined to transform the model's looks.

Improved handling

Improvements were not only cosmetic – handling
also benefited from a slightly wider rear axle. All-
round race-proven disc brakes, an option since
1958, were standardized.

Wire wheels had been available as an option on
the 2.4 and they particularly suited the Mark II for

which they could also be specified as a desirable extra. Not only did they greatly improve the model's looks but they also helped to keep the brake discs cool. The model proved to be particularly popular on the American market where the Mark II for several years topped the vote for the country's 'Best Imported Car.'

The existing 2.4 and 3.4 liter engine options were maintained but they were joined by a top-of-the-range 3.8 liter version. This was the engine already fitted in the XK150 sports car and the commodious Mark IX sedan. However, the version used in the passenger cars was the less powerful 220bhp unit, as opposed to the fiercer 265bhp one. Inevitably, the 3.8 proved to be the fastest of the Mark II range being capable of 125mph (201km/h). Inside the model was enhanced by a walnut veneer dashboard and comfortable leather upholstered seats, a feature of the marque to this day.

The 3.8 liter version was discontinued in 1967 when the engine was transferred to Jaguar's acclaimed XJ6 that appeared in 1968. However, the 2.4 and 3.4 lines were perpetuated in 240 and 340 guises with less opulent interiors and synthetic Ambla replacing the leather seats. These had ceased production by 1969 – by then Jaguar was concentrating its resources on the increasingly popular XJ6.

Specification	Jaguar Mark II (3.8 liter)
Engine location	Front, in-line
Configuration	Six-cylinder
Bore and stroke	87 x 106mm
Capacity	3781cc
Valve operation	Twin overhead camshafts
Horsepower	220bhp @ 5500rpm
Transmission	Manual four-speed
Drive	Rear
Chassis	Unitary
Suspension – front	Wishbones and coil spring
Suspension – rear	Cantilever sprung live axle
Brakes	Disc
Top speed	125mph (201km/h)
Acceleration	0-60mph (0-96km/h): 8.6 seconds

Left: The model's elegant tail. The enlarged wrap-around rear window which greatly improved driver visibility is just visible. The rear axle was 3.5in (89mm) wider than previously, which improved roadholding. The rear lights were also larger than those fitted to the Mark I and the below-bumper skirt deeper.

Left: Jaguar's famous mascot was designed by The Autocar's *celebrated artist, Frederick Gordon Crosby, and was offered from the 1939 season as an optional extra on the SS Jaguar range. This revised version appeared in 1955, and was offered as a factory accessory on the 2.4. It was designed for the hood rather than the radiator cap.*

Daimler SP250

**Top speed
120mph**
193km/h

*Right: The Daimler's
functional cockpit featured
comfortable bucket seats.
This a 1964 B specification
car with automatic
transmission.*

*Below: Looking like
nothing else on the road,
the glass-fiber-bodied
SP250 was a relatively
small car to be powered by
a 2.5 liter engine.*

 After more than 50 years of producing
luxurious and dignified sedans and
limousines, in 1959 Daimler experienced
a personality change when it introduced a 120mph
(193km/h) glass-fiber-bodied sports car. Announced
at the 1959 New York Motor Show, it was initially
known as the Dart, but was renamed the SP250
after protests from Chrysler, whose Dodge marque
owned the Dart name.

The model's arrival reflected a change in the
top management of Daimler's BSA parent. In 1956
the profligate 12-year reign of Sir Bernard Docker
came to an end. His replacement was motorcycle
magnate Jack Sangster and he promoted Edward
Turner from his Triumph motorcycle concern to the
post of Daimler's chief engineer. He was
accordingly responsible for the SP250 which was
intended to give Daimler a slice of the lucrative
American sports car market.

The lines of the glass-fiber bodywork were
unusually distinctive and dominated by twin rear
fins that were all the rage in America at the time.
The use of this material contributed to the model
turning the scales at a respectable 2218lb (1006kg).

Left: A 1964 SP250 with its distinctive V radiator motif, intended to underline the presence of a V8 engine under the hood. This was an unusual configuration in Britain, but popular in America which was where the model was targeted.

Below: Edward Turner's fine 2.5 liter V8 engine with cast iron block, alloy head, and, unusually, short alloy pushrods to help keep weight to a minimum to allow the revs to rise. The crankshaft was a five-bearing counterbalanced unit.

Beautifully flexible V8 engine

Because this was a wholly new concept, there were no components carried over from Daimler's traditional closed cars. A conventional box-section chassis was employed and the SP250 was powered by a beautifully flexible and economical 2.5 liter V8 engine, an unusual configuration for the British motor industry, although it would have struck a chord with transatlantic customers.

Daimler had a long tradition of producing cars with semi-automatic transmission and the SP250 was its first model since the late 1920s to be fitted with a manual gearbox. However, automatic transmission was available at extra cost.

Then in 1960 Daimler was acquired by Jaguar and there could clearly be no long-term future for the SP250 as it was now competing with the in-house E-Type. Despite this, in April 1961 the B specification cars made their appearance. These possessed stronger sills to prevent body flexing and resultant cracking. The bodywork was also strengthened. The final variant, the C spec cars of 1963, were better equipped but production ceased in January 1964 after a total of 2650 examples had been completed.

However, in 1963 Jaguar had united its Mark II sedan body with the SP250's engine and the resulting V8 250 survived until 1968, the year in which the medium-sized Jaguar was discontinued. With its demise, all traces of Daimler's brief excursion into the performance sector had been firmly extinguished.

Specification	Daimler SP250
Engine location	Front, in-line
Configuration	V8
Bore and stroke	76 x 69mm
Capacity	2548cc
Valve operation	Pushrod
Horsepower	140bhp @ 5800rpm
Transmission	Manual four-speed
Drive	Rear
Chassis	Box section
Suspension – front	Wishbones and coil spring
Suspension – rear	Half-elliptic spring
Brakes	Disc
Top speed	120mph (193km/h)
Acceleration	0-60mph (0-96km/h): 10.4 seconds

Austin-Healey 3000

**Top speed
114mph**
183km/h

*Right: A Mark III 3000
produced for the 1964
model year – this was a
more civilized offering with
a revised dashboard with
wood veneer, central console
complete with cubby box,
and wind-up windows. The
seats were also improved,
including the smaller
occasional rear ones.*

*Below right: A Mark II car
with factory hardtop and
the sliding side screens in
place. This example has
non-standard vents cut into
the front fenders to permit
hot air to escape from the
engine compartment. The
wire wheels were also a
desirable optional extra,
but usually disc wheels
were fitted as standard.*

*Opposite: A Mark II car of
1961. Produced between
1961 and 1963, it is instantly
identifiable by the radiator
grille's vertical bars; its
Mark I predecessor's were
horizontal. There is also a
small Mk II badge placed
beneath the winged Austin-
Healey motif.*

The rugged Big Healey of the 1960s, with
no-nonsense specifications and a
consistent rallying record, owed its
origins to the Healey 100 of 1952 which was the
brainchild of successful pre-war rally driver Donald
Healey. He had initially produced, in Warwick
between 1946 and 1952, a range of Riley-engined
models that were costly, heavy but potent.

The single-minded Cornishman soon realized
that he ought to create a smaller, cheaper, open
sports car of a type that was introducing America to
the delights of two-seater motoring. The 1.8 liter
Austin-engined Healey 100 accordingly made its
debut at the 1952 London Motor Show. It was
immediately commandeered by Leonard Lord,
chairman of the newly formed British Motor
Corporation that was a merger of the Austin and
Morris motor businesses.

Overnight Donald's roadster became the Austin-
Healey 100, so styled to reflect the fact that it was
capable of 100mph (161km/h) and was BMC's
corporate sports car. It was produced in this form
until 1956 when the four-cylinder engine was
replaced by a 2.6 liter six. Renamed the 100/6 and
available in two- and more popular two-plus-two
seater guises, it was, if anything, slower than the
model it replaced! Fortunately this shortcoming
was rectified by the adoption, from the 1958
season, of a six-port cylinder head.

In 1957 production was transferred from
Austin's Longbridge factory to MG's Abingdon
works and two years later the engine's capacity was
increased to 3 liters. Arriving for 1960, the
appropriately renamed 3000 greatly benefited from
the bigger-bored 132bhp engine. It was capable, in
overdrive top, of speeds approaching the 115mph
(185km/h) mark. This speed required the fitment of
front disc brakes.

Although raced and rallied by BMC on both
sides of the Atlantic, in the event these rugged,
reliable but pushrod-engined cars were invariably
outpaced by the consistently faster 3 liter Ferraris
with overhead camshafts.

The last of the line

The Mark II 3000 of 1961 was briefly offered with triple carburetors although it reverted to twins in 1962. The last of the line, the Mark III of 1963, was only produced in two-plus-two form – by then the engine was boosted to 150bhp.

The Big Healey died in 1968, following the absorption of BMC by the Leyland Corporation. The new owner was reluctant to continue paying royalties to an outside contractor who built what had become an outdated design.

Although Donald Healey attempted to fill the gap left in America by the 3000's demise with the smaller Jensen-Healey of 1972/76, it proved to be a pale shadow of the original.

Specification	Austin-Healey 3000 Mark I
Engine location	Front, in-line
Configuration	Six-cylinder
Bore and stroke	83 x 88mm
Capacity	2912cc
Valve operation	Pushrod
Horsepower	124bhp @ 4600rpm
Transmission	Manual four-speed with overdrive
Drive	Rear
Chassis	Platform
Suspension – front	Wishbones and coil spring
Suspension – rear	Half-elliptic spring
Brakes	Front disc, rear drum
Top speed	114mph (183km/h)
Acceleration	0-60mph (0-96km/h): 11.5 seconds

Volvo P1800

**Top speed
105mph**
169km/h

*Right: The P1800ES had a
similar instrument layout to
that of the original car, but
the units were modernized
and a padded steering
wheel was introduced.*

*Below: The P1800S could
perform as well over rough
roads as on the world's
newly opened freeways. It
offered two-seater motoring
with space for the
occasional rear passenger.*

A car that was destined to gain
immortality as the transport used by
Simon Templar, *The Saint* of the
television series of the same name, the P1800 was
an uncharacteristic product for a company better
known for solid, reliable sedans.

Like Daimler's unexpected Dart, the P1800 was
conceived by the Swedish Volvo company as a way
to tap the potential of the American performance
car market. The model was the brainchild of
freelance engineer, Helmer Petterson, who in 1957
succeeded in convincing Volvo's president, Gunnar
Engellau, of the need for such a car to supplement
its range of solid, well-regarded sedans. It did,
however, take some time for the concept to be
transformed into a production model. The
distinctive styling was the work of Petterson's son,
Pelle. The coupé's tail fins were to be an enduring
feature of the design, long after they had ceased to
be fashionable.

However, the Swedish company had no spare
capacity in which to produce the P1800 and in
1958 it approached the German Karmann concern
with a view to Karmann assembling the model for
them. When the deal fell through, Volvo came to

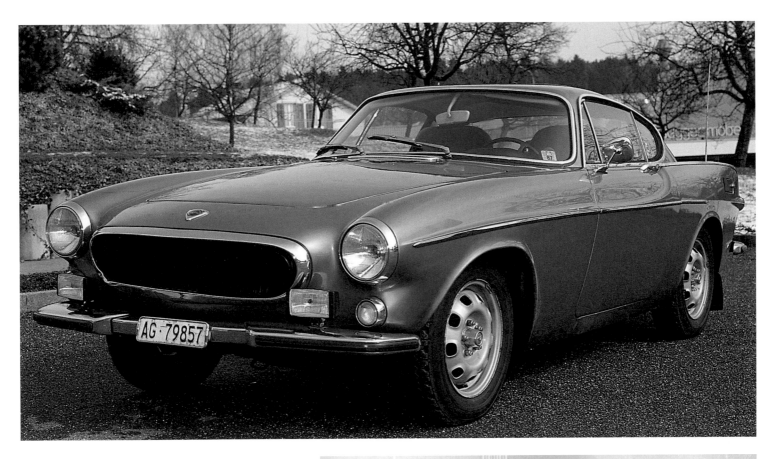

Britain and the result was that the shells were manufactured by Pressed Steel at its plant at Linwood in Scotland. They were then delivered to Jensen at West Bromwich and the cars completed there alongside the Big Healey bodyline.

Respectable top speed

Announced at the 1960 Brussels Motor Show, it was powered by a twin-carburetored 1.8 liter engine, boosted to 100bhp, that came courtesy of Volvo's P120 Amazon sedan. So endowed, this distinctive sports coupé had a respectable top speed in excess of 105mph (169km/h). A two-seater with some space in the rear for two children or a single adult, the provision of seat belts was an unusual feature for the day.

Production did not begin until early in 1961. Unfortunately quality problems resulted in Volvo taking over the P1800's final assembly from 1963, although the bodies were still UK-sourced. The model, with its engine boosted to 108bhp, increasing to 115bhp from 1966, was designated the 1800S, for Swedish built. However, in 1970 body manufacture was also transferred to Volvo's Torslanda factory.

In the meantime engine capacity had been upped to 1986cc in 1969, and when the model was

Specification	Volvo P1800
Engine location	Front, in-line
Configuration	Four-cylinder
Bore and stroke	84 x 80mm
Capacity	1780cc
Valve operation	Pushrod
Horsepower	100bhp @ 5500rpm
Transmission	Manual four-speed
Drive	Rear
Chassis	Unitary
Suspension – front	Wishbones and coil spring
Suspension – rear	Radius rods and coil spring
Brakes	Front disc, rear drum
Top speed	105mph (169km/h)
Acceleration	0-60mph (0-96km/h): 12.5 seconds

revised that year it was renamed the P1800E, the suffix standing for *Einspritzung*, which is the German word for fuel injection. This was an indication that a Bosch Jetronic system was employed and the engine now developed 130bhp. Production eventually ceased in 1972 after some 40,000 examples had been completed.

The 1800ES sports estate version, the final manifestation of the line, appeared in 1971. Just 8078 examples were completed before production ceased in 1973.

Above: A P1800E, showing its matt black radiator grille and composite wheels (the centers were aluminum alloy and the rims steel). 1800E badges were introduced on the tail panels while extractor vents also appeared on the rear fenders to service a new through-flow ventilation system.

1961–1970
The Coupé Comes of Age

Sales of fast cars boomed in the 1960s as a new post-war generation of young buyers came of age. Although Britain continued successfully to export its open two-seaters, the growing popularity of the high speed aerodynamically refined coupé was exemplified by Porsche's 911, along with Ferrari's exclusive V12-engined berlinettas and the delectable products of its new Lamborghini rival.

Datsun's popular 240Z, significantly also a closed car, highlighted the growing strength of Japan's motor industry. And America gave birth to the muscle car which harnessed V8s of growing capacity and power. But how long could the boom last?

Jaguar E-Type

**Top speed
150mph**
241km/h

Below: The Series III E-Type, introduced in 1971, was the first recipient of Jaguar's long-awaited 5.3 liter V12 engine. Identifiable by its enlarged radiator grille and flared wheel arches, this example has been fitted with optional wire wheels – usually discs were used. It was similarly produced in coupé form.

Without question one of the world's outstanding sports cars, the 3.8 liter E-Type sprang from Jaguar's Le Mans-winning D-Type and caused a sensation on its announcement at the 1961 Geneva Motor Show.

Appearing first in hardtop coupé form with a useful rear opening door, a roadster soon followed. Certainly the E-Type's looks were sufficient to ensure immortality. Jaguar claimed a top speed of 150mph (241km/h) but, in truth, only a few carefully assembled examples were capable of this figure. The $2800 price tag ensured that the model was destined for a long production run, and in fact it survived in this form until 1971.

Independent rear suspension, created for the impending Mark X sedan, featured for the first time on a Jaguar sports car, while all-round disc brakes, honed on the motor racing circuits, were fitted front and rear.

Triumph of styling

Stylistically the E-Type's lines were a triumph for Jaguar's aerodynamicist Malcolm Sayer, who also had the bodies of the sports racing C and D-Types to his credit. For once Jaguar's chairman, William Lyons, who usually styled the company's products, took a back seat.

Like the E-Type's XK120 predecessor, the new model found immediate favor in America where it was known as the XK-E, and no less than 80 per cent of production was exported there.

For 1966 the E-Type was fitted with a 4.2 liter engine which did not push the top speed but improved bottom end torque. An all-synchromesh gearbox replaced the unrefined Moss unit which lacked synchromesh on the bottom cog.

The original version was strictly a two-seater but 1966 saw the arrival of a 2+2 E-Type coupé which offered rear seating for two small children.

This extended the model's appeal. On the debit side, the redesign caused a dilution of those impeccable lines and increased weight.

The American market

A Series II E-Type arrived for 1969. It was revised to take account of American safety and emissions regulations. It was outwardly identifiable by its forward-mounted open headlamps, which dispensed with the previous perspex covers, and an enlarged radiator intake. The interior was also revised with tumbler switches replacing the more attractive but projecting lever-type units. But under the hood detoxing the engine for the US market meant 171 rather than 265bhp and a top speed of 'only' 125mph (201km/h).

The Series II was discontinued in 1971, when the Series III version appeared on the 2+2 chassis powered by Jaguar's long-awaited 5.3 liter V12 engine. Less of sports car, more of a grand tourer, it survived until 1975. By then the twin effects of soaring fuel prices and advancing age spelt the end of what had become a motoring legend in its own lifetime.

Below: The superlative lines of a 1962 E-Type coupé are shown to good effect. Unusually, this particular example raced at Le Mans.

Bottom left: The 'office' of a 4.2 liter E-Type with the original flick switches that survived until 1969.

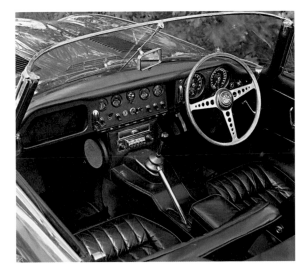

Specification	**Jaguar** E-Type (3.8 liters)
Engine location	Front, in-line
Configuration	Six-cylinder
Bore and stroke	87 x 106mm
Capacity	3781cc
Valve operation	Twin overhead camshafts
Horsepower	265bhp @ 5500rpm
Transmission	Manual four-speed
Drive	Rear
Chassis	Monocoque/squared tubular front sub-frame
Suspension – front	Wishbones and torsion bar
Suspension – rear	Wishbone and coil spring
Brakes	Disc
Top speed	150mph (241km/h) but see text
Acceleration	0-60mph (0-96km/h): 7 seconds

Above: One of the rare and desirable 'Lightweights,' this very original example, delivered in December 1963, was used by Dick Wilkins as a road car, no doubt to the consternation of his fellow motorists! It was later sold to Tony Harrison, who hill-climbed it. It has clocked up very few miles since new.

Right: Something special, the 3.8 liter engine of car number 11 above with alloy block, wide angle cylinder head, and Lucas fuel injection. The latter system was renowned for the noise it generated! Those cars that are run in current historic races have been converted to Weber carburetors. Dry sump lubrication featured.

Although the E-Type had sprung from the sports racing D-Type, it was first and foremost a road car. However, this did not deter a number of owners from campaigning the new Jaguar on the racetrack, the most successful of whom was American millionaire Briggs Cunningham. In 1962 he entered an E-Type coupé for the Le Mans 24 hour race and, sharing the driving with Roy Salvadori, they attained a creditable third placing.

Introduction of the 'Lightweight'

The factory responded by producing what it described as the 'Special GT E-Type' which has since been known as the 'Lightweight,' although this was never an official designation. They were capable of speeds approaching 170mph (274km/h), some 35mph (56km/h) faster than the production models and very much quicker off the mark.

In all 18 examples were completed and, at about 2220lb (1007kg), they weighed some 500lb (227kg) less than the road car. This was because, where practical, steel elements were replaced by aluminum ones. For instance, the monocoque tub and body panels were made of aluminum. Under the hood the 3.8 liter XK engine had an aluminum block in place of the cast iron original, although this was not a wholly satisfactory arrangement as it lacked rigidity. This meant that reliability, a key tenet of the Jaguar racing philosophy, was compromised.

Alterations to the camshafts, a special cylinder head, and the provision of fuel injection meant that the Lightweight's engine developed 296bhp, some 35bhp more than the norm.

Although these were sports racers, they could also be used as road cars. Only roadsters were built, and the cars were run in GT class events with their hardtops in place which improved their aerodynamic efficiency. The Lightweights were supplied to Jaguar distributors and private owners who had a good track racing record. They were run in European events and as far afield as America. But the result of the 1963 Sebring 12 hour race foretold the future when the two Lightweights were decisively outclassed by the V12-engined GTO Ferraris, which took the first six places, leaving the racing E-Types to occupy a lowly seventh and eighth positions. They were, nevertheless, the first British cars home.

The last of these potent E-Types was delivered to its owner in January 1964 and thus Jaguar's involvement with the car ceased. But they continued to be raced enthusiastically on British circuits and in club events. Of the 12 cars completed, all but one survive and these rare E-Types are now widely sought by Jaguar enthusiasts around the world.

Above: Cockpit of the Low Drag Coupé illustrated at the bottom of this page. Created for racing, it was never campaigned by the factory, but it was when acquired in 1963 by Dick Protheroe who registered it, memorably, CUT 7.

Left: This is one of three Lightweights owned by American millionaire racing driver Briggs Cunningham. He ran at Le Mans in 1963 but had to retire. He also owned another car which for a time used this registration number, so there is some doubt regarding its history.

Left: Jaguar's Low Drag Coupé. Four were planned but only this one was built for the World GT Championship. Work began in 1962 and the lines were the design of aerodynamicist Malcolm Sayer.

Triumph TR4, TR5, TR6

**Top speed
121mph**
195km/h

*Below: Triumph sports cars
with a 1966 TR4A,
complete with Michelotti's
ingenious 'Surrey-top,' in
the foreground with a
similarly enhanced 1965
TR4 behind and a 1972 TR6
in the background.*

 Triumph met the fresh challenges of the 1960s with the TR4 which benefited from an impressive new Michelotti body that survived, in essence, until its ultimate descendant, the TR6, was discontinued in 1976.

In 1959 Triumph had launched its Herald sedan and much of its success was credited to the styling, which was the work of the Italian Giovanni Michelotti. So when the TR3A, whose lines dated back to the TR2 of 1953, was updated, it was not surprising that he was commissioned to undertake the work.

Launched at the 1961 London Motor Show, the TR4's mechanicals were essentially the same as those of its predecessors, although an all-synchromesh gearbox was employed. This meant essentially the same 2138cc engine, although the car was 12in (305mm) longer and had a wider track. Top speed remained at 102mph (164km/h).

Engine boosted

The TR4 sold a respectable 40,000 examples before the TR4A arrived for the 1965 season. Although outwardly similar, mechanically there was a radical change with the arrival of semi-trailing arm independent rear suspension, as pioneered on Triumph's 2000 sedan of 1962. The long running engine was boosted by changes to the profile of the camshaft to increase top speed to 110mph (177km/h) but at the expense of fuel consumption.

Specification	**Triumph** TR5
Engine location	Front, in-line
Configuration	Six-cylinder
Bore and stroke	74 x 95mm
Capacity	2498cc
Valve operation	Pushrod
Horsepower	150bhp @ 5500rpm
Transmission	Manual four-speed
Drive	Rear
Chassis	Box section
Suspension – front	Wishbones and coil spring
Suspension – rear	Semi-trailing arm and coil spring
Brakes	Front disc, rear drum
Top speed	121mph (195km/h)
Acceleration	0-60mph (0-96km/h): 8.9 seconds

Even more radical, its TR5 successor of 1968 was fitted with a 150bhp, fuel-injected, 2.5 liter, six-cylinder engine and was capable of over 120mph (193km/h). And a 0-60mph (0-96km/h) figure of 8.9 seconds made it noticeably quicker off the mark.

Unfortunately the fuel injection system proved to be unreliable and those cars sold on the American market were fitted with carburetors. Even though it was rooted in the 1950s, there was still some mileage in this sports car, and in 1969 the TR6 appeared – it looked like a new model. In fact the TR4 sub-structure survived but it was enhanced with new front and rear ends essayed by the German Karmann company.

The TR6, which was destined to remain in production until 1976, was the most popular TR to date and 94,619 were produced. While top speed remained about the same, acceleration was improved thanks to a more highly tuned engine.

Sadly the 2 liter TR7 coupé which replaced it in 1976 was some 10mph (16km/h) slower! Intended as British Leyland's corporate sports car, it proved to be ill conceived, visually uninspiring, and unreliable. A better-looking convertible version followed in 1979 and there was the short-lived 3.5 liter V8-engined TR8 of 1980. But although some 112,000 TR7s were built, the once highly regarded initials had lost much of their luster.

Above left: Cockpit of a TR6 with a new steering wheel introduced for the 1973 season. Detail changes were also made to the instruments at the same time. In truth this layout was essentially the same as that created by Michelotti when he designed the TR4's body back in 1961 and it was only mildly modified over the years.

Left: The driving compartment of the 1966 TR4A opposite with a new wood-veneered dashboard introduced in the spring of 1965 for European customers. It had already been offered in the American market. The layout of its TR4 predecessor was retained. Triumph also took the opportunity to relocate the handbrake to the top of the transmission tunnel – it had previously been mounted alongside it.

AC Cobra

**Top speed
138mph**
222km/h

*Below: An AC 289 of 1966,
this example has been in the
same ownership since new.
Produced for the European
market, this was AC's
version of the Cobra, but
under a different name. The
lines of the Ace, on which it
was based, are readily
apparent in the styling.*

One hundred miles an hour (161km/h) coming up in 14 seconds is still a very respectable acceleration figure today – in the 1960s it was truly sensational. The AC Cobra, in which a lusty American V8 engine replaced a British power unit of a mere 2 liters capacity, was one of the truly great performance cars of the post-war years.

The Cobra was rooted in AC's Ace of 1954, an open two-seater sports cars with a tubular chassis and all-independent transverse leaf suspension. This behaved best when powered by a 2 liter Bristol engine, which was an alternative to the Thames Ditton's company's own 2 liter six, although the last of the line used a 2.5 liter Ford Zephyr unit.

Then American racing driver Carroll Shelby approached AC with a view to extending the Ace's life with a 260cid (4.2 liter) V8, courtesy of Ford of America. He proposed that left-hand-drive cars should be built without engines at AC's factory and then shipped to California where he would install their power units. The resulting car would be called the AC Shelby-Cobra, the name having come to him in a dream!

AC Shelby-Cobra in production

The British company agreed to this proposal and the car was announced in the fall of 1962. After the first 75 had been completed, the original engine was replaced by a 289cid (4.7 liter) unit. Performance of this Mark II was excellent for its day, top speed being 138mph (222km/h).

But the engine transplant displayed the limitations of the 1954 vintage suspension and Shelby initiated, with Ford input, the uprated Mark

KYW 858D

Left: All beef and muscle: a 427 Mark III Cobra, shod with the appropriate Halibrand alloy wheels. Left-hand-drive, of course.

Below left: The Mark III engine with the Shelby-fitted rocker covers which replaced the original pressed steel ones.

Below: UK Cobra guru Rod Leach at the wheel of the impressivly powerful 427. The front fender vent allows hot air to escape from the engine compartment.

III Cobra of 1965 with a wider chassis and all-round wishbones and coil spring suspension. A 427cid (6.9 liter) V8 was now employed and the Halibrand alloy wheels required even wider wheel arches. In this form what was now called the Shelby-Cobra was capable of 165mph (265km/h). It continued to be sold until 1968.

Right-hand-drive Cobras had been available on the British market since 1964. The Mark III, though fitted with the 4.7 liter V8, was marketed as the AC 289 in Britain between 1966 and 1968 because AC did not own the rights to the Cobra name.

After a hiatus, in 1983 the Cobra concept was revived in Britain. Initially the 4.9 liter AC Mark IV could not be called a Cobra but in 1986 permission for use of the name was forthcoming from Ford, which by then owned it. The car remains in limited production at the time of writing (2002), no less than 40 years since this ingenious Anglo-American sports car was first conceived.

Specification	AC Shelby-Cobra Mark II
Engine location	Front, in-line
Configuration	V8
Bore and stroke	4.0 x 2.87in (101 x 72mm)
Capacity	289cid (4735cc)
Valve operation	Pushrod
Horsepower	300bhp @ 5700rpm
Transmission	Manual four-speed
Drive	Rear
Chassis	Tubular steel
Suspension – front	Transverse leaf spring and wishbones
Suspension – rear	Transverse leaf spring and wishbones
Brakes	Disc
Top speed	138mph (222km/h)
Acceleration	0-60mph (0-96km/h): 5.6 seconds

Above: Chunky, muscular, and a direct descendant of AC Cobra of the 1960s, the CRS, announced for the 2000 season, differed from its predecessors in using a carbon-fiber body in place of the aluminum previously employed. The 5 liter Ford V8 engine developed 225bhp. The CRS was available in road-ready form or in tuned and tautened racing guise.

The AC company acquired a new owner in 1996, South African businessman Alan Lubinsky, and he was determined that the company would not rest on its laurels. In 1998 it unveiled the Mark IV-based Superblower which, as the name suggested, was powered by a supercharged version of the Ford 4.9 liter V8. With a top speed of 165mph (266km/h), acceleration was electrifying with 60mph (96km/h) arriving in 4.2 seconds. The price, however, was some $98,000.

Carbon fiber body

The 2000 season saw the arrival of the Cobra CRS. This retained the model's traditional chunky and purposeful look, but it differed from its predecessors in that instead of having the usual open two-seater aluminum body, it was made of light but immensely strong carbon fiber. In consequence the CRS turned the scales at 2380lb (1080kg) and it cost some $28,000 less than the metal-bodied car. The Ford V8 produced a healthy 225bhp which resulted in a 0 to 60mph (96km/h) time of 5.3 seconds. Both racing and roadgoing versions were on offer.

The 2001 season saw the appearance of a further variation of the evergreen classic in the shape of the 212 S/C. Launched at the 2000 British Motor Show, it was essentially a re-engined CRS. Although the traditional open two-seater lines were retained, AC forsook the usual Ford V8 for the twin turbocharged 3.5 liter Lotus unit of a similar specification to that used in the Lotus Turbo. The model's name reflected the power unit's 3506cc capacity expressed in cubic inches.

It is no coincidence that John Owen, AC's chief engineer, previously worked for Lotus where he headed the design team that conceived the V8. He was, therefore, no stranger to the engine, its performance capabilities and potential.

Drive is taken through a six-speed Tremec manual gearbox. Power steering is a refinement, but the 212 remains at heart a near 50-year-old concept with its twin tubular chassis and all-round wishbone suspension which dates from the Cobra 427 of 1965.

In addition AC also produces a more luxurious variation on the open two-seater theme in the shape of the Ace that was launched for the 1998 season.

Similarly powered by a Ford V8, it is also available in twin-cam 4.6 liter form, courtesy of the Mustang. The '4.9' is also used in the Aceca coupé unveiled at the 1998 British Motor Show. This is a genuine four-seater with 9.8in (250mm) added to its wheelbase. AC thus offers a quartet of distinctive, fast cars for the enthusiast who wants to combined tradition with out-and-out performance.

Above: A change of emphasis; the well-appointed, refined Aceca coupé arrived for the 1999 model year.

Left: Despite its state-of-the-art body material, the dashboard of the CRS is pure 1960s.

Below left: Lotus's twin turbocharged 3.5 liter V8 used in its Esprit is employed by AC in the 212 S/C.

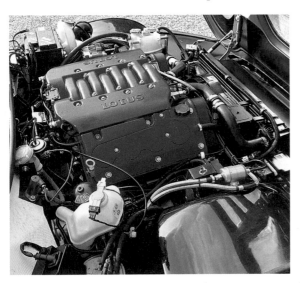

Specification	AC 212 S/C
Engine location	Front, in-line
Configuration	V8
Bore and stroke	83 x 81mm
Capacity	3506cc
Valve operation	Twin overhead camshafts per cylinder bank
Horsepower	350bhp @ 6500rpm
Transmission	Manual six-speed
Drive	Rear
Chassis	Twin tubular
Suspension – front	Wishbones and coil spring
Suspension – rear	Wishbones and coil spring
Brakes	Disc, ventilated at front
Top speed	155mph (249km/h)
Acceleration	0-60mph (0-96km/h): 3.9 seconds

Mini Cooper S

**Top speed
98mph**
158km/h

*Right: The immaculate
but crowded engine
compartment of the 1275
Cooper S shown below. The
component to the left of the
engine is the brake servo.*

*Below: This Austin 1969
Cooper S MkII can be
identified by the enlarged
radiator grille which was
also shared with the Morris
versions.*

The lion-hearted little car that scored a
resounding three wins in 1960s Monte
Carlo Rallies, the Cooper S was the
competition version of Alec Issigonis's legendary
Mini. Created for the British Motor Corporation,
the Mini bristled with ingenuity. Its 848cc engine
was transversely mounted and the gearbox was
ingeniously located in the sump from where it
drove the front wheels.

A small car in which every inch of interior
space was used to the maximum effect, Issigonis
never envisaged that the roadholding advantages of
front-wheel drive could be successfully harnessed
for use on the racetrack and rally course. But he
had not reckoned with John Cooper of the Cooper
Formula 1 team which had won the World
Manufacturers Championship in 1959 and 1960. He
proposed a faster version and the Mini Cooper was
born in 1961 powered by a 55bhp, 997cc, twin-carb
version of BMC's versatile A Series engine.

This was enlarged to 998cc in 1963 and it
paved the way for the even more potent Mini
Cooper S of 1963 with a 1071cc engine. Initially
developing 70bhp, this was a 90mph (145km/h) car
although it became progressively faster as it
evolved. Outwardly similar to the standard Cooper,
it retained the white roof by which that variant was
usually distinguished.

ODL 975H

Definitive Cooper S

In March 1964 this was replaced by a choice of 970cc (although it only lasted for 11 months) and 1275cc versions, the latter being regarded as the definitive Cooper S. These all used the Mini's rubber-based suspension, although this was replaced by the interconnected Hydrolastic system for the 1965 season.

By then the S had already attained international recognition. Skilfully prepared by BMC's Competition Department based at MG's Abingdon factory, in 1964 Paddy Hopkirk won the Monte Carlo Rally outright and BMC took the team prize. Timo Makkinen repeated the feat in 1965 and these triumphs were consolidated when the car achieved a one, two, three victory in 1966, although this was overturned by the organizers on a technicality. However, there were no mistakes in 1967 when the Cooper S was again victorious.

But Minis were beginning to feel the effect of sure-footed opposition from Ford. Then in 1968 BMC was taken over by Leyland and the famous Competitions Department was closed down. The 1275cc Cooper S ceased production in 1971, two years after the Cooper had been discontinued.

However, the 1275cc Mini Cooper concept was revived in 1990 by the Rover Group, BMC's latter-day descendant, and the new BMW-built Mini of 2001 also includes a Cooper version in tribute to its now legendary forebear.

Specification	Mini Cooper S (1275cc)
Engine location	Transverse
Configuration	Four-cylinder
Bore and stroke	70 x 81mm
Capacity	1275cc
Valve operation	Pushrod
Horsepower	76bhp @ 5800rpm
Transmission	Manual four-speed
Drive	Front
Chassis	Unitary
Suspension – front	Wishbone and rubber
Suspension – rear	Trailing arm and rubber
Brakes	Front disc, drum rear
Top speed	98mph (158km/h)
Acceleration	0-60mph (0-96km/h): 10.9 seconds

Left: Interior of the 1965 Monte Carlo-winning 1275cc Morris Mini Cooper S with enhanced instrumentation and more supportive seats than usual.

Below: The 1965 Monte Carlo Rally-winning Cooper S. The car was subsequently extensively rebuilt and won the 1982 Lombard-RAC Golden 50 rally.

Aston Martin DB4 GT Zagato

**Top speed
152mph**
244km/h

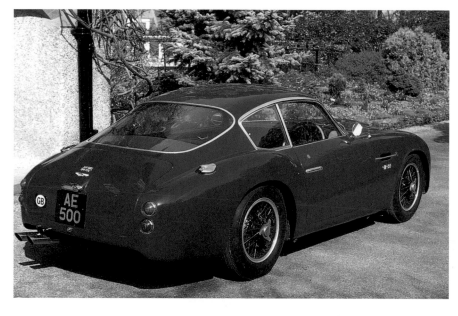

In October 1958 Aston Martin unveiled its acclaimed Touring-styled DB4 and a lighter, shortened, faster GT version followed a year later. Then, at the 1960 London Motor Show, the memorable and even more potent DB4 GT Zagato appeared. It was so named because it was bodied in Italy by the Zagato styling house of Milan.

Visually stunning

The work of the talented young Ercole Spada, 'the Zagato,' as it was invariably known, was a visually stunning competition car although it was also available in roadgoing form.

Under the hood was a high specification version of the DB4's twin-overhead-camshaft 3.6 liter engine. Originally developing 240bhp, the GT version was boosted to a claimed 302bhp, actually 267, thanks to 9:1 rather than 8.2 compression ratio, special high lift camshafts, twin sparking plugs per cylinder and triple Weber carburetors in place of the original twin SUs. Running on a 9.7:1 compression, the Zagatos' engines were further boosted to 285bhp.

At 2800lb (1270kg), the tubular-framed, purposeful, alloy coupés were about 100lb (45kg) lighter than the factory GTs and could attain over 150mph (241km/h). Once completed, the cars were returned to Aston Martin's Newport Pagnell works for trimming, although a few examples were completed by Zagato.

Like the factory DB4 GTs, there were only two seats in the front. The space usually occupied by the rear seat was occupied by a platform for the storage of luggage.

Above: A 1962 right-hand-drive Zagato, arguably the best and most original of the cars as it was purchased new in October of that year by J.E. Beck of Cheshire, who kept it for many years. Note the absence of a rear bumper.

Right: The Zagato's lines shown to advantage. The transparent headlamp covers were fitted in the interests of aerodynamic efficiency. All the cars differ slightly in details and, of the 19 cars built, all survive. The only 'missing' car was discovered in Italy in 1974.

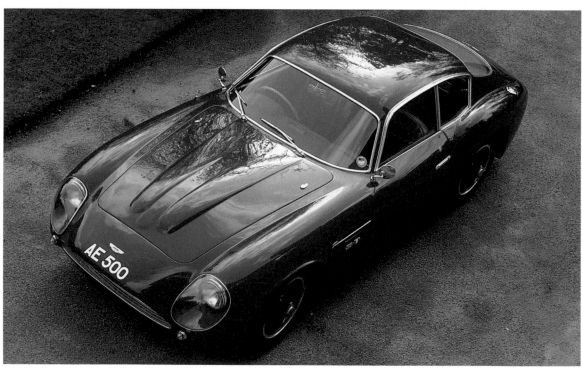

Over the next three years a total of 19 cars was completed, each one differing slightly from the others. Production was almost evenly split with ten right-hand-drive examples built while the remainder were left hookers. Perversely, one chassis was bodied by Bertone.

Essex Racing Stables

Aston Martin had withdrawn from sports-car racing in 1959 so the Zagatos were campaigned on the racing circuits during 1961 and 1962 by privateers, most significantly John Ogier's Essex Racing Stables which ran two of them memorably registered 1 VEV and 2 VEV. While the cars invariably finished in GT races in Britain and on the Continent, they were unable to hold their own against the might of Ferrari's GTOs.

Although production ceased in 1963, this was not quite the end of the story. In 1991 Aston Martin decided to utilize four unused chassis numbers that had been allocated to the original series. Zagato

Specification	Aston Martin DB4 GT Zagato
Engine location	Front, in-line
Configuration	Six-cylinder
Bore and stroke	92 x 92mm
Capacity	3670cc
Valve operation	Twin overhead camshafts
Horsepower	285bhp @ 6000rpm
Transmission	Manual four-speed
Drive	Rear
Chassis	Platform
Suspension – front	Wishbones and coil spring
Suspension – rear	Trailing link, Watt's linkage/coil spring
Brakes	Disc
Top speed	152mph (244km/h)
Acceleration	0-60mph (0-96km/h:) 6.2 seconds

produced a further four cars under the Sanction II designation, outwardly almost identical to the originals and with only detail differences to their specifications. Otherwise they remained true to the 1960 classic design.

Above left: Cockpit of a left-hand-drive Zagato. The seven instruments can be clearly seen through the wood-rimmed steering wheel. The seats, which are adjustable for rake, are supportive while the pedals are well positioned.

Above right: The Zagato's engine with the DB4 GT's twin-plug cylinder head serviced by distributors driven off the bulkhead end of each camshaft. The triple Weber carburetors on the far side of the engine use a cool air intake box.

Left: Strictly a two-seater, the Zagato still looks good some 50 years after its first appearance. Made of light alloy, it is vulnerable to damage. Note the Z monogram ahead of the air intake on the front fender, so there can be no doubt of the body's origins!

Above: Incredibly this Zagato was completed in 1991. It is one (chassis no 196) of the four Sanction II cars and is almost indistinguishable from the originals. The absence of bumpers leaves the lines unsullied but makes them vulnerable when parking. This desirable quartet sold for between $1,000,000 to $1,050,000 apiece and their classic status is now assured.

For a factory to resurrect a model, 24 years after it ceased production, must be an unprecedented initiative, even within the multifarious and unpredictable world of the global motor industry.

The Zagato Sanction II project dated from 1987, prior to the company's acquisition that year by Ford, and was initiated by Aston Martin's joint chairmen, Victor Gauntlett and Peter Livanos, who had always been aware that there were four unused chassis numbers in the DB4 GT Zagato series.

They decided to apply them to a quartet of Zagatos that would be produced to resemble the original cars as closely as was feasible and be of comparable build quality. As they were to be built by the original manufacturer, they could not be regarded as replicas.

Four DB4 chassis were accordingly uprated to short wheelbase GT specifications by Aston Martin specialist Richard Williams of Cobham, Surrey. These were then dispatched to Zagato's Milan premises, along with Williams' own original Zagato which was dismantled so that the local workforce could acquaint themselves with the construction techniques of the early 1960s.

Light green livery

The resulting cars were unveiled at Williams' premises in July 1991. Outwardly indistinguishable from the originals, they were finished in authentic light green livery. Only placing one of them next to an original car would reveal that the Sanction II Zagatos have 15in (381mm) rather than 16in (406mm) wheels.

There were some underbody changes too. The four 1991 cars have 4.2 rather than 3.7 liter engines, although authentic twin sparking plug cylinder heads were retained. Minor changes were made to the manifold configuration of the triple Weber carburetors to improve gas flow, while alternators replaced the original dynamos.

Modest changes were made to the front and rear suspension with the intention of improving roadholding which was also aided by the fitting of

Above left: The interior is gloriously 1960s and the instrumentation exactly the same with the exception of the ammeter which, instead of 0-30, reads 0-50 because an alternator has replaced the original dynamo. The black leather-trimmed bucket seats are relatively small, but comfortable.

Above right: The Sanction II's engines are of 4.2 rather than the original 3.7 liter capacity but the twin-plug cylinder heads are correct. Although triple twin-choke Weber carburetors are fitted, the 45DCOE units have been replaced by DCO1/SP ones.

Left: This left-hand-drive Zagato, chassis 0188/L, has a unique nose and hood which were visually related to the production DB4. The headlights are thus forward-mounted instead of being recessed behind aerodynamically efficient transparent covers. This Zagato was raced in historic events in the 1970s by O'Rourke.

radial tires in place of the original crossply covers. The interiors were indistinguishable from the originals, complete with wood-rimmed steering wheels and speedometers reading to 160mph (257km/h). There was nothing to prevent these cars from attaining the 150mph plus (241+km/h) top speed of the originals, although whether their owners would wish to extend such valuable collectors' pieces fully must be open to question!

But this quartet of coupés are more than worthy of the Zagatos of the 1961-63 era. And it is unlikely that any other car maker will be similarly tempted to follow Aston Martin's example and wind back the clock to recreate one of its most alluring and memorable sports racers.

Specification	Aston Martin DB4 GT Zagato Sanction II
Engine location	Front, in-line
Configuration	Six-cylinder
Bore and stroke	98 x 92mm
Capacity	4212cc
Valve operation	Twin overhead camshafts
Horsepower	352bhp @ 6000rpm
Transmission	Manual four-speed
Drive	Rear
Chassis	Platform
Suspension – front	Wishbones and coil spring
Suspension – rear	Live axle, coil spring and Watts linkage
Brakes	Disc
Top speed	152mph (245km/h)
Acceleration	0-60mph (0-96km/h): 5.5 seconds

Ferrari 250 GTO

**Top speed
185mph**
298km/h

*Right: The GTO's engine
with the 12 stacks of the
inlet ports for the six Weber
carburetors readily
apparent. With weight an
ever-present consideration,
the cam covers were made
of magnesium.*

*Below: The semi-circular
air intakes could be covered
and were opened to increase
air flow to the engine at
slow speeds. The apertures
below the headlamps direct
air to the brakes.*

One of the rarest (just 39 were built) and
today the most collectible and expensive
of Ferraris, the legendary GTO was
created for the newly introduced GT World
Championship of 1962. A sports racer that could
also be used as a road car, it was capable of a
blistering 185mph (298km/h).

The car was engineered by Giotto Bizzarrini,
who was later to be responsible for Lamborghini's
enduring V12 engine. Unusually he not only laid
out the chassis but also the sensational lines of the
Ferrari's berlinetta body, a task usually undertaken
by Pininfarina.

The resulting design was not only supremely
elegant but utterly distinctive, for Bizzarrini also
recognized the importance of improving a car's
performance by aerodynamic refinement and he
accordingly undertook airflow experiments in Pisa
University's wind tunnel. The results were
confirmed during testing at the Modena and Monza
circuits and even on the Italian *autostradas*, no
doubt to the delight of other motorists.

Distinctive rear spoiler

The Scaglietti-built body's distinctive rear spoiler
helped to kept the wheels of the 295bhp 3 liter V12
on the road. This proven and reliable power unit
was inherited from the GTO's open sports-racing
Testa Rossa predecessor.

The car was the ultimate development of
Ferrari's 250 GT of 1955, which was produced in
short wheelbase form for the racetrack from 1959.

The GTO title stood for *Gran Turismo Omologato* – in other words homologated, a racing stipulation which required that 100 examples of a particular car be constructed. After some controversy with the authorities, Enzo Ferrari got around the problem by proclaiming that he had been producing 3 liter GTs since 1955!

Although the overwhelming majority of GTOs were 3 liter powered, there was a trio of 4 liter models. It was typical of Ferrrari that while much attention was lavished on the engine and body, the tubular chassis featured conventional wishbones and coil springs and the essentials of a cart-sprung rear which had not been much updated since 1947.

Created for the new 3 liter GT World Championship, the GTO not only gave Ferrari victory in 1962 but also in 1963 and 1964. The latter year proved to be the last for this potent and, it should be said, beautiful and purposeful car.

Success on the racing circuits

The GTO had proved itself invincible on the GT racing circuits and an example was placed second at Le Mans in 1962. It was only displaced in the mid-1960s when rear-engined sports racers, following in the wheeltracks of Formula 1 cars, gained the upper hand.

In 1965 the Maranello company decided to concentrate all its efforts on Formula 1 and prototype sports car racing. Ferrari therefore bowed out from GT competition after a highly successful decade, mostly spent on top.

Above: The GTO looks just as good from the rear. The large air outlet positioned on the rear fender allowed hot air generated by the back tires and brakes to escape more quickly.

Below left: The instrument panel was dominated by a revolution counter; all the dials can be easily seen through the spokes of the lovely Nardi aluminum and wood steering wheel.

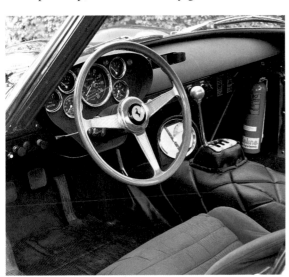

Specification	**Ferrari** GTO
Engine location	Front, in-line
Configuration	V12
Bore and stroke	73 x 58mm
Capacity	2953cc
Valve operation	Twin overhead camshafts per bank
Horsepower	295bhp @ 7400rpm
Transmission	Manual five-speed
Drive	Rear
Chassis	Tubular steel
Suspension – front	Wishbones and coil spring
Suspension – rear	Half-elliptic springs, radius arms and Watts linkage
Brakes	Disc
Top speed	185mph (298km/h)
Acceleration	N/A

Above: As can be seen, the bodywork of the GTO 64 differed radically from the previous year's design.

Below: The same car on the move at a Goodwood Festival of Speed event. Note the absence of Ferrari's familiar prancing horse mascot.

Ferrari had announced the rear-engined 250 LM sports racer in the fall of 1963. It was intended that this would replace the GTO in GT events. But not enough of them were produced to qualify, so Ferrari continued to campaign the GTO, although the 1964 version differed outwardly from the previous season's cars.

These changes, which echoed those adopted on the Pininfarina-styled LM, were effected to reduce weight and improve the coupé's aerodynamics. Precious kilograms were also saved by slightly shortening the car at both its front and rear ends, and the thinnest possible aluminum sheet was used. The bodies were once again built in Modena by Scaglietti.

The most obvious changes were at the front where the air intake was now wider and elongated horizontally. This resulted in a less visually attractive and distinctive nose, and Ferrari's famous prancing horse symbol was removed from the aperture. The three distinctive semi-circular engine cooling slots were also dispensed with, although vents were retained – situated out of sight below the radiator intake.

Restricted visibility

The cars were also slightly lower than the 1962 originals. This required the provision of a new windshield; there was a recessed small rear window. However, visibility was less than perfect because of the extended aerodynamically honed cockpit sides. Inside alterations were made to the seating and the layout of the instrumentation. While the abruptly truncated tail was similar to the original, alterations to improve the coupé's drag coefficient resulted in a visually less satisfactory rear profile.

By contrast, the chassis and engine underwent only detail modifications. Suspension remained essentially the same, although the ratings of the front springs were changed. And even though one journalist mistakenly reported that the '64 GTOs were fitted with independent rear suspension, the original conventionally sprung rear axle was perpetuated. Under the hood the V12 developed between 296 and 302bhp but the power curve varied somewhat from the 1963 line.

Four existing GTOs were rebodied and there were also three new cars. The model proved itself still competitive, an example being placed second in the Nürburgring 1000 kilometre race. Ferrari took the first three places at the 1964 Le Mans event with 275P prototypes but GTOs still showed their mettle by attaining fifth, sixth, and ninth positions. Significantly, a Shelby Ford Cobra Daytona coupé came in fourth, ahead of the first GTO, and this was the model that would wrest the GT Championship crown from Ferrari in 1965.

Nevertheless, the GTO stands out as one of the greatest of Ferrari's front-engined racers, and it remains a sought-after five-star car for most collectors, but one that is almost invariably unobtainable. Such is Modena's allure!

Below: Some GTO 64s have smooth hoods instead of sporting a cold air intake such as that fitted to the car opposite. Here historic racing driver and restorer Tony Merrick is at the wheel of this desirable Ferrari at the 1993 Goodwood Festival of Speed. There were, in all, seven such cars.

Porsche 911

**Top speed
130mph**
209km/h

Right: A 911S shod with the distinctive Fuchs five-spoke forged alloy wheels introduced to the model in 1967 – they were an option on the standard version. They had the virtue of being 5lb (2.2kg) lighter than the usual steel variety.

Below: A Targa top on a 1973 911, a halfway house between a convertible and fixed-head coupé. It had proved to be a popular option ever since 1969. Introduced in 1965, it originally featured a removal rear window.

 One of the world's greatest sports cars, Porsche's legendary, unconventional, yet utterly distinctive 911 was introduced at the 1963 Frankfurt Motor Show. Today, some 40 years on, it remains in production and the current model is recognizably a descendant of the original. However, its top speed of 174mph (280km/h) is some 40mph (64km/h) faster than the first of the line. Acceleration has been similarly enhanced.

The 911 has been produced in countless variations for both road and track, and is the descendent of a line that began with a single model which entered production back in September 1964.

Work on the project had begun in 1958 and followed the theme established with the 356. It was an aerodynamically refined coupé powered by a rear-mounted, air-cooled, horizontally opposed engine. But there the resemblance ended because the 911's power unit did not possess a trace of its predecessor's Volkswagen ancestry. The purpose-designed 2 liter six-cylinder engine, which developed 130bhp, employed chain-driven single-overhead camshafts in place of pushrods. However, torsion bar suspension was inherited from the 356, although it was used at the front in conjunction with struts.

Arrival of the Targa

Until the 1967 season there was only one model in the 911 family but then came the more powerful 160bhp 911S which was shod with distinctive Fuchs alloy wheels. No convertible was offered at this stage, but the 911T, for Targa, arrived for the 1969 season. This had a fixed rear window and detachable roof panel, an initiative which was widely copied by other sports car manufacturers. Powered by a detuned 110bhp engine, it was offered with semi-automatic transmission.

In the 1969 model year fuel injection arrived on the 911S and the newly introduced 911E. The 911's first increase in engine capacity, to 2.2 liters, came

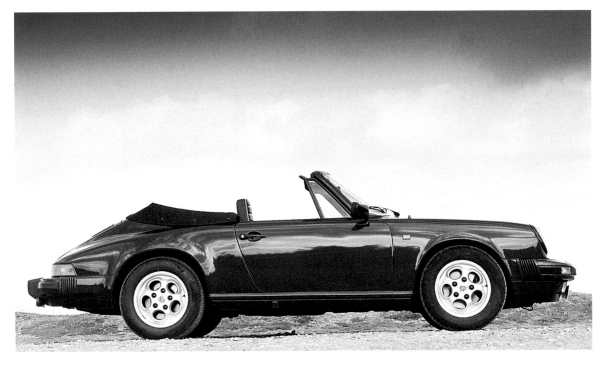

Above left: The Carrera RS's engine had its capacity enlarged to 2687cc by increasing the bore of the existing 2.3 liter unit to 90mm. It developed 210bhp.

Above right: The sought-after Carrera RS of 1973 which could reach 60mph (96km/h) in under six seconds. A mere 1600 examples were built.

Left: A 1984 Carrera Cabriolet. The roof can be raised and lowered single-handed. Later, for 1986, came similarly equipped open Turbos.

in 1970. There was another rise, to 2.4 liters, for the 1972 season and the following model year saw the return of the Carrera. This RS version had a 210bhp engine and was capable of a spirited 150mph (241km/h).

The 1974 models were distinguished by another rise in engine capacity, to 2.7 liters, although the Carrera broke ranks and sported a 2.9 liter power unit which developed 230bhp.

A turbocharged 911 with a 3 liter engine followed for the 1975 model year and this variant can be found on page 166. This engine, although in unblown form, was extended to the Carrera for the 1976 season and was fitted in detuned 180bhp form in the mainstream cars of the 1978/79 model years.

Specification	Porsche 911 (2 liter)
Engine location	Rear, in-line
Configuration	Six-cylinder
Bore and stroke	80 x 66mm
Capacity	1991cc
Valve operation	Single overhead camshaft
Horsepower	130bhp @ 6100rpm
Transmission	Manual five-speed
Drive	Rear
Chassis	Unitary
Suspension – front	MacPherson strut and torsion bar
Suspension – rear	Semi-trailing arms and torsion bar
Brakes	Disc
Top speed	130mph (209km/h)
Acceleration	0-60mph (0-96km/h): 8.9 seconds

Above: A Carrera 2 of 1993, identifiable by its five-spoked alloy wheels which appeared in 1992 and which replaced the seven-spoked units of the 1990-91 era. The so-called 964 series of the 911, introduced for 1989, were powered by a 3.6 liter 250bhp engine. It was replaced for the 1994 season by the radically revised 993 series.

Right: A 1995 Carrera 2 cabriolet with Tiptronic automatic transmission. This 993 series interior is identifiable by its redesigned steering wheel which incorporated an airbag – one was also added for the passenger. The dashboard has not really changed significantly since the 911's arrival in 1963.

The next increase in engine capacity came with the Carrera for the 1984 season, the 3.2 liter unit, a very 'torquey' engine, developed 231bhp and was destined to endure until 1989.

Unlike the 356 that had been available in cabriolet (open) form since its inception, the 911 had only been produced, the Targa excepted, in coupé guise. It was not until 1982, no less than 19 years since the 911's announcement, that the Cabriolet made its appearance, and it has been an integral part of the model line ever since. Originally designated the 911SC, it continued as a Carrera for 1984 and the option was extended from the 1986 season to the Turbo.

Four-wheel drive joined the Carrera line for 1989, a model year in which its engine capacity was increased to 3600cc. Yet another mechanical change was the replacement of the torsion bars, a feature of the 911 since its inception, by all-round coil springs.

The body underwent further revision for the 1994 model year with newly contoured bumpers and flared wheel arches. The cars were powered by 3.6 liter engines, but there were further changes in the offing prompted by the arrival of Porsche's cheaper, mid-engined, 2.4 liter Boxster convertible for 1997.

Radical re-design

When the current version of the 911 arrived for the 1998 season it shared no less than 36 per cent of its components with its smaller capacity stablemate. This was nothing short of a root and branch re-design of the famous model.

The new shell is 45 per cent more rigid than its predecessor which means more interior room. Its distinctive headlamp covers extend to incorporate the side lamps and flashing turn signals are also shared with the Boxster. Quarterlights, a body feature that the 911 had inherited from the 356, have been deleted.

An even more radical departure is the engine

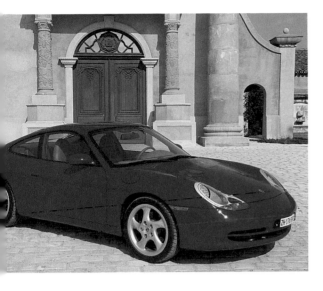

Specification	**Porsche** 911 Carrera 2
Engine location	Rear, in-line
Configuration	Horizontally opposed six-cylinder
Bore and stroke	96 x 78mm
Capacity	3387cc
Valve operation	Twin overhead camshafts
Horsepower	300bhp @ 6800rpm
Transmission	Manual six-speed
Drive	Rear
Chassis	Unitary
Suspension – front	MacPherson strut
Suspension – rear	Wishbone and strut
Brakes	Disc
Top speed	174mph (280km/h)
Acceleration	0-60mph (0-96km/h): 5.1 seconds

which is of a slightly smaller capacity than its predecessor. The 3.4 liter 'flat' six is water-cooled, so dispensing with air cooling that dated back to the 356. It similarly shares the Boxster's layout of twin overhead camshafts, four valves per cylinder, and twin front-fender-located turn signals.

Suspension is common to both models and is mounted front and rear on aluminum sub-frames to reduce noise levels. There are MacPhersont struts at the front with strut-sprung wishbones at the rear.

The mainstream model is the Carrera 2 and, like other variations on the contemporary 911 theme, it is a far more refined product that its predecessors, although Porsche has succeeded in retaining its sports car credentials. It is also available in four-wheel-drive form as the Carerra 4 while a Cabriolet and Turbo complete the range. The 911 will celebrate its 50th birthday in 2003, making it the world's most enduring and celebrated performance car.

Above left: The 911 was radically revised for the 1998 season and the resulting 996 series was developed in conjunction with Porsche's cheaper, mid-engined Boxster. It shared many components with the new two-seater, most obviously the headlamp units. It was also a quieter car than previously because the 3.4 liter engine was water- rather than air-cooled.

Left: A second-generation Targa arrived with 993 series 911 Carrera for 1996. Unlike its predecessor, which featured a manually removable roof panel, this version used an electrically controlled roof, which contained an ultra-violet filter to protect the occupants from the sun's glare. At the touch of a button the panel retracted beneath the fixed rear window, so leaving the roof completely open.

Chevrolet Corvette Sting Ray

**Top speed
142mph**
228km/h

*Right: The 'Ray's engine
was a 327cid V8, introduced
in 1962. Developing
250bhp, a more powerful
365bhp unit was available
at extra cost.*

*Below: Well proportioned
and distinctive, a 1963
Corvette roadster. The
dummy hot air outlets were
opened up in 1965 to duct
heat away from the engine.*

 The Corvette Sting Ray with its glass-fiber body, finely chiselled lines, and concealed headlights came of age in the 1963 season. For, apart from its V8 engine, there were no legacies from earlier 'Vettes, and the car was based on a new all-independent suspension chassis to the benefit of roadholding.

Its memorable and distinctive aerodynamically-honed styling was the work of William Mitchell, General Motors' head of styling, who was much more susceptible to European influences than his predecessor Harley Earl. And while the Sting Ray possessed its own distinctive personality, the stylistic subtleties of Jaguar's superlative E-Type were readily apparent (Mitchell was an enthusiastic owner/driver of one).

Further visual input came from two of Mitchell's experimental cars, the 1958 Stingray two-seater racer and XP-720 coupé of 1959. The latter was significant because the '63 Corvette was

to be offered in coupé form in the Continental European manner and the style has been an enduring feature of the line ever since.

'Father of the Corvette,' Belgian-born engineer Zora Arkus-Duntov, was intent that the Sting Ray would offer better interior accommodation than its predecessor, along with better handling. This was achieved, despite the fact that the car had a shorter wheelbase, at 98in (2489 mm), than the 1953-62 generation's 102in (2590mm). To allow for this, there was a new box-section chassis and rear transverse leaf spring/radius rod independent suspension demanded by the body's design.

Speed in excess of 140mph

The engine was the previous year's 327cid (5.3 liter) V8 which was to be available in 250 and 365hp guises during the Sting Ray's production life. The latter powered the model to over 140mph (225km/h). Fuel injection, introduced in 1957, remained as an option until 1966.

There were further engine enhancements in the pipeline and in 1965 a 396cid (6.5 liter) V8 appeared. This was the year in which the Corvette was also provided with all-round disc brakes. Yet a further engine option arrived for 1966, in the form of a 427cid (7 liter) V8; however, less desirably, the model's increased weight dropped its top speed to 135mph (217km/h).

Outwardly the classic lines remained essentially unchanged during the 'Ray's six-year production life, although the coupé underwent a small but

significant modification from the 1964 season. Mitchell had initially insisted on a divided rear window but this was deleted on the grounds that it restricted visibility. But he has had the last word because today collectors are queuing up to buy pre-1964 examples…

The line was discontinued in 1967 after some 180,000 Sting Rays had been completed. A legend was in the making.

Above: The Corvette acquired a coupé body with the Sting Ray. This 1963 car is identifiable by its now highly desirable divided rear window which was deleted in 1964. The fact that the doors intrude into the roof is a nice touch.

Specification	**Chevrolet** Corvette Sting Ray (327cid)
Engine location	Front, in-line
Configuration	V8
Bore and stroke	4.0 x 3.25in (101 x 82mm)
Capacity	327cid (5358cc)
Valve operation	Pushrod
Horsepower	250bhp @ 4400rpm
Transmission	Manual three-speed
Drive	Rear
Chassis	Perimeter
Suspension – front	Wishbones and transverse leaf spring
Suspension – rear	Radius rod and transverse leaf spring
Brakes	Drum
Top speed	142mph (228km/h)
Acceleration	0-60mph (0-96km/h): 5.9 seconds

Ford GT40

**Top speed
160mph**
257km/h

*Right: The mid-located
Ford V8 engine, this
example exhibiting Cobra-
related Shelby origins.*

*Below: A desirable race-
bred road car. Note the
scuttle-mounted gas tank
and single windshield wiper.*

Created by Ford with the express aim of
winning the Le Mans 24 hour race, the
Anglo/American GT40 did precisely that
and took the checkered flag there in four successive
years from 1966 to 1969.

However, Ford's Le Mans triumphs were not
lightly won and it took no less than three years to
develop a winning car. Ford was a company used
to producing value-for-money, mass-produced
sedans, and it lacked any experience of creating
such a racer. So it acquired the rights to the
innovative Lola GT, which had run, albeit
unsuccessfully, at the 1963 Le Mans race. Radically
its 4.2 liter Ford V8 engine was mounted
longitudinally behind the driver in the manner of
contemporary Formula 1 cars.

Using this ingenious concept as a starting point,
Ford proceeded to develop the design at Slough,
Berkshire in a facility managed by John Wyer,
formerly of Aston Martin. The trio of cars that

Left: Because the GT40 is such a desirable car, its numbers have increased over the years! However, this is a 1966 example converted for road use. It was destined for Shelby American but was returned to Ford Advanced Vehicles because of troubles relating to its documentation.

Below: The original chassis for this car was scrapped when it was damaged during testing at Silverstone and it was rebuilt around a Mark III one. Note the coupé's low lines, it is just 40in (1016mm) high.

appeared at the 1964 Le Mans event were thus closely related to the Lola, although they were powered by an alloy version of Ford's V8. The GT40 name was adopted because on the road the coupés stood a mere 40in (1016mm) high.

Although spectacularly fast, one was timed at 187mph (301km/h), all the cars suffered from teething troubles, after which Ford transferred the GT40's development to America and placed the project under the control of Carroll Shelby, creator of the AC Cobra.

The original V8 was replaced by a 7 liter unit. Six examples of what was designated the Mark II were run at the 1965 Le Mans event but all succumbed to mechanical failures.

Radical modifications

Further radical modifications followed and in 1966 Ford was triumphant and took the first three places in the 24 hour classic. The following year the Mark IV, with a lighter stronger chassis made of an aluminum honeycomb sandwich material, was also victorious. At this point Ford decided to quit while it was ahead. However, GT40s prepared by John Wyer took the checkered flag at Le Mans for the next two years under the sponsorship of Gulf Oil.

In the meantime Wyer had produced a roadgoing version of the Mark III powered by a 4.7 liter V8. Introduced in December 1965, it cost $9300 and closely resembled the sports racer, apart from a reprofiled nose, twin headlamps which

replaced the single units, and a taller tail that incorporated overheated luggage compartments located either side of the gearbox. Even this tamed version could attain 160mph (257km/h).

Production ceased in 1968, by which time just 31 examples of these fabulous street machines had been completed.

Specification	**Ford** GT40 Mark III (4.7 liters)
Engine location	Mid, in-line
Configuration	V8
Bore and stroke	101 x 72mm
Capacity	4736cc
Valve operation	Pushrod
Horsepower	306bhp @ 6000rpm
Transmission	Manual four-speed
Drive	Rear
Chassis	Steel semi-monocoque
Suspension – front	Wishbone and coil spring
Suspension – rear	Trailing arm, wishbones and coil spring
Brakes	Disc
Top speed	160mph (257km/h)
Acceleration	0-60mph (0-96km/h): 5.3 seconds

Sunbeam Tiger

**Top speed
120mph**
193km/h

*Right: One of the few
outward giveaways, the two
badges on the front fenders
indicate that this is not a
standard four-cylinder
Alpine.*

*Below: Although it went on
sale in Europe from the
1965 season, inevitably
most Tigers crossed the
Atlantic as it was created
with the American market
in mind. Otherwise this
Sunbeam was pure Alpine IV.*

 The AC Cobra was the inspiration for the
Sunbeam Tiger that transformed the open
two-seater Alpine into a 120mph
(193km/h) sports car. In its original form the Alpine
of 1959 was powered by a 1.5 liter engine which
endowed it with 90mph plus (145km/h+)
performance. Created for the American sports car
market, it had to compete with the likes of MG and
Triumph. It also suffered commercially from the
dawning of the muscle car era and the increased
performance that came in its wake.

The outcome, in April 1964, was the Sunbeam
Tiger, inspired by the company's 1925 land speed
record car of that name. The man behind it was Ian
Gerrad, who was Rootes West Coast sales manager.
He enlisted Carroll Shelby's assistance and Shelby
shoe-horned Ford's 260cid (4.2 liter) V8, which
had just been fitted to the first of the Cobras, under
the Series II Alpine's hood. A second prototype was
built by Ken Miles who was Rootes' chief
development engineer in America.

Results were sufficiently encouraging for
Rootes to proceed with the project and the Tiger's
assembly was entrusted to Jensen. Outwardly the
car appeared little different from its Alpine Series
IV stablemate, which remained in production, the
substitution having been effected with remarkably
little modification.

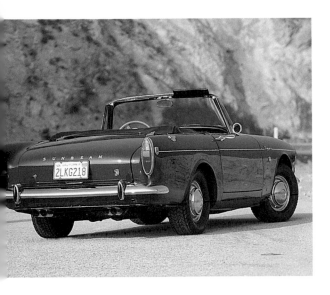

Specification	**Sunbeam** Tiger
Engine location	Front, in-line
Configuration	V8
Bore and stroke	3.8 x 2.87in (96 x 73mm)
Capacity	260cid (4261cc)
Valve operation	Pushrod
Horsepower	141bhp @ 4400rpm
Transmission	Manual four-speed
Drive	Rear
Chassis	Unitary
Suspension – front	Wishbones and coil spring
Suspension – rear	Half-elliptic spring
Brakes	Front disc, rear drum
Top speed	120mph (193km/h)
Acceleration	0-60mph (0-96km/h): 9.4 seconds

Revised steering gear

A rack and pinion steering gear replaced the original recirculating ball unit, and there was a cross-flow radiator and a new Salisbury rear axle. Changes were also made to the spring rates and a Borg-Warner manual four-speed gearbox was fitted, although it was soon replaced by a Ford all-synchromesh unit.

Fuel consumption was in the region of 18mpg (15lit/100km) but this was not a problem because the Alpine III had already been fitted with twin fuel tanks to increase its range. The V8 transformed the Alpine's performance – it was capable of about 120mph (193km/h) and 60mph (96km/h) arrived from standstill in under 10 seconds. Initially only available for export, right-hand-drive versions were introduced in March 1965.

In 1967 came the 125mph (201km/h) export only Tiger II powered by the Mustang's 289cid (4.7 liter) V8 complete with an egg-crate radiator grille and side stripes. However, in that year Chrysler obtained control of Rootes and it did not wish to continue producing a car powered a rival engine. Production therefore ceased in mid-1967. By then 6495 examples of the Tiger I and just 571 examples of its successor had been completed.

Above left: The 260 badge on the trunk lid of this 1965 car describes the capacity, in cubic inches, of the Ford V8 engine which powered the Tiger. The two exhaust pipes were another giveaway although the twin fuel tanks were shared with the Alpine IV. Steel wheels were fitted as standard with wires available at extra cost.

Left: The Tiger's smart wood-veneered dashboard which was fitted to most of the cars; originally PVC had sufficed. Note the length of the gear lever. Originally a short control, similar to that used on the AC Cobra, was fitted, but this made engaging first and third gears uncomfortable for Tiger drivers. So Ford introduced this more ergonomically acceptable lengthened stick.

Gordon-Keeble

**Top speed
137mph**
220km/h

*Right: The crowded engine
compartment of a 1965
Gordon-Keeble, which, in
addition to the 5.3 liter
Corvette V8 engine, had to
accommodate twin brake
servos and two cooling fans.*

*Below: Bertone styling,
Chevrolet power, and
British craftsmanship
combined in this acclaimed,
fast, glass-fiber-bodied
grand tourer. The badge
featured a tongue-in-cheek
tortoise emblem.*

 Although the Gordon-Keeble of 1964
experienced a somewhat protracted
gestation period, when it appeared the
137mph (220km/h) grand tourer looked like a sure-
fire winner. This was thanks to its assured Italian
styling and reliable, guaranteed performance from a
5.4 liter V8, which came courtesy of its Chevrolet
Corvette contemporary.

The marque took its first name from John
Gordon, who ran Slough-based Peerless Motors. In
1957 the company launched the glass-fiber-bodied,
Triumph TR3-engined Peerless GT which survived
until 1960. It was subsequently produced, until
1962, under the Warwick name.

In the meantime Jim Keeble, an Ipswich garage
proprietor, was asked by an American customer to
install a 4.6 liter Chevrolet V8 engine into a
Peerless. As a result of the ensuing dialogue,
Gordon and Keeble decided to market the reworked
concept, which was named the Gordon GT.
Ambitiously, it was displayed at the 1960 Geneva
Motor Show.

Its understated, well-proportioned, two-door,
four-seater Bertone body was the work of Giorgetto
Giugiaro. Later, in 1968, he created the renowned
Ital Design styling house. The body concealed a
space-frame chassis with a de Dion rear axle; under
the Gordon's hood was the Corvette's V8.

Although there were plans for the car to enter
production in September 1960, unfortunately there
was a four-year hiatus before the Gordon-Keeble

Left: The deep framed windows and slender pillars ensured excellent visibility. Note the twin gas tanks, with fillers on each rear fender – each one contained 13.2 gallons (50lit) of fuel.

Below: The well equipped cockpit with rev counter, speedometer, oil pressure and water temperature gauges in front of the driver. Buttons for the electric windows adjoin the gear lever on the central console.

GK1 was launched in March 1964. It was outwardly similar to the show car, but the original metal body had been replaced by a glass-fiber one. The car was built in Eastleigh, Hampshire at a factory located at Southampton Airport.

By this time the capacity of the Corvette V8 had increased to 5.3 liters. The result was a reliable, flexible GT with excellent traction, handling, and brakes. Quiet, yet rapid, it was able to reach 60mph (96km/h) in a mere 7.5 seconds.

Breaking the mold

Weighing 3164lb (1435kg), thanks to its choice of body material and tubular chassis, its build quality was commended by commentators. Williams and Pritchard of London made the molds and the first 12 hulls. But there were many who believed that the body was constructed of steel or aluminum, which also reflected well on the factory that was responsible for the shell's manufacture.

The only fly in the ointment was that the fact that the Gordon-Keeble sold for just $3920. It was seriously underpriced and the original company only survived until March 1965, by which time 93 examples had been completed. Although it was revived later that year as Keeble Cars and the price was raised to $5680, the opportunity that had existed in 1960 had all but disappeared. The production of these now Southampton-built cars only continued until 1967. Although the rights to the design were acquired by American John De Bruyne and two rebadged examples were duly exhibited at the 1968 New York Motor Show, the promised cars never entered production. In all just 99 Gordon-Keebles were built.

Specification	Gordon-Keeble
Engine location	Front, in-line
Configuration	V8
Bore and stroke	101 x 82mm
Capacity	5355cc
Valve operation	Pushrod
Horsepower	300bhp @ 5000rpm
Transmission	Manual four-speed
Drive	Rear
Chassis	Space-frame
Suspension – front	Wishbones and coil springs
Suspension – rear	De Dion axle and coil springs
Brakes	Disc
Top speed	137mph (220km/h)
Acceleration	0-60mph (0-96km/h): 7.5 seconds

Pontiac GTO

**Top speed
110mph**
177km/h

The GTO was the car that ushered in America's muscle car era. Destined to revitalize Pontiac's sales in the booming youth market of the 1960s, such was the success of this outwardly deceptive model that the rest of the American motor industry wasted little time in following suit.

It was in January 1963 that Pontiac advertising executive Jim Wagners (or engineers John DeLorean and Bill Collins depending on who was telling the story) decided to insert a 389cid (6.4 liter) V8 under the hood of Pontiac's newly minted Tempest line.

Development undertaken in secret

The only trouble was that Pontiac was a division of General Motors and there was a corporate ban on engines larger than 330cid (5.4 liters) powering an intermediate model such as the two-door Tempest. Development work was consequently undertaken in secrecy with prototypes fitted with '326' V8s although, in reality, they carried the larger capacity 389 unit.

Pontiac got around the corporate diktat by making what it named the GTO. The appellation was filched from the Ferrari of the same name, the initials standing for *Gran Turismo Omologato*, an option in the Tempest Le Mans series.

The model, introduced for 1964, was available in sports coupé, hardtop, and convertible forms. It used the 389 unit with distinctive chromed valve covers, enhanced by a 'hotter' camshaft and High Output cylinder heads which were crowned by a Carter four barrel carburetor. Available in two states of tune, the standard was 325hp and there was an optional 348 version.

Selling for a highly competitive $3400, the GTO could reach 60mph (96km/h) in around 4.5 seconds and top speed was in excess of 110mph (177km/h). Such performance had not previously been available at this price.

The following year's GTO underwent a reskin and was easily identifiable by its vertically

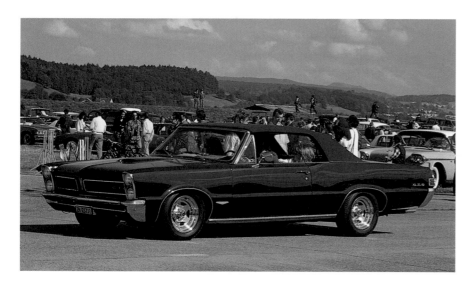

Above: The Pontiac GTO was reskinned for the 1965 season, and was better looking than the rather angular original. It is easily identifiable by the stacked headlamps that were taken from larger Pontiacs.

Right: The GTO name lingered on until 1974, its performance image being a victim of the depression fueled by the oil price rise. This is the GTO 400 version of the two-door Pontiac Le Mans. Note its curious hood scoops.

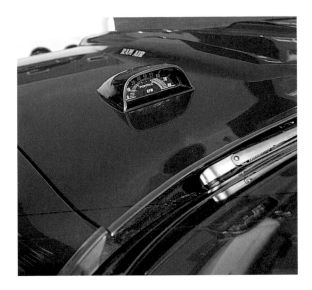

Specification	Pontiac GTO
Engine location	Front, in-line
Configuration	V8
Bore and stroke	4.06 x 3.75in (103 x 95mm)
Capacity	389cid (6374cc)
Valve operation	Pushrod
Horsepower	325bhp @ 4800rpm
Transmission	Manual three-speed
Drive	Rear
Chassis	Box section
Suspension – front	Wishbones and coil spring
Suspension – rear	Trailing links and coil spring
Brakes	Drum
Top speed	110mph (177km/h)
Acceleration	0-60mph (0-96km/h): 6.9 seconds

Above left: An optional hood-mounted revolution counter appeared on the GTO 400 during the 1967 model year.

Left: The GTO convertible for the 1967 season was essentially the same as the previous year's cars, apart from more visible rear lights.

Below: The impressive cockpit with bucket seats, floor gear change, and GTO initials proudly emblazoned on the dash.

mounted twin headlamps which replaced the horizontal ones. Otherwise the mechanicals remained the same although the 389's outputs were modestly increased to 335 and 360hp.

There was an impressive and distinctive new GTO for 1966 and demand was such that Pontiac built no less than 96,946 of them in a single year which was a production record for any muscle car. Similarly powered by a 389 engine, this was a 120mph (193km/h) model. The second generation GTO was uprated for the 1967 season with the V8 enlarged to 400cid (6.5 liters). Top speed was now 125mph (201km/h).

The last of the line, the GTO of the 1968-72 era, retained the 400 V8 but also offered an optional 455cid (7.4 liter) unit. But by then Pontiac was concentrating resources on its increasingly potent and popular Firebird line.

Shelby Mustang GT-350

**Top speed
119mph**
191km/h

The sporty Mustang of 1964, the fastest-selling model in Ford's post-war history, spawned a rare and successful track-ready derivative in 1965 in the form of the GT-350.

Commissioned by the company and prepared by Carroll Shelby, creator of the AC Cobra, it was built to challenge the rival Chevrolet Corvette in Sports Car Club of America events and simultaneously to hone Ford's performance image.

Power was boosted to 306bhp

Taking the 2 + 2 GT Mustang coupé as his starting point, Shelby retained the 271bhp 289cid (4.7 liter) V8 but power was boosted to 306bhp by the fitment of a bespoke Holley carburetor, a high rise aluminum inlet manifold, and new exhaust system. A Borg-Warner aluminum four-speed close-ratio manual gearbox was employed.

Suspension was uprated and adjustable Koni shock absorbers added. Perversely, the unassisted steering box was removed and replaced by a higher geared powered unit. Inside the trim was discarded and replaced by two competition front seats with the spare tire taking the place of the rear squab.

As for the name of the conversion, legend has it that this was born during a meeting held at Shelby American's modest factory at Venice, California. When he asked about the distance to a nearby engineering shop, a colleague paced out the gap and declared it to be some 350 feet. So the GT-350 was born…

Shorn of its corporate badges, the Shelby Mustang was unveiled in January 1965 and was offered in two guises. There was a potent 360bhp GT-350R which was intended for racing, but the overwhelming majority of cars were the more tractable GT-350S street machine.

Above: A 1965 Shelby Mustang in obligatory white. The interior is black. Based on the fastback model, the cars were delivered from Ford minus hood, exhaust system, and back seat, the conversion work being undertaken at Shelby's factory in Venice, California.

Right: The 1965 GT-350 bore a closer resemblance to the production Mustang than 1966 cars. They had plastic rear quarter windows and scoops behind the doors to cool the rear brakes. In both cases the Ford badges were removed.

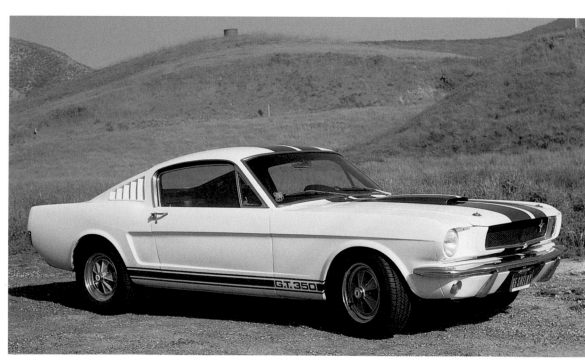

There was just one exterior finish specified, white, which is America's racing color, with blue striping that ran along the cars' sills and proclaimed the *GT-350* designation. There were also extra matching 'Le Mans' stripes added to a car's center-line. Other identifying features were side air scoops introduced ahead of the rear wheel arches while small triangular rear side windows replaced the original louvers.

Racing success

Some 680,000 standard Mustangs were built in 1965 and Shelby's production accounted for a mere 562 examples, of which perhaps 30 were racers. But they did everything expected of them and won that year's SSCA's B-Production National Championship and repeated the success over the next two years.

1966's cars were rather tamer than the originals and the color range was expanded to embrace red, blue, green, and black which were complemented by black or gold racing stripes. Just 2380 were built in 1966 and this included 936 which were rented that year to lucky customers by Hertz. They were invariably returned with telltale signs of racing activity in evidence!

Specification	Shelby Mustang GT-350
Engine location	Front, in-line
Configuration	V8
Bore and stroke	4.0 x 2.87in (101 x 73mm)
Capacity	289cid (4735cc)
Valve operation	Pushrod
Horsepower	306bhp @ 6000rpm
Transmission	Manual four-speed
Drive	Rear
Chassis	Unitary
Suspension – front	Wishbones and coil spring
Suspension – rear	Half-elliptic springs
Brakes	Front disc, rear drum
Top speed	119mph (191km/h)
Acceleration	0-60mph (0-96km/h): 6.5 seconds

Below: A distinctive plain grille with the famous Mustang motif moved from its customary central position to the side.

Iso Grifo

**Top speed
171mph**
275km/h

*Right: The heart of the
Grifo, an American V8
which provided plenty of
performance at a reasonable
price. This is a 7 liter
Chevrolet Corvette unit, but
this was later replaced by a
smaller capacity Ford one.*

*Below: The fine lines of the
Grifo's Bertone body helped
to sell a model that was one
of the fastest cars in the
world. The hot air vents
helped keep the engine and
rear brakes cool.*

Seizing on the concept of a potent
American V8 shoe-horned into a stylish
coupé body, in 1963 the Italian Iso
concern produced the Grifo which was one of the
fastest GTs of its day and could attain speeds in
excess of 180mph (290km/h).

Milan-based motorcycle manufacturer Iso was
the creator of the Isetta bubble car; in 1955 it sold
the design to BMW and there was to be a seven-
year hiatus before it produced another vehicle. In
1960 founder Renzo Rivolta attended the London
Motor Show and he was influenced there by the
Bertone-styled, Corvette-V8 engined Gordon-
Keeble. The result was the 1962 Rivolta GT with
body lines similarly essayed by Bertone and
powered by a 5.4 liter 300bhp Chevrolet V8. Its
chassis was engineered by Giotto Bizzarrani,
formerly of Alfa Romeo and Ferrari, and the
transmission was of transatlantic origin, being Borg
Warner or, later, Powerglide automatics. A five-
speed ZF manual gearbox was also available.

This paved the way the following year for the
lighter and faster two-seater Grifo which used a
shortened version of the Rivolta's chassis. It was,

once again, Bertone-bodied although it was far
more stylish that its rather soberly styled
predecessor. In addition to the mainstream coupé, it
was also available with a sun roof, a Targa-type
top, and as a full roadster.

7 liter version introduced
This initially used the Chevvy V8; the 365bhp
version was capable of 158mph (254km/h).
However, it was also successively available in 350,

300 and 340hp states of tune. A top-line muscular 7 liter version followed in 1969 which used the Corvette 427 engine, and a 7.4 liter unit followed in 1970. The latter version was fitted with modified bodywork, developed no less than 460bhp and could attain 186mph (299km/h) flat out. Later, in 1973 and 1974, 'smaller' 5.7 liter Ford V8s replaced the Chevvy units.

There was also a sports-racing Grifo A3/C which Bizzarrini produced at his own plant at Livorno. When Iso ceased its racing activities at the end of 1965, he continued to produce the car, which was variously named the Bizzarrini GT Strada or GT America, until 1969.

The Grifo proper ceased production in 1974, by which time 412 examples had been completed. But in 1998 Pietro Rivolta, the founder's son, announced plans for a new Grifo with Zagato-styled composite body and a Ford 4.5 liter V8. Sadly this latter-day car has failed to materialize.

Above: Looking as good from the rear, the twin exhaust pipes reveal the presence of V8 power…

Below left: The Grifo's left-hand-drive interior was very light, thanks to the large rear window.

Specification	**Iso** Grifo (7 liters)
Engine location	Front, in-line
Configuration	V8
Bore and stroke	108 x 95mm
Capacity	6998cc
Valve operation	Pushrod
Horsepower	390bhp @ 5200rpm
Transmission	Manual four-speed
Drive	Rear
Chassis	Unitary
Suspension – front	Wishbones and coil spring
Suspension – rear	De Dion axle, radius arm and coil spring
Brakes	Disc
Top speed	171mph (275km/h)
Acceleration	0-60mph (0-96km/h): 7.1 seconds

Lamborghini Miura

**Top speed
171mph**
274km/h

In 1966 the Miura supercar, in which a sensational body was united with innovative mid-engined mechanicals, set the seal on the credibility of the three-year-old Lamborghini marque.

It was the only make to challenge Ferrari's pre-eminent position as Italy's foremost supercar builder. Tractor manufacturer Ferruccio Lamborghini's first model, the 350GT for 1963, was powered by a magnificent 3.5 liter quad-cam V12 engine, designed by former Ferrari engineer Giotto Bizzarrani. Yet although the Touring-designed body was elegant, it lacked that special elusive quality that Lamborghini was seeking.

It arrived in abundance with the Miura. Daringly, Lamborghini's young chief engineer Giampaolo Dallara transferred the 350bhp V12, by then extended to 3.9 liters, from the front of the car to the middle of it. But rather than positioning it longitudinally, Ford GT40-style, he adventurously opted for a transverse configuration in the manner of the British Mini. The five-speed gearbox was similarly located in the engine's sump.

Below: Often hailed as the world's first supercar, the Miura's Bertone body was as stunning as its mid-engined mechanicals that were inspired by Ford's sports-racing GT40. The cabin was of monocoque construction while the hood and engine cover were made of aluminum and, accordingly, unstressed. Note the cooling ducts for the transversely mounted V12 engine.

Stunning styling by Bertone

These revolutionary mechanicals were cloaked in a stunning Bertone coupé body, the work of 26-year-old Marcello Gandini. The resulting car was displayed at the 1966 Geneva Motor Show where its name was revealed as the Miura. This was in tribute to Don Eduardo Miura, a breeder of fighting bulls – Ferruccio Lamborghini, who was born under the Zodiac sign of Taurus the bull, being drawn to names with taurine associations.

Entering production early in 1967, the Miura was a mere 41in (1041mm) high, and was utterly distinctive and beautifully proportioned with a tail that could be mistaken for no other on account of the innovative engine location.

If you can't stand the heat...

The heat generated by the V12 was a major problem, however, so a series of louvers, that were likened to the slats of a venetian blind, were introduced to permit some rear visibility and, principally, to allow the hot air to escape. However, this meant inserting a window between the cockpit and engine compartment to separate the occupants from the twin bugbears of high temperature levels and noise.

At the front, the swivelling headlamps were set in what looked suspiciously like eyelashes but which were in fact disguised ducts that directed cooling air to the front brakes.

Top speed was over 170mph (274km/h) and the Miura combined out and out performance with the handling expected from a mid-engined machines.

In 1969 the even more powerful Miura S with 375bhp on tap was unveiled but the ultimate version was the SV of 1971 with 385bhp, wider track and rear wheels and, in consequence, back fenders. The original 'eyelashes' were also banished. Destined for a relatively short life, the last SV was built late in 1972. There would be a two-year hiatus before the Miura was replaced by the equally spectacular Countach.

Left above: The Miura's headlights rapidly elevated when they were switched on. The color of the 'eyelashes' changed with the paint color.

Left below: The only way in which the V12 could be transversely mounted was to locate the gearbox Mini-style in the sump.

Below: The cockpit was well equipped, but it was a little on the small side and noisy because of the close proximity of the engine.

Specification	**Lamborghini** Miura
Engine location	Mid, transverse
Configuration	V12
Bore and stroke	82 x 62mm
Capacity	3929cc
Valve operation	Twin overhead camshafts per bank
Horsepower	350bhp @ 7000rpm
Transmission	Manual five-speed
Drive	Rear
Chassis	Steel box section
Suspension – front	Wishbones and coil spring
Suspension – rear	Wishbones and coil spring
Brakes	Disc
Top speed	171mph (274km/h)
Acceleration	0-60mph (0-96km/h): 6 seconds

Improved handling

The design of the suspension remained essentially the same, but it was subtly improved and refined. Handling improved as a consequence. At the front the car was slightly lower than before which improved the aerodynamics and countered a tendency for the SV's nose to lift at high speeds.

The magnificent V12 engine was also an improvement on the original. Its S predecessor had reshaped combustion chambers, high lift camshafts, and larger carburetors. This improved output to 370bhp. Yet further changes were made to the SV's valve timing with different valves and further changes to the carburetors. Another difference was a new sump to correct excessive oil surge on fast cornering. Previously Miuras had occasionally suffered from this problem which resulted in bearing failure.

While every Miura sold was a coupé, a single open version was made but, alas, it never entered production because the company lacked the necessary capital. In 1968 Bertone produced a single car as a design study which, although it used many of the original body panels, featured changes to the cockpit and its tail.

However, this car did not disappear, as is the fate of many such design exercises. It was acquired by the International Lead Zinc Research Organisation. Assisted by Bertone, many original metal parts, such as inlet and exhaust manifolds, sump, bumpers, and door handles, were replaced with zinc ones.

Above: The lines of a 1969 Miura S shown to good effect. This example lacks the headlamp 'eyelashes' which were also deleted on its SV successor. The right-hand hood grille conceals the fuel filler cap.

Below: The Miura was only 3ft 5in (1041mm) high. This is a 1972 SV model. While the driving position was fine for drivers of average height, it was not so good for taller people.

In all only 150 examples of the SV were built. Apart from the modifications already mentioned, the factory took this opportunity to correct many of the shortcomings owners had experienced with the earlier Miuras. As a consequence the SV is the best of the breed and, in retrospect, it seems unfortunate that its manufacture was halted early, particularly as its Countach successor did not enter production until 1974.

The SV's chassis was notably stronger than those of its predecessors. While the Miura's sensational lines remained essentially the same, beneath the surface heavier gauge sheet steel was used in the unitary hull because the original had a tendency to flex, particularly when the driver was hard down on the accelerator.

Although the last Miura was delivered to Italian industrialist Luigi Innocenti on January 15 1973, this was not quite the end of the story. One further example was completed in 1975 from existing parts for dedicated Canadian Lamborghini enthusiast Walter Woolf. He took the car over in April and that really was the end of the line.

In all 765 Miuras were completed during six years of production. There were 475 examples of the original car, 140 Miura Ss and 150 SVs. But in the meantime, Ferruccio Lamborghini had lost control in 1972 of his company, having sold his tractor business to Fiat. Such is the vulnerability of the supercar manufacturer.

Below: The Miura's lines are extraordinarily impressive and remained essentially the same on the SV. Lamborghini's famous badge displaying a fighting bull is prominent.

Chevrolet Camaro Z-28

**Top speed
126mph**
203km/h

*Below: There were no Z-28
emblems on the 1967
version – these arrived in
1968 – but the racing
stripes were a distinctive
feature. The rear spoiler
was an optional extra.*

The success of the Shelby-prepared Ford
Mustangs in Sports Car Club of America
events had not escaped the attention of
rival General Motors. Its response was the Z-28
version of the Chevrolet's newly introduced
Camaro coupé of 1967, which was capable of
speeds nudging the 130mph (209km/h) mark.

But the SCCA's rules specified that for
TransAm races the engines of competing cars could
not exceed 305cid (5 liters) – the Mustang had been
eligible because it was powered by a 289cid (4.7
liter) unit. Unfortunately Chevrolet's smallest V8
was of 327cid (5.3 liter) displacement. The answer
was to rework its internals so reducing the engine's
capacity to 302cid (4.9 liters).

Corvette cylinder heads

Corvette parts were incorporated, namely its big
port cylinder heads. There was a special camshaft
and the hydraulic tappets were replaced by solid
lifters. There was a baffled sump and high pressure
oil pump. A Holley four-barrel carburetor, complete
with a special manifold, was fitted.

At this time General Motors – Chevrolet's
parent – did not permit its divisions to be directly
involved in racing, so the development of the car
was placed in the hands of front-line drivers Roger
Penske and Mark Donohue who would also race it.

The regulations required that 1000 examples of
a street-ready model needed to be sold before it
could be certified to compete. The Z-28 was based
on the mainline Camaro but fitted with the new
302cid (4.9 liter) V8. Other enhancements included
uprated suspension, wider wheels, and higher ratio
steering, all for an extra $400. It was only available
with a four-speed Munci manual gearbox; this was
a no-nonsense specification, automatics and air
conditioning options were not listed.

The Z-28 was soon proving its worth in the
SCCA events for which it had been created. After a
faltering 1967 season, it wrested the title from
Mustang in 1968, winning 10 out of 11 races in the
series. It was the same story in 1969 when
Donahue again took the championship.

*Right: A 1978 Z-28 with T-
bar twin hatch roof fitted
with tinted glass. This is the
high performance version,
identifiable by its distinctive
livery with black-throated
pointed hood air scoop and
louvers let into the front
spoiler. Under the hood was
a 350cid (5.7 liter) V8
which developed 170 or 185
horsepower.*

Specification	**Chevrolet** Camaro Z-28 (350cid)
Engine location	Front, in-line
Configuration	V8
Bore and stroke	4 x 3.50in (102 x 89mm)
Capacity	350cid (5735cc)
Valve operation	Pushrod
Horsepower	360bhp @ 6000rpm
Transmission	Manual four-speed
Drive	Rear
Chassis	Unitary
Suspension – front	Wishbones and coil spring
Suspension – rear	Half-elliptic spring
Brakes	Front disc, rear drum
Top speed	126mph (203km/h)
Acceleration	0-60mph (0-96km/h): 5.9 seconds

The model was reskinned and its lines sharpened up that year, but its replacement in 1970 had a new coupé body that looked mean, purposeful, and distinctive. A change in the TransAm rules meant that 350cid (5.7 liter) units could be used and Chevrolet promptly installed the 350 engine from its Corvette stablemate.

Best-selling Camaro

Although the winning Penkse/Donohue duo had departed for America Motors and the championship that year went to Ford, this Z-28 proved to be the fastest and best-handling of the line. And the regular Camaro became one of Chevrolet's best-sellers, surviving in this form until 1981.

Above left: The cockpit of a comprehensively instrumented 1993 model.

Below: A purposeful-looking 1985 European Version Camaro Z-28.

Ferrari Daytona

**Top speed
174mph**
280km/h

*Below: Last of the great
front-engined Ferrari
berlinettas, for the time
being at least, the Daytona's
Pininfarina-styled body is
regarded as one of the
design house's finest
creations. The sense of
balance between the long
hood, its lines uninterrupted
by projecting headlights,
and the relatively small
passenger area is
outstanding.*

Ferrari's first generation of fabled V12-engined berlinettas came to an end in 1973 with the demise of the big and memorable Daytona which was capable of no less than 174mph (280km/h). When the prototype was unveiled at the 1968 Paris Salon, what was then described at the 365 GTB/4 was hailed as the fastest road car in Ferrari's history.

Interestingly, the Daytona name was not an official one but the car was so christened by the press following Ferrari's victory in the 1967 Daytona 24 hour race.

Pininfarina had produced a magnificent and distinctive coupé body in which the headlamps, for aerodynamic considerations, were located behind clear plastic covers within the finely chiseled nose. However, they were subsequently found not to conform to regulations in the all-important American market so retractable units were introduced above the originals.

The seat of power

The long hood concealed an all-alloy, 4.4 liter, four-cam, V12 engine; although this followed the layout of Ferrari's earlier power units, it was essentially new in execution. The dry sump unit came complete with six Weber carburetors and it developed an impressive 352bhp. The five-speed ZF gearbox was in unit with the transaxle.

There was the usual tubular chassis with all-independent suspension and disc brakes but this was a heavy car with a long wheelbase and it turned the scales at 3600lb (1633kg).

Although Pininfarina had been responsible for the design and construction of the prototype, the bodies of the production cars, which appeared a year after the model's Paris debut, were built in Modena by Scaglietti. Audaciously, there was only room for two occupants.

Performance and handling was up to Maranello's usual demanding standards. And while the brakes were sufficient for road use, they displayed their limitations on racing versions that were capable of speeds approaching 200mph (321km/h). Examples ran at Le Mans in 1971 and 1972 when Daytonas attained creditable fifth placings on both occasions, and in the latter year also occupied sixth to ninth positions.

A convertible (spider) version of the model was unveiled at the 1969 Frankfurt Motor Show and it also displayed sensational lines. Although the berlinettas inevitably predominated, about 150 open cars were built.

When Daytona production ceased in 1973, some 1350 examples had been completed. It was replaced by the mid-engined 365 GT4BB, the legendary Boxer. But if the public thought that it had seen the last front-engined Ferrari, it was very much mistaken…

Above: Despite the Daytona's size, there is only room for two people; the view down that long hood is memorable.

Left: Although the great majority of Daytonas were coupés, there were some convertibles which are greatly sought after.

Below left: Beneath that substantial air cleaner are six Weber carburetors. The twin oil filters are remarkably accessible.

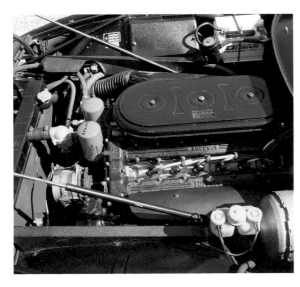

Specification	Ferrari 365 GTB/4 Daytona
Engine location	Front, in-line
Configuration	V12
Bore and stroke	81 x 71mm
Capacity	4390cc
Valve operation	Twin overhead camshafts per bank
Horsepower	352bhp @ 7500rpm
Transmission	Manual five-speed
Drive	Rear
Chassis	Tubular steel
Suspension – front	Wishbones and coil spring
Suspension – rear	Wishbones and coil spring
Brakes	Disc
Top speed	174mph (280km/h)
Acceleration	0-60mph (0-96km/h): 5.4 seconds

Above: Ferrari prepared this right-hand-drive Daytona for UK Ferrari importers Maranello Concessionaires to race in 1972.

Below: A NART Daytona in the paddock; it dramatically raised the model's profile in the American market.

Although the Daytona had particularly proved its worth at Le Mans, it was also successfully campaigned in America, which was appropriate in view of its (unofficial) model name. In truth, Ferrari seemed a little reluctant to lend support to owners who wanted to race what was essentially a road car. But its hand was forced to some extent by the fact that, in late August 1971, no less than 500 examples had been completed. This meant that the Daytona became eligible for Group 4 racing in the Special Grand Tourer series.

Competition versions

At this point Ferrari's importers in Britain, France, Belgium, and Switzerland pressed Maranello to produce competition versions of the car. But it was American importer Luigi Chinetti, who in 1972 was appointed the company's East Coast representative, who was in the forefront of racing the model.

The reality was that the America-designated Daytonas became available well after the European specification cars had been marketed. Sales began modestly in 1971 but it was only the following year that they began to gather any momentum.

Unlike Europe's Daytonas, which had optional air conditioning, this feature was standard, if not overly efficient, on those cars sold on the American market. They were also distinguished by the fitting of every conceivable option, from leather upholstery to electrically operated radio antennas.

It was against this background that in 1971 the factory began to support, albeit reluctantly, the racing effort. Back-up was not provided by Ferrari's racing workshop but by the company's separate 'customer facility' in Modena and its 'competition Daytona' did not become a reality until 1972.

Chinetti's North America Racing Team (NART) had already run at the Daytona 24 hour and the Sebring 12 hour races, in 1970, but without success. But works involvement from 1971 saw a 12th placing at Sebring, and Chinetti co-drove a Daytona to eighth position at the circuit in 1972. A NART-entered example also won its class at Watkins Glen.

Five special cars were prepared for the 1973 season with 450bhp engines, and uprated brakes and suspension. Chinetti achieved a second place and first in class at the 1973 Daytona event, paradoxically in NART's non-works enhanced car, and another example was placed fifth and second in class. In addition there was a class win at Le Mans and a sixth overall placing.

However, with the arrival in 1973 of the mid-engined Boxer, the works turned its attention away from front-engined cars like the Daytona. Of course, private individuals continued to campaign Daytonas on the track, so providing another strand in the history of this fabulous Ferrari.

Above: A notable feature of the production Daytona was that its twin headlamps were concealed behind transparent cowlings. However, in the Daytona, chassis 15681, that Maranello entered for Le Mans in 1972 (the only occasion it was raced by the company), the lights were exposed to view.

Left: The cockpit of the Maranello Daytona prepared for the 1972 Le Mans race where it was driven by Peter Westbury and John Hine. Noise levels in the cockpit were high because the twin pipes of the unsilenced exhaust emerged just below the driver's door! The Ferrari only survived until the eighth hour, when it was withdrawn when lying in 29th position because of a blown cylinder head gasket.

Morgan Plus 8

**Top speed
125mph**
201km/h

*Right: The magnesium
alloy wheels which were
fitted to the Plus 8 right
from its introduction in 1968
were still doing sterling
service 20 years later.*

*Below: Ancient and modern
– the Plus 8's lines were
firmly rooted in the 1930s
but an alloy V8 engine
resided under the hood.*

 It has got the looks of a pre-war sports car but the performance of a 21st century one. The current 130mph (209km/h) Morgan Plus 8 dates from 1968 and demand for this model, with its unique combination of attributes, shows no sign of abating.

It comes as no surprise to find that the Plus 8's origins stretch back to 1935 which was when Morgan recognized that the days of its famous three-wheeler line, introduced back in 1910, were numbered. So it introduced the 4/4 which in turn spawned the Plus 4 of 1951. Initially this used a 2 liter Standard engine, but it was subsequently powered by the closely related Triumph TR 2.2 liter unit which endured until the TR4A was discontinued in 1967.

However, the impending arrival of the six-cylinder TR5 placed Morgan in a predicament because the elongated engine could not be squeezed into the Plus 4 without major structural surgery. Salvation came in the shape of Rover which in

1965 had acquired the rights to an ex-Buick alloy 3.5 liter V8 engine and successfully reworked it for its own use. Although the unit's compact configuration meant that it could have been shoe-horned into the Morgan's original underhood space, the Plus 8, which made its debut at the 1968

London Motor Show, actually had a 2in (50mm) longer wheelbase. It was also slightly wider than its predecessor, to the benefit of roadholding, because of its new alloy wheels and tires.

Otherwise it was the same mixture as before; hand-built ash-framed steel-paneled bodywork mounted on a Z-frame chassis with Morgan's famous sliding pillar independent front suspension and a conventional half-elliptic sprung rear axle endowed with a limited slip differential.

With a sparsely furnished but comfortable cockpit, the two-seater Plus 8 was capable of 125mph (201km/h), a significant 30mph (48km/h) faster than the Plus 4 it replaced.

Sports Lightweight

An alloy-bodied Sports Lightweight appeared for 1976 and the following year the original separate Moss gearbox was replaced by Rover's unit-construction five-speed unit. The V8 engine itself was extensively revised in 1982, and fuel injection became available as an option from 1984 and was later standardized. In 1990 the power unit's capacity was increased to 4 liters.

Further more radical changes were made for the 1998 season. Bodies were now made entirely of aluminum, the cockpit was enlarged and the doors modestly lengthened. An additional top-of-the-range model appeared in the shape of a 4.6 liter V8, although the 4 liter car was also available. And the alloy wheels were replaced by wires.

The Plus 8 remains very much in production, an indication of the ongoing vitality of this British family-owned concern.

Specification	Morgan Plus 8 (3.5 liters)
Engine location	Front, in-line
Configuration	V8
Bore and stroke	89 x 71mm
Capacity	3529cc
Valve operation	Pushrod
Horsepower	160bhp @ 5200rpm
Transmission	Manual four-speed
Drive	Rear
Chassis	Z section
Suspension – front	Sliding pillar
Suspension – rear	Half-elliptic spring
Brakes	Front disc, rear drum
Top speed	125mph (201km/h)
Acceleration	0-60mph (0-96km/h): 6.8 seconds

Below left: An example of a 1970 Plus 8. Its exposed spare wheel is another pre-war inheritance.

Below right: The 1970 model also boasted this revised, functional dashboard.

Datsun 240Z

**Top speed
125mph**
201km/h

*Right: The 240Z's 2.4 liter
engine, a strong, reliable
power unit with seven-
bearing crankshaft, cast
iron block, and alloy
cylinder head. The twin
carburetors are SU units.*

*Below: A British-
specification 240Z
distinguished by the rubber
spoilers front and rear. The
turn signals have been
awkwardly positioned
above the bumper to meet
UK regulations. This
example dates from 1973.*

Datsun successfully shrugged off its
image as a mass-producer of well
equipped but dull sedans when, in 1969, it
launched the 125mph (201km/h) 240Z that was
destined to become the world's most popular sports
car, snatching the crown from the MGB.

Conceived to occupy the void left by Britain's
ageing sports car lines in America, the project's
starting point was a sports coupé designed for
Datsun in 1963 by German-born US-domiciled
freelance stylist Albert Goertz, who was
responsible for the acclaimed lines of BMW's 507
roadster of the 1950s.

Using the Jaguar E-Type coupé as his starting
point, he reduced its dimensions to those
approximating the Porsche 911. It was
provisionally powered, like the Jaguar, by a twin-
overhead-camshaft engine but, when this proved
troublesome, work on the project was suspended.

And there the story might have ended, had it
not been for Datsun's rival Toyota which in 1965
produced its not dissimilar 2000GT. The appearance
of this car prompted Datsun to reactivate the sports

car concept. The essentials of Goertz's styling were
retained, but the complex twin-cam power unit was
replaced by an engine that was uniquely conceived
for the emerging Z car.

This was a 2.4 liter six-cylinder version of the
overhead-camshaft four which had powered the
company's 1967 510 sedan. Interestingly, ohc
engines were still relatively scarce at this time and
were usually reserved for more expensive models.

Left: The Z's well-equipped interior. Instrumentation was good, as was leg room, but the degree of seat recline was limited by the luggage shelf. The seats were nicely shaped but rather thinly padded. Note the 'dead pedal' rest for the driver's left foot.

Below: The 240Z was replaced in 1978 by the 280ZX, bigger, broader, and heavier, but outwardly less attractive, than the original. Surviving until 1983, there was a choice of 2 and 2.7 liter engines. But somehow the magic of the original had been lost.

A four-speed gearbox was fitted to those 240Zs sold in America but in other markets, including Britain, a five-cog unit was employed.

The all-independent suspension was similarly adventurous and took the form of all-round struts. A further progressive feature was rack and pinion steering which was a well established feature of European cars of the day, but not Japanese ones.

Only available as a coupé

The 240Z, so named to reflect its engine capacity, differed from most British sports cars in that it was only produced in closed form. Strictly a two-seater, like the E-Type it had an opening tailgate. And there was also plenty of luggage space.

On the road the model performed best on long straight roads and was able to cover mile after mile at 100mph (161km/h). And 60mph (96km/h) from a standing start was attainable in just 8 seconds which made it quicker than a Porsche 911 or Triumph TR6.

The 240Z remained in production until 1973; of the 156,000 or so built, some 85 per cent were sold in the United States. It was replaced by the 260Z and, later, the 280Z which were better equipped but heavier and, consequently, slower.

In short the first of the Z cars did everything expected of it and underlined to the motoring world that Japan was able produce well-engineered, marketable cars at a price the public could afford.

Specification	Datsun 240Z
Engine location	Front, in-line
Configuration	Six-cylinder
Bore and stroke	83 x 73mm
Capacity	2393cc
Valve operation	Single overhead camshaft
Horsepower	151bhp @ 5600rpm
Transmission	Manual five-speed, see text
Drive	Rear
Chassis	Unitary
Suspension – front	MacPherson strut with lower link
Suspension – rear	MacPherson strut with lower wishbone
Brakes	Front disc, rear drum
Top speed	125mph (201km/h)
Acceleration	0-60mph (0-96km/h): 8 seconds

Aston Martin V8

**Top speed
170mph**
274km/h

Right: The top-of-the-range Vantage, a 1978 car. The model is immediately identifiable by its closed radiator grille. Its impressive top speed of 170mph (274km/h) made it one the world's fastest cars.

Below: This DBS V8 dates from 1970 and is easily distinguished by its twin headlamps. They were replaced by single units in 1972. Styled by William Towns, the lines were destined to survive for 20 years.

Mainstay of the marque for no less than 20 years, the V8 was one of Britain's great performance cars, able to attain 170mph (274km/h). It was magnificently styled and carefully handbuilt at Aston Martin's famous Newport Pagnell factory.

Launched in 1969 and successor to the DB6 which remained in production until 1971, what was initially named the DBS appeared in 1967. It was no less than 4in (102mm) wider than the DB6. Styled by William Towns, it had been designed to accommodate a new 5.3 liter alloy V8 engine but this was not completed in time so it continued to be powered by the existing 4 liter twin-cam six.

What was named the DBS V8 sedan, although it was clearly a coupé, duly arrived two years later, and it was powered by the long-awaited engine. This was fuel-injected but, like Rolls-Royce, Aston Martin did not disclose the brake horsepower it developed. Capable of 160mph (257km/h), there was the option of a manual five-speed ZF gearbox or three-speed automatic transmission. However, the latter was by far and away the most popular choice with customers.

New owners

Then in 1972, Sir David Brown (knighted 1968), who had owned Aston Martin since 1947, sold the firm to Company Developments, a property business. In consequence the model was shorn of its DB prefix and was renamed the V8. The original twin headlamps were replaced by a single lamp design and this new nose was to endure for the rest of the car's manufacturing life. A Volante (open) version appeared in 1978.

A more powerful Vantage version with a disclosed 380bhp on tap had arrived in 1977, identifiable by a blanked-off radiator intake and rear spoiler, that was capable of a creditable 170mph (274km/h).

But Company Developments had succumbed to bankruptcy in 1974 and there were to be no less than three changes of ownership before Aston Martin was acquired by Ford in 1987. Both the V8 and Vantage continued to undergo development. In 1982 the company was forced to disclose the horsepower generated by the basic V8 engine because it became a requirement of German import regulations. It proved to be 305bhp, which was probably rather less than most owners had imagined.

In 1986 came a version bodied in Milan by Zagato in tribute to the legendary DB4 GT Zagato of 1960. There were 75 in total, 50 coupés and 25 convertibles. A top speed of over 180mph (290km/h) was attainable. The last V8 was completed in December 1989 although its Virage successor had made its debut at the previous year's British Motor Show. Although this duly entered production in 1990, it never attained the muscular vitality of its famous predecessor.

Above: A V8 Volante of 1979, introduced in the previous year. A power-operated roof and air conditioning were fitted.

Left: The luxurious interior of a 1978 V8 automatic. The instrumentation was comprehensive and included an oil temperature gauge and an ammeter.

Below left: The engine of the Volante shown above. Although the compartment appears rather congested, access to components is reasonably good.

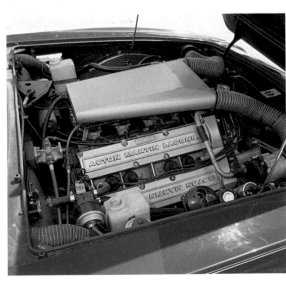

Specification	**Aston Martin** V8 Vantage
Engine location	Front, in-line
Configuration	V8
Bore and stroke	85 x 100mm
Capacity	5340cc
Valve operation	Twin overhead camshafts per cylinder bank
Horsepower	380bhp @ 5000rpm
Transmission	Three-speed automatic
Drive	Rear
Chassis	Platform
Suspension – front	Wishbones and coil springs
Suspension – rear	Radius arms, De Dion rear axle and coil springs
Brakes	Disc
Top speed	170mph (274km/h)
Acceleration	0-60mph (0-96km/h): 5.5 seconds

Jensen Interceptor FF

**Top speed
130mph**
209km/h

*Right: A hoodful of engine,
the Chrysler V8 was
dominated by the air filter
of the four-barrel Carter
carburetor.*

*Below: A 1968 Interceptor
FF, with identifying twin air
outlets. All models were
enhanced by stainless steel
trim. The alloy wheels were
later extended to the Mark
III cars.*

The 133mph (214km/h) Interceptor of
1967 was the last and most popular of the
West Bromwich-built Jensens. Also
produced in four-wheel-drive form, this FF variant
appeared 11 years before the Audi Quattro made
the configuration a marketing reality.

The Interceptor's origins are to be found in
Jensen's glass-fiber-bodied, Chrysler V8-engined
CV8 of 1962. Although capable of 130mph
(209km/h), its styling was controversial and its
appeal limited.

The Interceptor, announced at the 1966 London
Motor Show, replaced the CV8. From a visual
standpoint it differed radically from it. Not only did
the new car have a metal body, its styling, instead
of being undertaken in-house, was the work of the
Italian Touring concern.

A distinctive grand tourer with a large and
useful opening tailgate, the Interceptor's twin

tubular chassis was based on those of its CV8
predecessor, while its 6.2 liter Chrysler V8 hailed
from the same source. Automatic transmission was
fitted, although a four-speed manual 'box could be
specified for more sporting owners.

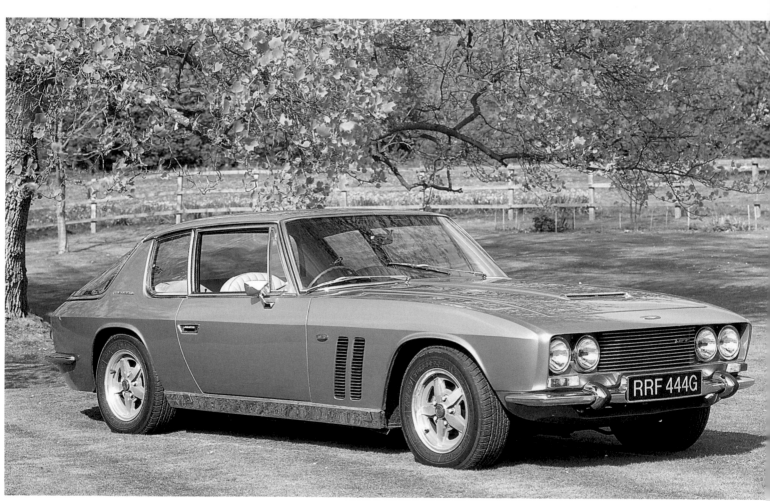

New alloy wheels

A Mark II version arrived for 1970 with a modified nose and interior changes; its Mark III successor for the 1972 season was identifiable by its new alloy wheels. These were also shared with the more expensive and larger 7.2 liter engined SP Interceptor. This was capable of 143mph (230km/h), but it only remained in production for a year.

The Interceptor FF, for Ferguson Formula, was a four-wheel-drive version which incorporated that company's long nurtured 4WD system. A further refinement was the pioneering use of Dunlop Maxaret anti-lock brakes.

Advertised as 'the world's most advanced car,' it was outwardly similar to the original, apart from an imperceptible 2in (51mm) that was added to its wheelbase. It was easily identifiable by the second cooling duct introduced in the front fenders. Traction was excellent and, as might be excepted, roadholding sensational.

But on the debit side was greater weight and mechanical complication, which reduced the FF's top speed to 130mph (209km/h), and caused some teething troubles. And at $8425, it was a significant $2160 more than the conventionally driven car.

The FF shared the updates applied to the mainstream Mark II and, briefly, Mark III before production ceased at the end of 1971. Only 224 had been completed. However, the conventionally driven Interceptor continued to sell strongly, and in 1972 the 7.2 liter engine, already being used in the SP, replaced the 6.2 liter unit.

Unfortunately the oil price rise of 1973 spelt disaster for the big, thirsty Jensen. Although the business struggled on, car production finally ceased in 1976, after 4112 Interceptors had been completed. Some further examples were built in the 1983-92 era but that really was the end of this ingenious, well conceived grand tourer.

Specification	Jensen Interceptor FF
Engine location	Front, in-line
Configuration	V8
Bore and stroke	108 x 86mm
Capacity	6276cc
Valve operation	Pushrod
Horsepower	325bhp @ 4600rpm
Transmission	Automatic three-speed
Drive	Four-wheel
Chassis	Twin tubular
Suspension – front	Wishbones and twin coil springs
Suspension – rear	Half-elliptic leaf spring
Brakes	Disc
Top speed	130mph (209km/h)
Acceleration	0-60mph (0-96km/h): 8.5 seconds

Left: The interior with its comfortable seats, distinctive central console, and lockable compartment behind the automatic transmission lever.

Below: The FF in profile with the large rear window readily apparent. When this hatch was opened in conjunction with the spring-loaded parcel shelf, access could be gained to the luggage compartment. Fittingly for a grand tourer, the Interceptor could carry plenty of suitcases.

Citroën SM

**Top speed
135mph**
217km/h

 Capable of 135mph (217km/h), the SM of 1970 – an extravagantly conceived Maserati-engined grand tourer – was destined to be the last flowering of the Citroën company, a business that was taken over in 1974 by its Peugeot rival.

The SM was a child of the buoyant 1960s. When Citroën planned a grand touring flagship for the following decade, it soon recognized that it did not possess a sufficiently large capacity engine to power such a prestigious model.

Instead of designing one, Citroën decided in 1968 to acquire the struggling Maserati concern and it wasted little time in adapting its 4.1/4.7 liter V8 for its special needs. Because French taxation penalized cars of over 15CV, the equivalent of 2.8 liters, the result was a V6 unit of 2.6 liters capacity. A purpose-designed five-speed manual gearbox was employed.

Announced at the 1970 Geneva Motor Show, the SM (S had been the project code and M stood for Maserati) was – by French standards – a large, complicated car that was clearly intended to place

Below: Bristling with hydraulic refinement, Citroën declared the front-wheel-drive SM the safest and most comfortable grand tourer of its day. The suspension maintained a constant height, regardless of load, and could be set for four different cruising positions depending on the state and type of road. The distinctive body lines reflected the results of aerodynamic testing.

Citroën head and shoulders above its rivals and contemporaries.

The styling was distinctive rather than attractive and, as ever, it was aerodynamically refined. The mechanicals were based on those of Citroën's enduring DS sedan. This meant, of course, front-wheel-drive and hydraulically charged self-leveling pneumatic suspension. Much else was hydraulically assisted with sophisticated power steering that also self-centered; cleverly, the inner pair of six headlights, concealed behind a transparent cover, turned with the wheels.

Left-hand-drive only

The intention was to build about 20 SMs a day. Although only made in left-hand-drive form, the model was available in Britain from 1972 where it sold for a pricey $7480. But drivers took some time to adapt to the steering and the Maserati engine, typically, provided good performance but without much refinement. In consequence it was found to be unduly noisy. And fuel consumption was an unhealthy 13mpg (17lit/100km).

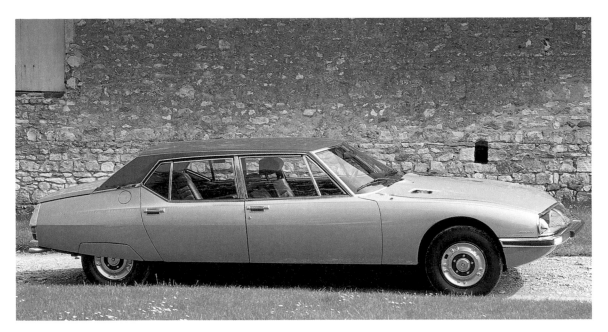

Left: Parisian coachbuilder Henri Chapron produced this four-door version of the SM which was exhibited at the 1972 Paris Motor Show. Only produced in prototype form, it was over 16ft (4877mm) in length.

Below: The Chapron SM convertible was named the Mylord. Previously the company had produced an open four-door car reserved for use by the French president. It remained in service long after the model had ceased production.

Although there was sufficient space for the driver and front passenger, rear seat accommodation was found to be unduly cramped. Despite these shortcomings, the SM sold well enough for the first two years of production, but the oil price rise of 1973 and the consequent increase in fuel costs spelt the end for the SM. Sales slumped and Citroën also succumbed to a take-over by Peugeot.

This was despite the addition, in 1972, of fuel injection, and the appearance in 1973 of a 3 liter version with automatic transmission.

It was all over by 1975 when SM production ceased and support was withdrawn from Maserati which was left to its own fate. Just 12,920 examples of the SM had been built in five years.

Specification	Citroën SM
Engine location	Front, in-line
Configuration	V6
Bore and stroke	87 x 75mm
Capacity	2670cc
Valve operation	Twin overhead camshafts per cylinder bank
Horsepower	180bhp @ 6250rpm
Transmission	Manual five-speed
Drive	Front
Chassis	Unitary
Suspension – front	Twin transverse arms with hydropneumatic struts
Suspension – rear	Trailing arm with hydropneumatic struts
Brakes	Disc
Top speed	135mph (217km/h)
Acceleration	0-60mph (0-96km/h): 9.1 seconds

Plymouth Road Runner Superbird

**Top speed
140mph**
225km/h

Right: The Superbird was fitted with a 440cid V8 as standard, but there was an optional and even more powerful 426 'hemi' available.

Below: You couldn't mistake it for anything else! The black vinyl roof was a standard fitment, along with the unmissable fixed rear stabilizer, the presence of which did not significantly affect the car's behavior.

OK, it looks as though it has just landed! But in 1970 this zany be-winged coupé was one of the fastest cars on America's roads and racetracks, being capable, in its most potent form, of 190mph (306km/h).

In 1968 Plymouth, Chrysler's bargain-basement car division, introduced the two-door, no-frills Road Runner coupé, the car being named after the Warner Brothers cartoon character of that name. It even possessed a distinctive beeb-beeb horn in tribute to its inspiration.

In what was to be dubbed the Muscle Car era, the 'Runner was based on Plymouth's new Belvedere model, and powered by the company's proven 383cid (6.3 liter) V8, enhanced to produce 325bhp. Aimed at the young driver to take to the racetrack, the 'Runner was progressively up-engined, surviving in this form until 1970. In that year its most extreme manifestation was unveiled in the form of the Superbird.

Created to meet NASCAR (National Association for Stock Car Auto Racing) homologation track

requirements, the authorities required that no less than 1000 Road Runner Superbirds had to be sold commercially to meet qualification regulations. Plymouth responded that it had orders for 2000 and, in due course, 1971 machines found owners.

As such small numbers were involved, aftermarket specialist Creative Industries was responsible for the aerodynamic modifications.

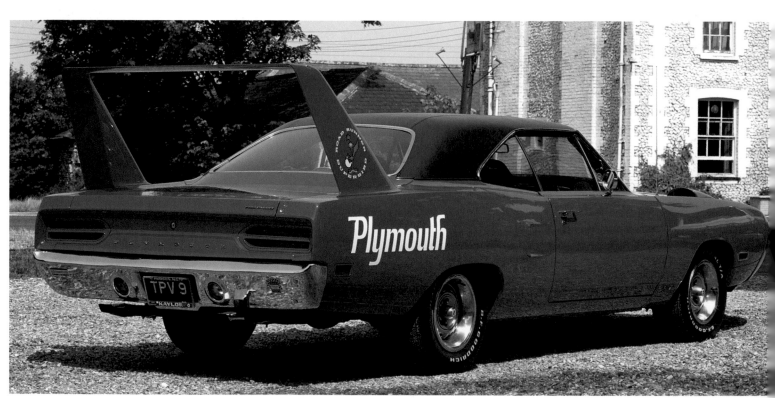

This required extending the front of the car by 18in (457mm) – the resulting chiseled nose incorporated pop-up headlamps behind glass-fiber flaps. The original recessed rear window was replaced by flush-fitting glass but, to hide evidence of this modification, all 'Birds were fitted with a black vinyl roof.

Outlandish spoiler

Much more apparent was a large spoiler mounted some 24in (610mm) above the car's trunk with the Road Runner decal featuring on the supports. But despite the 'Bird's outlandish looks, this aerodynamic extension did not prove to be wholly satisfactory. The modifications added weight and didn't really kick in until the Plymouth was traveling at 80 to 90mph (129 to 145km/h).

Most Superbirds were powered by a 375bhp version of the 440cid (7.2 liter) Super Commando V8 with either four-speed manual or TorqueFlite automatic transmission. There was an optional 390hp version and a top line 'hemi' 426cid (7 liter) with 425hp in harness.

While the street cars were good for 140mph (225km/m), those created for the racing circuits only used hemi power and were capable of about 50mph (80km/h) more.

Solely produced for 1970, revised legislation rendered the Superbird obsolete and Plymouth introduced a new Road Runner shape for 1971. Sales of the old line were slow although today they are much sought after by collectors.

Specification	**Plymouth** Road Runner Superbird
Engine location	Front, in-line
Configuration	V8
Bore and stroke	4.32 x 3.75in (110 x 95mm)
Capacity	440cid (7210cc)
Valve operation	Overhead valve
Horsepower	375bhp @ 4600rpm
Transmission	Manual four-speed
Drive	Rear
Chassis	Unitary
Suspension – front	Wishbones and torsion bar
Suspension – rear	Half-elliptic spring
Brakes	Drum
Top speed	140mph (225km/h)
Acceleration	0-60mph (0-96km/h): 4.9 seconds

Left: The Road Runner cartoon character from which the mainstream model took its name was a 'fun feature' of the car. This cheerful emblem appeared on the spoiler mounts and was repeated on the left-hand headlight flap.

Below: The Superbird's aerodynamically refined nose was made of glass fiber and also incorporated pop-up headlamps.

JCF 900N

1971–1980
Down but Not Out

The post-war boom came to an abrupt halt with the outbreak, in 1973, of the Arab-Israeli war. The result was a hike in oil prices with predictable consequences for the cost of fuel at the pumps.

The economic downturn that followed wrought havoc within Britain's uncompetitive motor industry and its rapid contraction effectively spelt an end to its increasingly dated range of sports cars.

In Germany rising fuel prices killed off BMW's pioneering 2002 Turbo sedan but the turbocharger was here to stay. A further technological milestone arrived in the form of a viable four-wheel-drive system, thanks to Audi's innovative, impressive and influential quattro coupé.

De Tomaso Pantera

**Top speed
150mph**
241km/h

Below: The outstanding lines of the Pantera's Ghia-styled body were one of its most enduring attributes, as this 1974 GTS bears witness. Note the recessed rear window.

 On paper the Pantera which in its most potent GTS form was capable of over 170mph (273km/h), was the ideal grand tourer, stylish, fast, and not overly expensive. Unfortunately, early examples were hopelessly unreliable but this Italian car proved to be remarkably enduring and survived for no less than 25 years.

Argentinian-born Alejandro De Tomaso left his native country and in 1955 arrived in Italy, home of his paternal grandfather. Establishing a business at Modena in 1959, he progressed from building racing cars to roadgoing GTs – the Pantera of 1970 was his first series production model.

Style guru

By this time De Tomaso had acquired the Ghia and Vignale styling houses and in 1969 Ford, wishing to maintain its performance credentials and underpin its Le Mans triumphs both at home and abroad, took a majority shareholding in all these disparate businesses.

Outwardly the mid-engined Pantera looked impressive, having been styled by American-born John Taajara, who had joined Ghia in 1958 and consequently found himself in De Tomaso's employ. Engineering was the responsibility of Giampaolo Dallara, latterly of Lamborghini, where he had responsibility for the celebrated Miura.

The Pantera, the name is Italian for Panther, was based on a steel sub-structure with a 5.7 liter Ford 310bhp V8 mounted in line, driving the wheels via a ZF five-speed gearbox. The latter unit reputedly cost more to produce than the engine!

Capable of 150mph (241km/h), European versions of the model could reach 60mph (96km/h) in an impressive 6.5 seconds although the US cars were half a second slower on account of the engine's de-toxing equipment.

The model was well received on its announcement at the 1970 New York Motor Show. But the cars, which were sold in America through Ford's Lincoln-Mercury dealers, were plagued with reliability problems which remained largely

Right: Frontal view of the left-hand-drive GTS shown above. Unusually for the day the rear tires were wider than those at the front. What look like air intakes behind the rear windows are fakes; the radiator was front-mounted and the carburetors drew their air through an opening on the rear deck near to the back window.

unresolved. As a result Ford cut its losses in 1973, although it retained the Ghia business and its respected name.

That year a more powerful version of the Pantera, named the GTS, was introduced. With its V8 boosted to 350bhp, top speed was a reputed 175mph (282km/h) and the 0-60mph (96km/h) acceleration figure for the US models was shaved to 5.6 seconds.

The rupture with Ford saw De Tomaso move to smaller premises in Modena and for the next 20 or so years a trickle of Panteras continued to be built there. This seemingly indestructible model was given a modest stylistic facelift in 1991 and a 4.9 liter Ford V8 replaced the long-running 5.7 liter unit. It continued to be listed until 1996, by which time it had been replaced by the equally shadowy Guara GT!

Above: Still looking good, a 1984 GTS which has acquired a rear wing, a popular Pantera extra.

Below left: Interior of the car shown above, a right-hand-drive example built for the UK market.

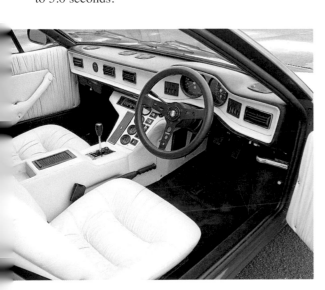

Specification	**De Tomaso** Pantera
Engine location	Mid, in-line
Configuration	V8
Bore and stroke	101 x 88mm
Capacity	5763cc
Valve operation	Pushrod
Horsepower	310bhp @ 5400rpm
Transmission	Manual, five-speed
Drive	Rear
Chassis	Unitary
Suspension – front	Wishbones and coil spring
Suspension – rear	Wishbones and coil spring
Brakes	Disc
Top speed	150mph (241km/h)
Acceleration	0-60mph (0-96km/h): 6.5 seconds

Panther J72

**Top speed
122mph**
196km/h

*Below: Unashamedly based
on the pre-war SS Jaguar
100, the build quality of the
J72 attracted many
admirers. Available in 3.8
and 4.2 liter six-cylinder
form, as well as in 5.3 liter
V12 guise, this example is
powered by the smallest
capacity engine. It is
identifiable by the absence
of a hood bulge on the
nearside.*

 Created for the worldwide playboy
fraternity, the Panther J72 was one of the
fastest accelerating cars of its day, the
V12 version being able to sprint to 60mph
(96km/h) in a mere 6.6 seconds. The car was the
brainchild of Robert Jankel, who had begun his
motoring career with the SuperSpeed Conversions
Ford tuning concern, prior to moving into the
fashion industry. The resulting cars thus
incorporated these rather eclectic ingredients.

Initially Jankel produced replica cars on a one-
off basis and before long orders began to mount.
The outcome, in 1971, was the creation of Panther
West Winds and the first Panther appeared in the
following year.

'The best replica yet' declared *Autocar* after
testing the J2, the first of the line, that had been
announced in June 1972. Inspired by the SS Jaguar
100 sports car of 1935, the reason behind the
choice of the big-cat Panther name was now
apparent. It was well designed and carefully built
with a hand-crafted aluminum body resplendent in
gleaming paint work. It sold for $6130, or about the
price of two E-Type Jaguars.

Built up around a chassis of square-section
tubing, beam axles were fitted rear *and* front with
all-round coil springs – each was located by a five
link system. Under the heavily louvered hood was a
Jaguar XK 3.8 liter engine which developed
240bhp in twin carburetored guise. This was
essentially the same unit that had powered the
Mark II sedan rather than the E-Type. It was mated
to an XJ6 all-synchromesh gearbox with overdrive
on top gear.

Connolly upholstery

The finish of the cockpit was very much in keeping
with the rest of the car, the seats being upholstered
in the best Connolly hides, with the material also
extended to the door panels and steering wheel.
The tastefully veneered dashboard was replete with
Jaguar instruments.

In this form the J2 was capable of 115mph
(185km/h). Generally the Panther lived up to
expectations, being easy to drive, comfortable and
ideal for motorways, even if on country roads the
limitations of the all-too-basic non-independent
suspension became apparent.

Improved acceleration

Subsequently the 3.8 engine was replaced by Jaguar's 4.2 unit and, best of all, the 5.3 liter V12 for 1974, which could be enhanced by fitting triple Weber carburetors. This not only pushed the top speed to about 122mph (196km/h), acceleration was also dramatically improved although, inevitably, at the cost of fuel consumption which was an overall 9mpg (25.6lit/100km). The price was $13,650. By the time production ceased in 1981 a total of 430 cars had been completed.

Unfortunately an over-extended Jankel succumbed to liquidation in 1979, although the Panther name continued until 1996, cars being latterly manufactured in South Korea.

Specification	Panther J2 (V12)
Engine location	Front, in-line
Configuration	V12
Bore and stroke	90 x 70mm
Capacity	5343cc
Valve operation	Single overhead camshaft per cylinder bank
Horsepower	250bhp @ 6000rpm
Transmission	Manual four-speed
Drive	Rear
Chassis	Twin rectangular steel tube
Suspension – front	Leading arm, Panhard rod and coil spring
Suspension – rear	Leading arm, Panhard rod and coil spring
Brakes	Disc
Top speed	122mph (196km/h)
Acceleration	0-60mph (0-96km/h): 6.6 seconds

Far left: The 3.8 liter Jaguar XK engine.

Left: The ultra traditional walnut-veneered instrument panel and leather-bound steering wheel.

Below: The hood pod followed the contours of the air filter to service the twin SU carburetors.

Lancia Stratos

**Top speed
140mph**
225km/h

*Right: Heart of the matter –
the Stratos' 2.4 liter Fiat-
built Ferrari engine.*

*Below: A mid-located
engine meant that the nose
could be aerodynamically
efficient. The pop-up
headlamps helped too.*

The Stratos typifies the 'homologation special', that is a model built in small numbers as a road car to qualify for competition, in this case the World Rally Championship. Immensely successful, the Stratos gave Lancia the rallying crown in three successive years from 1974 to 1976.

This is a car that began life as a Bertone styling exercise that appeared at the 1970 Turin Motor Show. The work of Marcello Gandini, who is better known for having styled the bodies of the Lamborghini Miura and Countach, it was based on the Lancia HF coupé sub-structure with its 1.6 liter V4 engine relocated behind the driver. Futuristic, wedge-shaped, and doorless, access to what its maker named the Stratos was by a single opening front flap.

It was seized upon by Lancia's competitions manager, Cesare Florio, who could visualize the essentials of a successful rally car in this concept vehicle. The trouble was that the Lancia engine was nearing the end of its competitive life. But an alternative was available because the company had recently, in 1969, been taken over by Fiat. This was the same year in which Italy's leading car maker had also acquired a controlling interest in Ferrari.

Ferrari power

Another 1969 initiative was Ferrari's mid-engined Dino coupé. Powered by a Fiat-built 2.4 liter V6 engine, it was also used in a Fiat of the same name. And this was the power unit that Florio chose for the Stratos.

The project took a further leap forward with a car displayed at the 1971 Turin show. Unlike the previous year's offering, it had orthodox doors and was based on a steel sub-structure with glass-fiber body panels. But the definitive Stratos had to wait until the 1972 event.

This version was a stubby, purposeful Bertone-refined wedge with a wheelbase of a mere 7ft 2in (2184mm). The Ferrari engine was mounted transversely behind the driver, and the car was able to attain a spirited and reliable 140mph (225km/h). The Stratos was first blooded in the 1972 Turin de Corse event, although suspension failure forced its retirement. However, it soon found its form.

Left: A Stratos in rallying guise. It gave the Lancia works team considerable success and the model also proved its worth in the hands of private teams. Strong and versatile, it had the virtue of being exceptionally fast, while also having excellent traction. Between 1974 and 1977 the Stratos were regularly fitted with four-valve cylinder heads which increased power to 285bhp.

Left: A 1975 Stratos in roadgoing mode. Although performance was guaranteed, on the debit side was unpredictable handling while the interior was somewhat cramped. But in the hands of a professional this did not matter, as was underlined by a victory in the 1979 Monte Carlo Rally when Darniche, a privateer, trounced Ford and other factory teams.

Its first victory came in the 1973 Spanish Firestone rally but production did not begin in earnest until 1974, so the cars ran in the prototype class because homologation was not achieved until that fall. From there on and for the next three years this Lancia proved to be virtually invincible.

When detuned for road use the Ferrari V6 produced a subdued 190bhp but it was perfectly tractable. The seating was rather cramped and, while forward visibility was fine, side views were restricted. Luggage space was minimal although the doors contained storage bins.

Stratos production ceased in 1975 by which time 492 had been completed, eight short of the required 500!

Specification	**Lancia** Stratos
Engine location	Mid, transverse
Configuration	V6
Bore and stroke	92 x 60mm
Capacity	2418cc
Valve operation	Twin overhead camshafts per cylinder bank
Horsepower	190bhp @ 7000rpm
Transmission	Manual five-speed
Drive	Rear
Chassis	Unitary
Suspension – front	Coil springs and wishbones
Suspension – rear	Coil springs and wishbones
Brakes	Disc
Top speed	140mph (225km/h)
Acceleration	0-60mph (0-96km/h): 5.9 seconds

Jaguar XJ12

**Top speed
140mph**
225km/h

*Right: Interior of the
coupé, marketed as the
XJ12C, pictured opposite.
Automatic transmission was
obligatory, a pity because a
manual box would have
been desirable on this
rather 'sporty' model.*

*Below: This sedan dates
from 1973 and is a Series 2
car, identifiable by the
raised bumper which
necessitated repositioning
the sidelights underneath.*

Smooth, turbine-like acceleration is the
principal characteristic of the V12 engine
and in 1972 Jaguar extended this power
unit to its acclaimed XJ6 sedan. The result was an
extraordinarily impressive car; the world's most
popular 12 cylinder-powered four-seater.

The 250bhp 5.3 liter unit with single cam heads
made its debut in the Series III E-Type of 1971. It
was extended to the hull of the XJ6 four-door sedan
which had been accorded the Car of the Year title
on its 1968 launch. It was a model which set new
levels of silent running and refinement for the
motor industry.

Able to attain 120mph (193km/h) in 4.2 liter
six-cylinder form, the XJ12 outwardly resembled
the six-cylinder car but was identifiable by a
vertically slatted radiator grille in place of the
original latticework one. This was enhanced by the
presence of a discreet centrally located V symbol.

Automatic transmission came as standard, but
this contributed to a prodigal average fuel
consumption figure of 10mpg (23.5lit/100km). The

figure was even worse on a long-wheelbase
version, the XJ12L, which arrived for the 1973
model year. This was also produced in Daimler
Double Six guise.

Able to cruise at 140mph (225km/h), this well
appointed Jaguar could reach 100mph (161km/h) in
under 20 seconds. Sadly sales of the model suffered
in the wake of the energy crisis of 1973-74. The
entire XJ range received a facelift in 1975. These

Series II XJ12s were only built in long wheelbase form and were identifiable by a squatter radiator grille and higher bumper line.

The V12 engine was uprated to 285bhp with the arrival of fuel injection and later in 1975 the model's name was changed to XJ5.3, diplomatically expunging the notion of 12 thirsty cylinders!

Pininfarina styling

The range received a further stylistic update, the work of Pininfarina, in 1979 with the Mark III XJs. Jaguar addressed the fuel consumption bugbear with the arrival, in 1981, of the HE, for High Efficiency, version. This employed new, more efficient cylinder heads, the work of Swiss engineer Michael May. Fuel consumption was now a more respectable 13mpg (17.6lit/100km).

The 1984 season saw the Sovereign name replace the XJ initials, and the model became the Jaguar V12 for 1990. Although a new version, coded XJ40, of the XJ6 was introduced in 1986, the V12 continued to be the sole engine fitted in the Series III body and this remained in production until 1993. The engine, enlarged to 6 liters, was then carried over to the XJ40 line. It was built until 1996 when the 12 finally made way for Jaguar's new V8.

Above: A 1974 coupé with its distinctive vinyl roof, fitted at the behest of the marketing department, not engineering!

Left: Broadspeed prepared XJ12Cs for Group 2 racing. Campaigned in 1976 and 1977, they did not achieve any measure of success.

Specification	Jaguar XJ12
Engine location	Front, in-line
Configuration	V12
Bore and stroke	90 x 70mm
Capacity	5343cc
Valve operation	Single overhead camshaft per cylinder bank
Horsepower	250bhp @ 6000rpm
Transmission	Automatic three-speed
Drive	Rear
Chassis	Unitary
Suspension – front	Wishbones and coil spring
Suspension – rear	Wishbone, drive shaft and coil springs
Brakes	Disc
Top speed	140mph (225km/h)
Acceleration	0-60mph (0-96km/h): 7.4 seconds

Maserati Bora

**Top speed
162mph**
261km/h

*Right: The Italian/French
Bora, Maserati's first
production mid-engined car,
with styling by Giorgetto
Giugiaro. This is a 1975
example. Power was
courtesy of Maserati's
proven V8 engine.*

*Below: The Bora possessed
the virtues of being a quiet,
powerful car with plenty of
room for its two occupants.
But on the debit side was a
poor heating and
ventilation system.*

 It was quite unlike any previous Maserati. The mid-engined Bora coupé, capable of over 160mph (257km/h), combined outstanding roadholding with remarkable refinement, the latter attribute not a characteristic always associated with the marque!

The model was conceived during Citroën's ownership of Maserati and it was for this reason that the Bora used hydraulically pressurized brakes. The pop-up headlamps were also hydraulically activated and the same went for the driver's seat and even the steering column.

The coupé body, commissioned in 1969, was the work of Ital Design and was visually enhanced by a stainless steel roof. The lines were both distinctive and attractive, but rear visibility was, alas, far from perfect because of the location of Maserati's 4.7 liter V8 engine. This was already being used in the conventional forward position in the two-seater Ghibli coupé. Longitudinally located in the Bora, it drove the rear wheels through a five-speed ZF gearbox.

Designated Maserati's Type 117, the car was announced at the 1971 Geneva Motor Show, although it was to be a further year before production got underway. An uncompromising two-seater, the model was found to be comfortable with excellent handling, as befitted the engine location, and it was surprisingly quiet. Criticisms were confined to the brakes which were thought to be too sensitive, and poor heating and ventilation. And the lusty 310bhp V8 was thirsty, consuming fuel at the prodigious rate of a mere 9 miles per gallon (25.6lit/100km).

Increased top speed

The upheavals of the 1970s saw a hefty rise in fuel prices and Citroën disposing of its Maserati asset. Bora production slumped from 56 cars produced in 1975 to a mere half dozen in 1976. Consideration was given to discontinuing the model, but instead the engine was enlarged to 4.9 liters which increased the top speed to 165mph (265km/h). It was destined to remain in production until 1978 by which time 571 examples had been completed.

The Bora lived on in the shape of its Merak derivative of 1972 which shared its body but was powered by a 2 liter version of the Citroën SM's V6 unit. This was a 127mph (204km/h) car, and in 1975 the lighter, faster Merak SS appeared with engine capacity upped to 3 liters. This was capable of 153mph (246km/h).

Much more popular than the Bora, some 1500 Meraks had been completed by the time that production ceased in 1983, making it the most popular Maserati of its day.

Specification	**Maserati** Bora (4.7 liters)
Engine location	Mid, in-line
Configuration	V6
Bore and stroke	91 x 75mm
Capacity	4719cc
Valve operation	Twin overhead camshafts per cylinder bank
Horsepower	310bhp @ 6000rpm
Transmission	Manual five-speed
Drive	Rear
Chassis	Unitary
Suspension – front	Hydraulic and coil spring
Suspension – rear	Hydraulic and coil spring
Brakes	Disc
Top speed	162mph (261km/h)
Acceleration	0-60mph (0-96km/h): 6.5 seconds

Above: *While having a distinctive tail, driver visibility was poor at the rear because of the mid-located engine. The simple rear bumper meant that the car was not allowed to be sold in America.*

Left: *A right-hand-drive Bora. Although the steering wheel was correctly positioned, the handbrake was not relocated and so was somewhat inaccessible.*

BMW 2002 Turbo

**Top speed
130mph**
209km/h

*Below: The Turbo with its
unmistakable front spoiler,
distinctive livery and
decals, lowered suspension,
and wider wheels and tires.
It was only produced in left-
hand-drive form.*

Europe's first turbocharged road car, the
performance of BMW's two-door 2002
sedan was a revelation with a top speed
(compared to the normally aspirated version)
increased by some 12mph (19km/h) to 130mph
(209km/h). Acceleration was similarly enhanced.

The starting point, certainly as far as the public
was concerned, for this exciting project was an
'experimental safety vehicle' that BMW unveiled in
1972. Although not intended for production, this
glass-fiber-bodied coupé had a theoretical top speed
of 155mph (249km/h). Powered by a turbocharged
version of the 2002's 2 liter engine, it developed
some 200bhp, about 70bhp more than the normally

aspirated unit. Its origins are to be found in a racing
engine which powered a BMW 2002 that won its
class in the 1969 European Touring Car
Championship. This was the first appearance of a
turbocharged engine in this event and, having
proved its reliability, BMW embarked on a program
to produce a roadgoing version.

Fortunes of war

Unfortunately the 2002 Turbo's launch at the 1973
Frankfurt Motor Show coincided with the outbreak
of the Arab-Israeli war. As a consequence oil and
fuel prices soared and the car only remained in
production for 10 months.

Invariably finished in white, there could be no doubt that it was something out of the ordinary because of its lowered suspension, wider wheels and tires which required arch extensions. There was no front bumper, in its place was a deep spoiler which was embellished with the word *turbo* in mirror writing so that other drivers would be in little doubt of what was about to overtake them! However, this feature came in for serious criticism from the usually sympathetic German press and BMW quickly dropped the idea. However, colorful and distinctive striping along the car's flanks was retained.

The KKK turbocharger installation differed from that of the 1972 mid-engined coupé in being mounted low down below the exhaust manifold, rather than above it. The result of this location meant that the model could only be produced in left-hand-drive form.

On the road, the turbocharger's presence only became noticeable above 4000rpm when the extra power seemed to arrive all at once. And because this was a pioneering installation, the Turbo also lacked flexibility.

A rapidly deteriorating world economy meant that when production ceased in 1974 only 1672 examples had been completed. BMW would not revive the concept until 1978, by which time the turbocharged road car was a proven concept, thanks to the Munich company's pioneering efforts.

Above: The rear spoiler and front and rear flared wheel arches were further Turbo features. Unlike the front of the car which lacked one, a bumper was fitted at the rear.

Left: A smaller padded steering wheel and extra instruments were just some of the Turbo's interior refinements. The fuel tank was also larger than usual.

Specification	BMW 2002 Turbo
Engine location	Front, in-line
Configuration	Turbocharged four-cylinder
Bore and stroke	89 x 80mm
Capacity	1990cc
Valve operation	Single overhead camshaft
Horsepower	170bhp @ 5800rpm
Transmission	Manual four- or five-speed
Drive	Rear
Chassis	Unitary
Suspension – front	MacPherson strut
Suspension – rear	Semi trailing arm, coil spring
Brakes	Front disc, rear drum
Top speed	130mph (209km/h)
Acceleration	0-60mph (0-96km/h): 6.8 seconds

Lamborghini Countach

**Top speed
175mph**
282km/h

*Right: Lamborghini's V12
was mounted longitudinally
in the Countach, and in its
Diablo successor. However,
it was less accessible than
the transversely mounted
engine in the Miura.*

*Below: The Countach's
wedge-shaped profile was
made possible by the mid-
position of the engine. This
is an LP400S model of
1981. What appear to be
the headlamps are in fact
flashing turn signals. The
real headlamps are of the
pop-up variety.*

Replacing a model of the stature of the
Miura should have represented a daunting
prospect for any car company, but then
Lamborghini is no run-of-the-mill motor
manufacturer. The new supercar made its debut in
1971 and was named the Countach, a regional
North Italian slang word which echoed the
appreciative exclamation of a worker when viewing
the new car for the first time.

Mid-engined like the Miura, the V12 unit was
enlarged to 5 liters, and positioned longitudinally
rather than transversely. Chief engineer Paolo
Stanzani also dispensed with its predecessor's sump
in gearbox design and instead decided to position
the five-speed unit in the center of the car,
alongside the driver. But with the drive at the rear it
was conveyed, via a sealed tube, within the
engine's sump.

Lamborghini once again turned to Bertone's
Marcello Gandini to design an appropriate body for
these unconventional mechanicals and he did not
disappoint. The result was a piece of automotive
sculpture of the highest quality, an audacious
wedge-shaped coupé with concealed headlamps
and memorable upward-opening doors.

Enthusiastic reception at launch

The first Countach was completed just in time to be
launched at the 1971 Geneva Motor Show where its
enthusiastic reception convinced Lamborghini that
this was the Miura's true successor. But it was to be
a further three years before the first production
Countach left the Saint' Agata Bolognese factory in
mid-1974. The enlarged V12 had disintegrated
during testing so the original 375bhp 3.9 liter unit
was reinstated.

Left: Rear view of the 400S. Although the rear spoiler makes a visual contribution to the car, contrary to appearances the Countach does not suffer from aerodynamic lift, and the spoiler adds drag, weight, and expense. Note the four exhaust pipes.

Below: A 5000QV bereft of a rear wing and probably the better for it. Outwardly identical to its predecessors, its performance was enhanced by a redesign of the V12 engine which was not only enlarged in capacity but featured four valves per cylinder.

The model was, nevertheless, faster than its predecessor; it could be wound up to about 175mph (282km/h) with 100mph (161km/h) arriving in a little over 13 seconds. And if the driver and passenger found some difficulty in entering or leaving the cockpit, no matter!

The original version survived until 1978 when it was replaced by the Countach S with wider Campagnolo alloy wheels – the arches were flared to accommodate them. A rear wing, which added to the car's aerodynamic aura, became a popular (if not a wholly necessary) extra.

More powerful engine

In 1982 the capacity of the V12 was upped to 4.7 liters and the car was now known as the LP5000S. Further changes were in hand and in 1985 the V12 was not only again increased in capacity, to 5.2 liters, but was also the beneficiary of twin-cam four-valve cylinder heads. Now producing 455bhp, the resulting 5000QV (for *quattrovalvole*) was faster, at 178mph (286km/h), and owners found it easier to drive than its predecessor on account of its torquier engine.

The QV was destined to have a four-year production life. In 1988 Lamborghini released the Anniversary model with mildly revised bodywork which celebrated 25 years as a motor manufacturer. Countach production ceased in July 1990, after a total of 1549 examples had been completed.

Specification	**Lamborghini** Countach (3.9 liters)
Engine location	Mid, in-line
Configuration	V12
Bore and stroke	82 x 62mm
Capacity	3929cc
Valve operation	Twin overhead camshafts per bank
Horsepower	375bhp @ 8000rpm
Transmission	Manual five-speed
Drive	Rear
Chassis	Tubular steel
Suspension – front	Wishbones and coil spring
Suspension – rear	Wishbones and coil spring
Brakes	Ventilated disc
Top speed	175mph (282km/h)
Acceleration	0-60mph (0-96km/h): 5.7 seconds

Above: A right-hand-drive Anniversary Countach, some 30 of which were sold in Britain. It is easily identifiable by its softer, smoother lines.

Below: Significant changes were made at the rear – stylist Marcello Gandini was particularly pleased with this aspect of his work.

Although the 5 liter V12 engine originally developed for the Countach was sidelined, there was a second example built and the story behind this provides yet another fascinating strand of the Countach story.

Lamborghini aficionado Walter Woolf, owner of the very last Miura, also played a significant role in the development of the much improved Countach S of 1978. A Canadian of Austrian birth and an oil equipment mogul, his commitment to motor sport was underlined by the formation, in 1976, of his own Formula 1 racing team.

In 1974 he had taken delivery of a red Countach, reputedly the first car off the line. Woolf was able to get the Sant' Agata factory to manufacture a second 5 liter engine of the type that had powered the prototype Countach and which had spectacularly disintegrated during testing in 1971. This special V12 had a capacity of 4971cc, internal dimensions of 85 x 73mm and developed 440bhp at 7400rpm. It was duly installed in the first of Woolf's Countachs which was also fitted with an innovative movable rear spoiler, squat Pirelli P7 tires and crudely extended wheel arches. And therein lay the genesis of the Countach S.

Public address system

When Woolf sold the car to a Japanese enthusiast he retained its special engine and installed it in a second Countach that he had acquired in 1976. This example was finished in his racing team's deep blue and gold livery with the colors repeated in the interior. It was also distinguished by the provision of a public address system which permitted the owner to hail other road users!

The 5 liter V12 engine was then again transferred to Wolf's third Countach in which the brakes were uprated, along with the clutch, to cope with the demands of the enlarged unit.

He was so impressed with the results of the

changes he had made that he paid for Giampaolo Dallara, creator of the Miura, who had left Lamborghini to join De Tomaso, to return to the works to enhance the production cars in the same way. The result was the much improved Countach S.

There was also a change of road wheels. Woolf had already fitted the so-called 'telephone dial' Campagnolo alloys, and the glass-fiber flares fitted to accommodate them, together with a front spoiler, all contributed to the visual enhancements that identify the model.

Although Lamborghini eventually increased the capacity of the V12 engine to 4754cc in 1982, it was of different dimensions to the original 5 liter unit. A third stretch took place in 1985 with the enlargement of the engine to 5167cc; four-valve cylinder heads were fitted.

Such is the role played by the wealthy and enthusiastic Walter Woolf in the unfolding Lamborghini story. In fact at one stage he nearly bought the firm but, fortunately in the light of future events, wiser counsels prevailed!

Below: The model's scissor doors are one of its most distinctive features. The engine air intakes were redesigned and replaced with these wider and lower intakes. Straked air scoops at the front which appeared again just ahead of the rear wheel arches were another detail refinement.

Porsche 911 Turbo

**Top speed
153mph**
246km/h

*Below: Something special:
a 1980 3.3 liter Turbo with
no chrome apparent, matt
black being something of a
Porsche specialty! The
wider wheels and enhanced
arches were established
Turbo features by then.
Less apparent is the
presence of drilled brake
discs arrested by Alcan
four-piston calipers.*

 When Porsche introduced its now
legendary 911 in 1962, it was capable of a
respectable 130mph (209km/h) top speed.
This figure progressively improved over the years
but the line received a significant boost in 1974
with the arrival of 911 Turbo that was capable of
153mph (246km/h). It was able to hit 100mph
(161km/h) in a mere 14 seconds.

Although Porsche's gargantuan Le Mans-
winning 917 sports racer of 1970/1 had been
further enhanced by a turbocharged engine, the
concept had not been immediately extended to road
cars. It fell to BMW to introduce, in 1973, the 2002
Turbo, which was Europe's first such street-ready
model. Driven by the need to homologate its
projected 935 racer in Group 4 competition, Porsche
proceeded with a turbocharged version of the 911
that appeared at the 1974 Paris Motor Show.

Tea-tray spoiler

Developed under the 930 designation, the 911
Turbo was instantly identifiable by its wider wheels
and accompanying flared arches while there was a
large 'tea-tray' spoiler at the rear which helped to
keep the back wheels firmly on the road.

Beneath was a mildly tamed race-bred, 3 liter,
RSR Carrera, KKK turbocharged, six-cylinder,
horizontally opposed, air-cooled engine. In this
form it developed 260bhp, a good 60bhp more than
the unblown 3 liter Carrera.

Fast but surprisingly flexible, the 911 Turbo
was a comfortable, well-appointed car with air
conditioning and electric windows fitted as
standard. It was produced in this form until 1978
when the engine's capacity was increased to 3.3
liters and a competition-proven intercooler was also
introduced which boosted the efficiency of the

turbocharger. Top speed was increased to 160mph (257km/h) while 100mph (161km/h) could be spirited up in a mere 12 seconds, which made this Turbo the fastest-accelerating road car of its day. Originally fitted with a four-speed gearbox, it was not until 1988 that an extra top cog arrived. This second generation Turbo was built until mid-1989, only to reappear in the spring of 1990 in revised Carrera 2 form.

The third generation Carrera Turbo arrived for 1994 with a 3.6 liter engine, twin KKK turbochargers, and four-wheel drive. Accordingly sure-footed, identifiable by a distinctive howl and exceptionally rapid, it was capable of an impressive 178mph (286km/h).

The current 911 Turbo, introduced for the 2001 season, is similarly driven, has a water-cooled engine and is also available with Tiptronic semi-automatic transmission. And its top speed nudges the 190mph (306km/h) mark…

Left: The 911 Turbo's air-conditioned interior was particularly well appointed. The revolution counter dominated the instrument display and was mounted right in front of the driver with the turbocharger boost gauge set into the bottom of the dial.

Below left: This 3.3 liter Turbo was easily distinguished by the new squared-off rear spoiler with its upturned rubber surround. In addition to generating downforce, it also housed the air-conditioning radiator and served the newly introduced intercooler which reduced the temperature of the turbocharged air and so improved engine efficiency.

Specification	Porsche 911 Turbo (3 liters)
Engine location	Rear, in-line
Configuration	Turbocharged horizontally opposed six-cylinder
Bore and stroke	95 x 70mm
Capacity	2993cc
Valve operation	Single overhead camshaft
Horsepower	260bhp @ 5500rpm
Transmission	Manual four-speed
Drive	Rear
Chassis	Unitary
Suspension – front	Wishbones and torsion bar
Suspension – rear	Semi trailing arm and torsion bar
Brakes	Ventilated disc
Top speed	153mph (246km/h)
Acceleration	0-60mph (0-96km/h): 6.4 seconds

Aston Martin Lagonda

**Top speed
145mph**
233km/h

Aston Martin's luxurious and futuristically-styled 145mph (233km/h) Lagonda sedan was a successful initiative which created a second product line to complement the company's hitherto exclusively sports car range.

Aston Martin owned the Lagonda marque, David Brown having acquired both businesses in 1947, and Lagondas remained in limited production until the demise in 1964 of the DB4-based Rapide. The name Lagonda was revived in 1974 for a low production run, but as a model, rather than a marque, designation. This was a four-door sedan based on an extended Aston Martin V8 chassis.

Only seven were built, and production ceased in 1976. However, it did provide the company with a platform on which to base its new car.

The firm had been placed in receivership in 1974 and a new management took over in the following year. It commissioned a body design from William Towns, who had styled the V8 coupé, and the result was a low and angular four-door sedan with concealed headlamps and a spacious trunk. The new Aston Martin was a daringly elongated car and, at 17ft 4in (5283mm), it was one of Europe's longest production models. It looked like nothing else on the road.

It was powered by a detuned version of the corporate 5.3 liter V8 engine with milder camshafts and larger valves. Three-speed automatic transmission was retained.

Sumptuous interior

The interior was sumptuously upholstered with buttoned leather squabs. But the truly revolutionary aspect of the design was a state of the art electronic dashboard. Perfecting this feature, and coping with the problems associated with it, nearly put paid to the entire project.

It was mostly for this reason that there was an two-and-a-half year hiatus before the first definitive Lagonda left Aston Martin's Newport Pagnell

Below: The Lagonda prototype of 1976. Only 4ft 3in (1295mm) high, it had plenty of trunk space, but rear passengers complained of a lack of leg room.

Right: The same car as above. The headlamps sit under electrically activated pop-up flaps. When the hood was raised, they remained in situ. The supplementary halogen fog and spot lights occupy the recess in the slot above the front bumper.

Opposite below: A 1987 Series 4 Lagonda. Towns' original sharp lines were somewhat softened. The original waistline rubbing strips were dispensed with and the pop-up headlamps were relocated in the nose.

Specification	**Aston Martin** Lagonda
Engine location	Front, in-line
Configuration	V8
Bore and stroke	85 x 100mm
Capacity	5340cc
Valve operation	Twin overhead camshafts per cylinder bank
Horsepower	280bhp @ 5000rpm
Transmission	Automatic three-speed
Drive	Rear
Chassis	Platform
Suspension – front	Wishbones and coil spring
Suspension – rear	De Dion axle and coil springs
Brakes	Disc
Top speed	145mph (233km/h)
Acceleration	0-60mph (0-96km/h): 8.9 seconds

factory early in 1979. By this time the price had risen in the inflationary 1970s from £24,570 ($34,400) to £49,933 ($69,900). This was a fast car, able, on a good day, to touch 148mph (238km/h) with 100mph (161km/h) arriving in a shade over 20 seconds.

There were few production changes during its life, with the exception of fuel injection which arrived in 1986. In the following year the body was refined with the angular lines replaced by gentler curves. The pop-up headlamps were dropped to be replaced by no less than six lights positioned within the nose, a spoiler was added, along with side skirts. Alloy wheels took over from the original steel discs.

Production ceased in January 1990 after a respectable 610 examples of this unconventional sedan had been completed. The Lagonda name, for the time being at least, remains in abeyance.

Above left: In October 1983 in-house Tickford launched the much enhanced Tickford Lagonda which was fitted with no less than two color televisions! But at $119,000 apiece there were few takers and only five examples were sold.

Porsche 928

**Top speed
135mph**
217km/h

*Right: Interior of a 1987
Series 2 928. The steering
wheel could be adjusted
vertically and, unusually,
the instrument binnacle
moved with it.*

*Below: As it was in the
beginning, a 928 of 1979
with its distinctive
'telephone dial' alloy
wheels and exposed pop-up
headlamps intended to
generate customer interest.*

Today the Porsche name is synonymous
with the enduring and enticing 911. But in
the 1970s its star was in decline as the
company pressed ahead with a range of
conventionally engined grand tourers, the flagship
of which was the 135mph (217km/h) 928.

This was a wholly new car with no legacy
passed on from previous models, although there
were family resemblances with its 924 and 944
contemporaries. All these new models were the
brainchild of Dr Ernst Fuhrmann, who had been
appointed Porsche's new chief executive in 1971.

The 928 was launched at the 1977 Geneva
Motor Show and promptly became Car of the Year
in 1978. A wide, smoothly contoured coupé with
opening tailgate, styled in-house by Anatole
Lapine, its lines appeared uncluttered by bumpers,
although they were in fact concealed beneath
deformable panels. Quite deliberately, exposed,
rather than concealed, pop-up headlamps were
specified and became a distinctive feature.

Powered by Porsche's first V8 engine, this 4.4
liter aluminum unit, with single camshafts per
cylinder bank, drove the five-speed differential-
mounted gearbox via a flexible driveshaft contained
inside the model's tubular backbone. There was
also the option of an automatic gearbox.

Left: A 928 Series 4 of 1988. It is identifiable by its reprofiled nose, which featured a combined unit housing spot, fog, and turn signal lights, and hinged rear spoiler. Both changes were intended to improve the coupé's aerodynamics.

Below: The Series 4 928 was replaced by the GTS for the 1992 season. Outward changes were few but included wider air intakes and new wheels which were shared with its 968 stablemate.

Yet for all the 928's ingenious specification and good performance – 60mph (96km/h) arrived in eight seconds – and despite near perfect road manners, commentators began to wonder whether that elusive and sometimes indefinable quality of character, so apparent in the 911, somehow eluded the 928.

Porsche, believing that more performance would remedy this problem, increased the V8's capacity in 1979 to 4.6 liters. Up went acceleration and top speed rose to 145mph (233km/h) yet that all-important Porsche ingredient still remained elusive.

Improving the 928

Dr Furhmann departed in 1980 and the 911 once again moved center stage. But this did not prevent the company from improving the 928 and in 1986 the 928-S4 appeared with sharper body lines, a new nose and the V8 stretched again, this time to 4.9 liters. More radically twin cam heads were introduced; all these ministrations produced 320bhp compared with the original's 234bhp. American customers had already had a preview of this engine, it having been fitted to US-sold 928Ss since 1985.

Now capable of 160mph (257km/h), Porsche succeeded in raising this to 170mph (274km/h) with the 928 GT of 1989. This had 330bhp on tap which made it Porsche's fastest road car.

The third and final increase in engine capacity, to 5.4 liters, came in 1991 with the arrival of the GTS. The model was discontinued in 1995, and its passing seemingly went unmourned, least of all by its manufacturer.

Specification	Porsche 928
Engine location	Front, in-line
Configuration	V8
Bore and stroke	95 x 78mm
Capacity	4474cc
Valve operation	Single overhead camshaft per cylinder bank
Horsepower	240bhp @ 5500rpm
Transmission	Manual five-speed
Drive	Rear
Chassis	Unitary
Suspension – front	Wishbones and coil spring
Suspension – rear	Semi trailing arm and coil spring
Brakes	Disc
Top speed	135mph (217km/h)
Acceleration	0-60mph (0-96km/h): 8 seconds

BMW M1

**Top speed
162mph**
261km/h

*Below: A cocktail of
influences with a body
styled by Giugiaro,
incomplete Lamborghini
engineering, and finish by
Baur in Stuttgart. This road
car, which was created so
the necessary 400 units
could be built for
homologation, dates from
1980. The elongated rear
deck indicates that the 3.4
twin-cam six is mounted
longitudinally ahead of the
ZF transaxle.*

 It looked like no other BMW and was
capable of over 160mph (257km/h).
However, only 456 lucky owners were
able to sample the delights of this race-ready mid-
engined coupé.

Initiated by Jochen Neerpasch, head of BMW
Motorsport, work began on the project, designated
E-26, in 1976. The intention was to produce a
850bhp Group 5 car to wrest the championship
from Porsche. To obtain homologation there would
have to be a roadgoing version, of which 400 were
required to be built over a 12-month period. There
was also a 470bhp variant with appropriately
tailored bodywork eligible for Group 4 GT racing.

BMW lacked the in-house facilities to
undertake the (albeit limited) production of such a
car, so the work was assigned to Lamborghini
which was also to be responsible for the
manufacture of the chassis. Styling was allocated to
Ital Design and it would also undertake the
construction of the glass-fiber shell.

The longitudinally-positioned engine was
BMW's 3.5 liter six-cylinder unit used in the 635
CSi coupé, but here enhanced with a twin overhead
camshaft/four valves per cylinder head. Output for
the road car was 277bhp, a not insignificant 65
more than the norm.

Unfortunately, the program encountered
unacceptable delays, which proved to be fatal,
while costs were rising alarmingly. In April 1978
BMW therefore cancelled its contract with
Lamborghini and later that year Baur in Stuttgart
began the assembly of the Ital-built bodies with
their tubular chassis. The work was finally
completed by BMW Motorsport which ensured a
quality of finish in keeping with the company's
other products.

Impressive road car

Formally launched at the 1978 Paris Motor Show,
the M1, which sold for 100,000DM, the equivalent
of $22,000, proved to be an impressive road car

able to sprint to 62mph (100km/h) in just 5.6 seconds. Although many Formula 1 drivers competed in the ProCar series of races for M1s, which were held prior to European grand prix events, the model's best placing in a sports racing event came in 1980 when Hans Stuck took third in that year's Nürburgring 1000km competition.

But the M1 never proved its worth against the real opposition because by the time it was homologated in 1981, it was beginning to date. It turned the scales at some 1985lb (900kg), which was about 440lb (200kg) more than its Porsche 936 rival. And in the competitive world of motor sport timing is all.

Left: Although only produced in left-hand-drive form, this is a British registered car. The engine produced 'only' 277bhp, thanks to 47mm inlet valves, 32mm exhausts, and a 9:1 compression ratio. This compared with 48.6mm and 32.5mm for the racing units and a CR figure of 11.5:1. All M1s were fitted with essentially the same gearbox, regardless of the type of engine employed.

Below left: The M1 dashboard was typically BMW while the pedals were slightly offset to accommodate the intrusion of the wheel arch into the foot well. However, tall drivers found the driving compartment a little on the cramped side. Through-flow ventilation was particularly praiseworthy.

Specification	BMW M1
Engine location	Mid, in-line
Configuration	Six-cylinder
Bore and stroke	93 x 84mm
Capacity	3453cc
Valve operation	Twin overhead camshafts
Horsepower	277bhp @ 6500rpm
Transmission	Manual five-speed
Drive	Rear
Chassis	Tubular
Suspension – front	Wishbones and coil spring
Suspension – rear	Wishbones and coil spring
Brakes	Disc
Top speed	162mph (261km/h)
Acceleration	0-62mph (0-100km/h): 5.6 seconds

Audi quattro

**Top speed
137mph**
220km/h

*Right: The instrument panel
of a left-hand-drive 1985
quattro included a display
to indicate whether the
center or rear differentials
were locked or not and a
turbocharger boost gauge.*

*Below: The lines of the
1985 quattro shown to
advantage. It incorporated
aerodynamic appendages
front and rear. The badge
on the lower door panel
represented the four car
companies that constituted
the pre-war Auto Union
concern, of which Audi is
the sole surviving member.*

 The 1980 quattro (the lower case 'q' is
Audi's preferred spelling) was not only a
crisply styled 137mph (220km/h)
turbocharged coupé, it was technically innovative
because all four of its wheels were permanently
driven. This was thanks to Audi's light and
ingenious system which instantly made the 4wd
concept a practical proposition in a road car. And
the motoring community was soon following in the
quattro's four-wheel-drive tracks.

The seeds of the idea had been sown three years
earlier when the company's engineers were
evaluating its front-wheel-drive sedans in Northern
Scandinavia. They were in company with another
Audi-designed machine – a pre-production
Volkswagen Iltris military vehicle that was due to
be launched in the following year. This easily
outpaced the Audi sedans on the snow, thanks to its
four-wheel-drive system.

This revelation was not wasted on Audi's chief
chassis engineer, Jörg Bensinger, and with the
encouragement of Walter Treser, Audi's manager of
advanced development and a former rally driver, in
May 1978 work officially began on what was to
emerge as the quattro.

Formidable rally contender

It was not only conceived to reinforce Audi's
already high technological profile; from 1979 four-
wheel-drive cars became eligible for the World
Rally Championship, and the company recognized
that the new model could be a formidable contender
for the crown. The intention was to build 10
quattros every working day, some 2000 a year, so
the 400 cars necessary for the new Audi to qualify
for homologation could be produced quickly. (It
was not, of course, the first four-wheel-drive car.

The concept was almost as old as the industry and had most recently been employed on the costly, heavy, and complicated Jensen FF.)

The model was the undisputed star of the 50th Geneva Motor Show of 1980. In 1977 Audi had introduced the world's first five-cylinder gasoline engine and at the beginning of 1980 this had been used in 170bhp turbocharged form in the flagship 200 model. The quattro was powered by this 2.1 liter unit. It featured a single overhead camshaft with two valves per cylinder and its output was boosted to 200bhp.

Using the Iltris system as a starting point, the Audi design team came up with an ingenious four-wheel-drive concept which dispensed with the heavy transfer box and drive shaft usually associated with the system. Like all front-wheel-drive Audis, the five-cylinder engine was mounted in line rather than adopting the more usual transverse layout. The gearbox was therefore attached to the back of the power unit in the manner of rear-drive cars.

On the quattro, power was transmitted through the gearbox in the usual way to a grapefruit-sized differential located directly behind the gearbox. From there it was conveyed to a conventional rear axle. But it was also transmitted forward, via a hollow gearbox output shaft, to the differential that drove the front wheels. This was the essence of the quattro system which was further enhanced by the latest low profile radial tires.

Specification	**Audi** quattro
Engine location	Front, in-line
Configuration	Turbocharged five-cylinder
Bore and stroke	79 x 86mm
Capacity	2144cc
Valve operation	Single overhead camshaft
Horsepower	200bhp @ 5500rpm
Transmission	Manual five-speed
Drive	Four-wheel
Chassis	Unitary
Suspension – front	MacPherson strut and coil spring
Suspension – rear	MacPherson strut and coil spring
Brakes	Disc, ventilated at front
Top speed	137mph (220km/h)
Acceleration	0-62mph (0-100km/h): 7.1 seconds

Above: Produced for the 1984 season, this short wheelbase Sport quattro of 1985 with a 396bhp engine was able to reach 60mph (96km/h) in a mere 4.5 seconds.

Left: The Sport's engine with large KKK-K27 turbocharger and Bosch LH-Jetronic fuel injection. Despite its high state of tune, it was remarkably docile in traffic.

Above: A quattro competing in the 1985 Portugal rally, by which time these sensational Audis were being challenged by Peugeot. Nevertheless, Walter Rohrl's car looked as though it was going to win until the gearbox, a five speeder, broke. Thereafter the quattros, equipped with six-cog units, ran in the Safari and Corsica events but failed to win.

Right: The 1990 season saw the 90 quattro offered with a new 20-valve 2.3 liter engine. Developing 136bhp, the body lines of the original coupé had been softened in 1988. This version was built by Baur of Stuttgart. Its maximum speed was 128mph (206km/h).

The model's all-independent strut suspension came courtesy of the Audi 200 and the two-door body, designed by Englishman Martin Smith, would emerge a year later as the front-wheel-drive Coupé GT.

Not only was the quattro a fast car, able to attain 137km/h (220km/h), its roadholding proved to be sensational. It soon found its way into showrooms around the world, and right-hand-drive versions appeared at the end of 1982. It also made its presence felt in the rally field. It should be said that these specially prepared works quattros were considerably more powerful than the road cars, their engines developing some 320/330bhp.

Audi had succeeded in wooing the Finnish rally driver Hannu Mikkola from Ford after he had experienced this revolutionary coupé at first hand. He immediately triumphed in two events – the 1981 Swedish and RAC rallies. The San Remo round was won by Michelle Mouton, who became the first woman to win a World Rally Championship competition.

In 1982 the model really found its form and Audi secured the Championship with Mouton winning three and Mikkola two. From 1983 the competition was run under Group B regulations,

and in 1984 the special shortened quattro Sport appeared with 13in (330mm) removed from the 8ft 3.4in (2522mm) wheelbase. The engine, with twin overhead camshafts and four valves per cylinder, developed in excess of 400bhp.

Audi again took the Championship in 1984. However, by 1985 Lancia and Ford opposition were getting the upper hand and a victory in that year's San Remo rally was the last win by a quattro in a championship event.

Evolution

The road cars were, however, continuing to evolve. Early in 1984 an automatic braking system was fitted, but it was not until the 1988 season that changes were made to the engine. Then the capacity of the five-cylinder unit was increased to 2226cc which brought it into line with the Audi 100. The only other difference, from a technical standpoint, was the provision of a more efficient Torsen center differential.

Further improvements were unveiled for the 1990 model year with the arrival of the rally-proven twin-cam 20 valve-unit which had 220bhp on tap. The model ceased production in 1991.

In the meantime the quattro four-wheel-drive system had been extended to Audi's other cars and by 1984 it had been applied across the model range. Such has been the success of the concept that in 2001 Audi calculated that over million of its customers had chosen four-wheel-drive, just 21 years after the quattro's momentous Geneva launch.

Above: Hailed on its arrival in 1994 as the world's fastest estate car, the Audi RS2, fitted with quattro four-wheel drive and jointly developed with Porsche, became an instant collectors' item as only 2200 were produced – 1700 in 1994 and 500 in 1995. With the 2226cc five-cylinder engine boosted to 315bhp, it was able to reach 163mph (262km/h).

Left: Audi maintained its reputation as the producer of world-beating estate cars with the arrival in 2000 of the RS4. It was powered by a 2.7 liter 380bhp engine although by this time the five-cylinder unit had been replaced by a V6 one. Top speed, in excess of 160mph (257km/h), remained about the same.

Lotus Esprit Turbo

**Top speed
175mph**
282km/h

Lotus's Esprit dates from 1975. It has stylistically and mechanically evolved over the past quarter century, and it can still show a clean pair of heels to most of the opposition with a top speed of 175mph (282km/h).

The result of a fruitful dialogue in 1972 between Lotus's founder, Colin Chapman, and Giorgetto Giugiaro of the Turin-based Ital Design, the Esprit was launched at the 1975 London Motor Show, as a mid-engined, crisply styled, glass-fiber-bodied coupé with Lotus's familiar backbone chassis and all-independent suspension. The engine was the corporate 2 liter, twin-cam four which developed 156bhp. Top speed was 124mph (200km/h), although Lotus claimed 138mph (222km/h).

An engine enlargement to 2.2 liters followed in 1980 and the Esprit Turbo arrived later that year. With 210bhp on tap, it was capable of 150mph (241km/h). The chassis had been redesigned to accept a new V8 engine then under development, although there would be a long wait for this unit.

The 1988 season saw the sharpness of Giugiaro's lines skilfully softened by the company's Peter Stevens. Later, in 1993, came a new nose and tail, power steering, and suspension revisions and a supplementary model, the Sport 300 (which reflected its bhp) with a larger turbocharger and wider wheels. This was followed in 1994 by the S4S with the Sport's mechanicals and a luxurious interior.

High performance league

Eventually, in 1996, the Esprit received its long-awaited 3.5 liter V8 engine which developed 349bhp with the aid of twin Garrett T25 turbochargers. At a stroke the model entered a new performance league with top speed soaring to over 175mph (282km/h) and 62mph (100km/h) arriving in a mere 4.5 seconds. However, the blown four-cylinder version remained in production as an entry-level 2 liter GT3, a model that survived, despite all the odds, until 1999.

Above: The Esprit Turbo in its original guise (in Essex Racing colors) sporting the Giugiaro-styled body dating from the model's 1975 introduction. Both wheels and brakes were uprated for the blown version.

Right: The Turbo received its long-awaited V8 engine in 1996, the model having had a visual facelift in 1988. Outwardly similar to its four-cylinder predecessor, this mid-engined Lotus offers praiseworthy performance and handling, although with specifications rooted in the 1970s.

Far left: The badge is the giveaway, particularly as the four continued in production.

Left: What treasure lurks under the rear deck – the longitudinally mounted turbocharged four.

Below: The Turbo acquired this new highly distinctive dashboard for the 1998 season.

For 1998 Lotus offered a bargain-basement Esprit, the GT, for a shade under $70,000 – $14,000 less than the original. Bereft of such items as the rear wing and air conditioning, both it and the Esprit V8 received a new roomier interior and dashboard.

The 1999 season saw the arrival of the supplementary Sport 350 – the most extreme Esprit ever – which was 176lb (80kg) lighter than the mainstream model. Production was limited to just 50 cars. Easily identifiable by its carbon-fiber rear wing, there were lightweight wheels and suspension and brake uprates. The interior featured carbon fiber and alloy in abundance.

So the Esprit continues to soldier on, but it is now showing its years. The end of the story cannot be far away, can it?

Specification	Lotus Esprit Turbo (3.5 liter)
Engine location	Mid, in-line
Configuration	Twin turbocharged V8
Bore and stroke	81 x 83mm
Capacity	3506cc
Valve operation	Twin overhead camshafts per bank
Horsepower	349bhp @ 6500rpm
Transmission	Manual five-speed
Drive	Rear
Chassis	Backbone
Suspension – front	Wishbones and coil spring
Suspension – rear	Upper and lower link and coil spring
Brakes	Disc
Top speed	175mph (282km/h)
Acceleration	0-62mph (100km/h): 4.5 seconds

1981–1990
The Revs Begin to Rise

This was a decade again dominated by an economic recession but this situation did not prevent Porsche from embarking, in 1983, on its costly, complex, and very rapid 959 coupé. And by the time that Ferrari offered its stark but sensational and even faster F40 in 1988, the industrialized world was once again basking in an era of apparent prosperity.

Further developments took place on the technical front with the revival, after an absence of some 50 years, of the supercharger. Its use in 1988 by such mainstream motor manufacturers as Ford and Volkswagen indicated that it could not be long before 'the blower' made a return to the higher echelons of the performance motor sector.

Bristol Beaufighter

**Top speed
150mph**
241km/h

*Right: Bristols have been
powered by Chrysler V8
engines since 1961 and the
Beaufighter Turbocharged
Convertible was fitted with
a 5.9 liter unit, its
performance enhanced by a
Rotomaster blower.*

*Below: The Beaufighter's
multi-purpose body was the
work of Zagato. Note the
four ventilation slots
located beneath the bumper
to aid engine cooling. The
substantial roll-over bar,
together with a steel gusset
beneath the floor, prevented
scuttle shake.*

Take brutal and angular Zagato styling
cloaking a substantial BMW-derived
chassis rooted in the 1930s, add a
turbocharged Chrysler 5.9 liter V8 engine, and you
have the essence of the impressively engineered
Bristol Beaufighter.

Rare, expensive, and appealing to a small but
discriminating clientele, Bristol is one of a handful
of Britain's post-war marques that has survived into
the 21st century. Originally it was an offshoot of
the Bristol Aeroplane Company. The 400, the first
of the line which appeared in 1947, used a potent 2
liter BMW-based six-cylinder engine. Progressively
enhanced, it remained in production until the
demise of the 406 model in 1961.

Its 407 replacement of 1962 was the first
Bristol to be powered by a Chrysler V8 engine, a
make and configuration that has been used in every
Bristol from then until the present day.

Remarkable speed

The Beaufighter of 1980 traces its origins back to
the Zagato-bodied 412 of 1975 which essentially
retained the mechanics of its 6.5 liter 411
predecessor. The two-door four-seater with its slab-
like hood was remarkably fast, being effortlessly
able to attain 150mph (241km/m). Unusually, it
was a convertible and came complete with a
substantial double roll-over bar. This subsequently
evolved, in 1976, into a 'convertible/sedan'.

It featured a fixed rear window although the
company helpfully informed its customers that 'the
entire roof section may be removed in about an
hour, with an ordinary tool kit…' It was then
replaced with a canvas roof. There was an
alternative targa-style detachable roof panel.

Wartime tribute

The 1978 season saw the 6.5 liter V8 replaced by a smaller capacity 5.9 liter unit; this Series 2 model was succeeded in 1980 by the Beaufighter, named as a tribute to the wartime torpedo-carrying strike aircraft produced by Bristol Aeroplane. Although outwardly similar to the 412, the 5.9 liter V8 was retained and its power was boosted some 30 per cent by the introduction of a Rotomaster turbocharger. Like Rolls-Royce, Bristol did not disclose the output of its engine.

These ministrations were sufficient to transform its performance, and while the 150mph (241km/h) top speed remained about the same, acceleration was much improved with 60mph (96km/h) arriving in under six seconds.

The targa style was discontinued and replaced by a solid top complete with sun roof. The occupants' comfort was assured by the electrically adjustable front seats, a noteworthy refinement for the day.

The Beaufighter was joined in 1987 by the Beaufort convertible which lacked the roll-over bar which characterized its 412 predecessor. Both models enjoyed long production runs, surviving for no less than 13 years before being discontinued in 1993. Happily, Bristol is still in business.

Above: The angular rear of the Beaufighter, complete with Bristol Cars' memorable, but unduly pessimistic, number plate!

Left: The car's badge is, appropriately, a representation of the coat of arms of the city of Bristol.

Specification	**Bristol** Beaufighter
Engine location	Front, in-line
Configuration	V8
Bore and stroke	101 x 90mm
Capacity	5900cc
Valve operation	Pushrod
Horsepower	N/A
Transmission	Automatic three-speed
Drive	Rear
Chassis	Box section
Suspension – front	Wishbones and coil spring
Suspension – rear	Live axle, torsion bars and Watts linkage
Brakes	Disc
Top speed	150mph (241km/h)
Acceleration	0-60mph (96km/h): 5.9 seconds

Renault 5 Turbo

**Top speed
124mph**
200km/h

Right: The 5 Turbo's mid-located 1.3 liter Garrett-turbocharged engine. This is the car which won the 1981 Monte Carlo Rally.

Below: The 1981 Monte Carlo Rally winner, driven by Ragnotti and Andrie, was a specially built rally car and its balance and traction proved their worth in the Alpine snows.

It superficially resembled Renault's ubiquitous 5 but closer inspection revealed that the Turbo's engine had been transferred from the front of the car to a mid-location. The result was a raucous turbocharged 124mph (200km/h) two-seater hailed by pundits as a 'Five on steroids.'

One of Renault's big sellers of the post-war years, the 5 supermini was launched in 1972. This front-wheel-drive hatchback, with its distinctive and seemingly ageless styling, was produced until 1984. By this time some 5.4 million had been completed. It was available with a variety of engines, from 782 to 1397cc.

France's largest car maker wasted little time in producing more potent versions, the most radical of which was the 5 Turbo of 1980. This, daringly, saw a union of the hatchback's body shell with a mid-located, in-line, 137bhp, turbocharged fuel-injected version of the model's 1370cc unit.

Different suspension

Suspension also differed from the original – instead of the usual rear trailing arms, it used a wishbone and coil springs layout courtesy of the Alpine A310/V6. Inside the interior featured space age color co-ordinated livery. There was no room for rear passengers but a little luggage could be stored under the hood and at the rear.

Roadholding was generally impressive, although not in the wet. The external giveaways were distinctive air intakes behind the doors and flared wheel arches. There was an altered front apron-cum-spoiler and the body was weight-saving as the roof, doors, and rear hatch were made of aluminum while the hood, bumpers, air dam, fenders, and roof spoiler were plastic moldings.

Success in the Monte Carlo Rally

There were some competition successes – an example won the 1981 Monte Carlo Rally at the first attempt. The model was replaced by the outwardly similar but more powerful Turbo 2 in 1983, by which time 1362 had been completed. Like its predecessor, this was also successful in the rally field. It could sprint to 60mph (96km/h) in a mere seven seconds and possessed excellent handling albeit with some rear end bias like its predecessor. Traction was good but ride quality was another matter – this was guaranteed to loosen the driver's deepest tooth fillings!

Only produced in left-hand-drive form, the Turbo 2 was built until 1986, two years after the mainstream 5 had ceased production. A mere 3576 examples were completed.

Above: The turbocharged Renault displaying its distinctive rear profile and hot air outlets.

Left: The enhanced cockpit of the Monte-winning Renault. Ragnotti had an eleventh hour tussle with Therier's Porsche.

Specification	Renault 5 Turbo
Engine location	Mid-located, in-line
Configuration	Turbocharged four-cylinder
Bore and stroke	76 x 77mm
Capacity	1370cc
Valve operation	Pushrod
Horsepower	160bhp @ 6000rpm
Transmission	Manual, five-speed
Drive	Rear
Chassis	Unitary
Suspension – front	Wishbones and torsion bar
Suspension – rear	Wishbones, anti-roll bar/telescopic dampers
Brakes	Disc
Top speed	124mph (200km/h)
Acceleration	0-60mph (0-96km/h): 7 seconds

Porsche 959

**Top speed
197mph**
317km/h

Right: Only produced in left-hand-drive form, the 959's interior shows some similarity to the 911 Turbo's. Despite its sophistication, this Porsche also has the virtue of being remarkably easy to drive.

Below: A 959 doing what it does best: traveling at speed. The relationship with the 911 is readily apparent. The air intakes are to help keep the massive discs cool.

It is the ultimate 911. Beneath those familiar body lines are a mind-blowing array of electro/mechanical gizmos which made the 959, for a time, the world's fastest production road car with a top speed of 197mph (317km/h).

Above all, the 959 was a reaffirmation by its makers of the spirit of the 911, with its unorthodox rear-mounted, air-cooled, flat-six engine. The 911 had taken a back seat between 1972-80, when Dr Ernst Fuhrmann was Porsche's chief executive and he decreed a switch to conventional front-engined cars such as the 928. But with the arrival of his successor, Peter Schultz, the 911 once again moved center stage and it has remained there ever since.

Porsche unveiled its four-wheel-drive *Gruppe B* car at the 1983 Frankfurt Motor Show. Aimed at Group B competition, this required that a minimum of 200 be produced for homologation purposes. Power came from a special 2.8 liter twin-turbocharged version of the 911's air-cooled flat-six engine which had competition-proven water-cooled cylinder heads.

This element of what was to be designated the 959 was resolved relatively quickly. Unfortunately the complex four-wheel-drive system took longer to develop than expected and the first example did not reach its patient customer until April 1987, three and a half years after the model was announced.

In the meantime an early version of the car had proved its worth on the demanding Paris to Dakar rally which it won in 1984. A further success followed in 1986. However, in that year, Group B, for which the 959 had been so carefully tailored, was banned in the wake of a series of fatal crashes.

Well worth waiting for

When the definitive 959 appeared, it proved well worth the wait. Deceptively easy to drive, at the heart of the four-wheel-drive system was the computer-controlled Porsche Control Clutch which distributed the correct amount of torque between the front and rear wheels.

For fast motoring, Porsche claimed a top speed of 193mph (311km/h); in fact 197mph (317km/h) was attainable when on-board computer control lowered the body to within 4.9in (124mm) of the ground. But uneven road surfaces could be accommodated with a 5.9in (150mm) setting and the car could be electrically jacked up to 7in (178mm) if the need arose.

Only produced in left-hand-drive form, demand was such that Porsche eventually produced 250 cars, 50 more than it had intended, the last example being delivered in 1988.

Specification	Porsche 959
Engine location	Rear, in-line
Configuration	Twin turbocharged horizontally opposed six-cylinder
Bore and stroke	95 x 67mm
Capacity	2849cc
Valve operation	Twin overhead camshafts per bank
Horsepower	450bhp @ 6500rpm
Transmission	Manual six-speed
Drive	Four wheel
Chassis	Unitary
Suspension – front	Wishbones and coil spring
Suspension – rear	Wishbones and coil spring
Brakes	Ventilated disc
Top speed	197mph (317km/h)
Acceleration	0-60mph (96km/h): 3.6 seconds

Left: Much of the 959's 2.8 liter, flat-six turbocharged engine cannot be seen when the lid is raised.

Below: *The fixed rear spoiler helps to keep the engine's 450 horsepower on the road.*

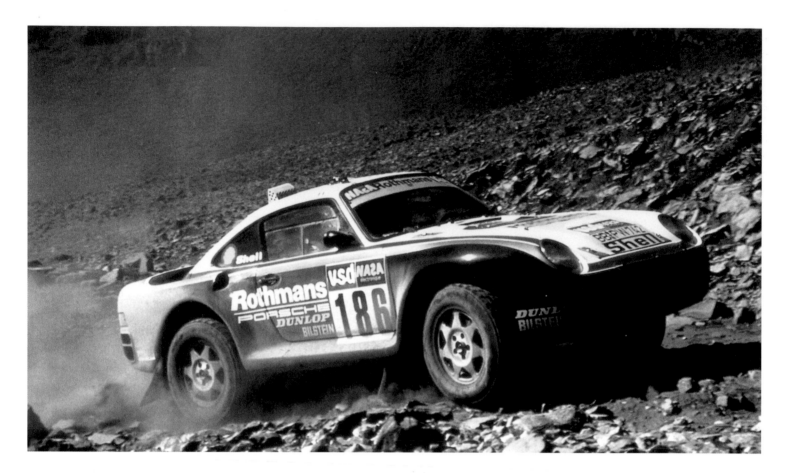

Above: A 959, driven by Metge and Lemoyne, during the 1986 Paris-Dakar Rally which it won. Note the high ground clearance – essential on such difficult terrain.

Below: Although only available in left-hand-drive form, some 959s were imported to Britain. The intakes behind the doors supplied air directly to the intercoolers.

Porsche also raced the 959 at Le Mans in 1986 although the competition car was allocated the 961 name. Work on this version had began soon after the model's triumph in that year's Paris-Dakar rally although, perhaps surprisingly, the modifications effected were relatively modest.

Outwardly the front intake was enlarged to accommodate a wider radiator. Once it had passed through the matrix, the air was expelled through a slot in the rear of the hood. At the back the stabilizer, that was a fixed unit on the road car, was made movable and it was also enlarged in size to increase downforce because the engine developed considerably more horsepower than the original.

Increased power

In truth, modifications to the turbocharged 'flat' six were relatively straightforward because it had been derived from the sports racing 956 engine. Turbocharger pressure was increased, alterations were made to the ignition and cooling and an open exhaust, bereft of a muffler, was fitted. After these ministrations by the Porsche engineers, it developed 640bhp at 7800rpm, an increase of 190bhp on the figure generated by the engine of the production 959.

A few changes to the suspension were effected with a view to tautening the system – as a result the 961 was 8.7in (220mm) lower than the rally 959, while 956 discs, complete with four piston calipers, replaced the originals. Wheels were 17in (432mm) in diameter rather than the 19in (483mm) first planned, which is why there appears to be plenty of space within the wheel arches!

As 959 production was not yet underway, in order to qualify for a Group B event a minimum of 200 cars would have had to have been built. As a result the 961 ran as a prototype in the IMSA-GTX class. In the race the car was driven by Réné Metge, who had twice taken the embryo 959 to victory in the Paris-Dakar race, and Claude Ballot-

Lena, a Le Mans veteran. It had the distinction of being the first four-wheel-drive car to run in the celebrated 24 hour classic race.

Timed at a speed of 207mph (333km/h), the Porsche started 26th in a field of 50 cars. It ran faultlessly throughout, apart from a tire blowing out in front of the pits, forcing Metge had to run an entire lap on the rim. Despite this, the 961 was not only placed seventh, but it also won its class, having averaged 112mph (181km/h) and covered 2694 miles (4335km).

With Group B banned soon afterwards, this success in the 24 hour classic event augured well for the 959 in the all important American market because it meant the competition version would run in IMSA races on the other side of the Atlantic. But, in the event, successes on US circuits were few and far between.

Left: A competition version of the 959, indicated by the presence of an anti-roll cage that reinforced the car's roof in the event of a crash.

Below: The front of the 959 was made from an elastic polyurethane known as Pur-Rpim, which was strengthened by a 15 per cent ground fiberglass mix. It was first used on the 944 Turbo and 928. The 959 hood, by contrast, was aluminum alloy.

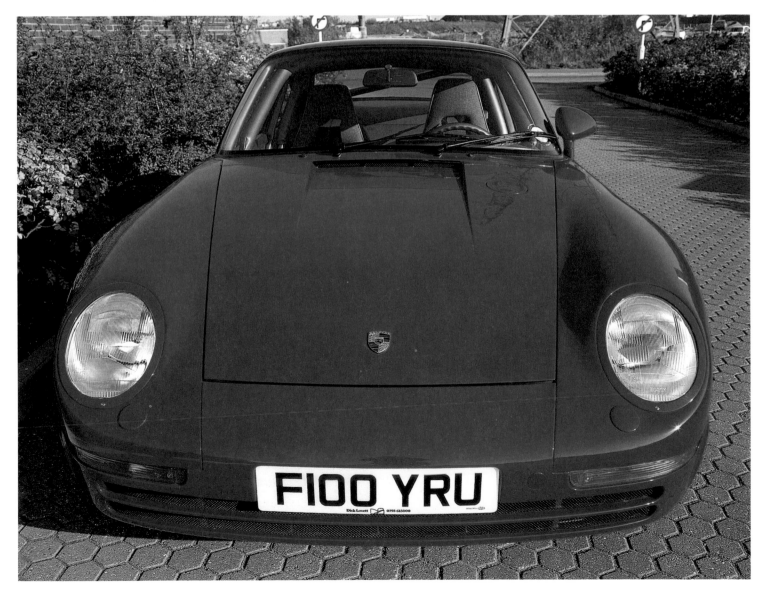

F100 YRU

Ferrari Testarossa

**Top speed
181mph**
291km/h

*Right: A left-hand-drive
Testarossa. Most of the
bodywork, apart from the
roof and door pressings,
was made of aluminum.
Aerodynamics were aided
by electrically activated
pop-up headlamps.*

*Below: The Testrossa's
outwardly similar 512R
successor of 1992. Its flat
12 engine was boosted from
390 to an impressive
422bhp. However, the
chassis was new and wider
rear tires than previously
were fitted.*

The impact of Lamborghini's visually
astounding Countach was not wasted on
Ferrari and in 1984 it responded with the
stylistically stunning Testarossa, a supercar that was
capable of over 180mph (290km/h).

Named in honour of Ferrari's celebrated 1957
sports racer, the Testa Rossa (Italian for red head),
it was the successor to the 4.9 liter 512BB
Berlinetta Boxer of 1973 which was the second
Ferrari road car to benefit from the presence of a
competition-bred horizontally opposed 12-cylinder
engine. The first had been its 365 predecessor.

Mounted on a tubular steel chassis, the
Testarossa was similarly powered by a mid-located
'flat' 12 that was positioned in the usual Ferrari
manner, in line and ahead of the rear suspension.
But although its 4942cc capacity was the same as
its predecessor's, and despite their outward
resemblance, the two alloy units had few parts in
common; this engine produced 390bhp, some
50bhp more than the Boxer's. As usual twin
overhead camshafts with four valves per cylinder
and mechanical fuel injection were fitted, although
a revised system appeared for the 1987 season.

If there was a superficial resemblance between
the two engines, the Pininfarina-designed and built
body differed radically from the Boxer. This was
because the radiator was moved from the front of
the car and replaced by twin units located on either
side of the mid-located engine to improve its
cooling efficiency. Nevertheless, a frontal cooling
grille was retained which allowed air to reach the
front brakes and which also serviced a condenser

for the air conditioning which was a standard and welcome fitment.

Most tellingly, the relocated radiators also allowed Pininfarina to extend the stunning cooling fins to the front doors and these became the model's most readily remembered feature – one that was often copied by other manufacturers, although never as successfully. As a result the Testarossa was the widest car of its day, measuring no less than 78in (1981mm) in width.

Outstanding handling

As ever only offering accommodation for two, there was additional luggage space behind the comfortable seats. Yet despite its size the Testarossa was a far more usable car that the Boxer, its controls being light which belied the presence of a more powerful engine. Handling, in the finest Ferrari traditions, was outstanding.

Announced at the 1984 Paris Motor Show, production began in 1985 when 568 cars were built. Next year 819 examples were built, mass production by Ferrari standards, but even so there was a year's worldwide waiting list for the car that was only gradually satisfied.

Destined to remain in production until 1992, the Testarossa reasserted Ferrari's pole position as the manufacturer of the world's finest supercar.

Specification	Ferrari Testarossa
Engine location	Mid, in-line
Configuration	Horizontally opposed 12-cylinder
Bore and stroke	82 x 78mm
Capacity	4942cc
Valve operation	Twin overhead camshafts per cylinder bank
Horsepower	390bhp @ 6300rpm
Transmission	Manual five-speed
Drive	Rear
Chassis	Tubular
Suspension – front	Wishbones and coil spring
Suspension – rear	Wishbones and coil spring
Brakes	Ventilated disc
Top speed	181mph (291km/h)
Acceleration	0-60mph (0-96km/h): 5.6 seconds

Left: A 1987 Testarossa engine looking remarkably like its 512BBi predecessor, although it shared very few parts with it.

Below: A 512M of 1995 – a second reincarnation of the Testarossa – with its distinctive exposed headlamps. The 4.9 liter flat 12 engine was re-worked.

MG Metro 6R4

**Top speed
110mph**
177km/h

Below: The 6R4's fittings were the result of extensive wind tunnel testing by aerodynamicist Bernie Marcus. Underneath, the familiar lines of the Metro were clearly discernible. Alas, this four-wheel-drive car never lived up to its ambitious specifications.

Created for the short-lived Group B racing category, the four-wheel-drive mid-engined MG 6R4 Metro of 1984 was a world away from the best-selling Austin supermini on which it was based. The 6R4 only bore a superficial resemblance to the production Metro because it employed four-wheel drive, the development of this fearsome two-seater having been entrusted to Formula 1 constructors Williams Grand Prix Engineering.

The resulting car was unveiled in May 1985. Powered by a purpose-designed 3 liter V6 engine with twin overhead camshafts and four valves per cylinder, the unit was unusual for not being turbocharged in a field of competition which favored blown power units.

It was mounted back to front in the Metro, with the forward end of the engine facing the hatchback and with the gearbox attached conventionally behind it and therefore in the middle of the car. From there the permanently engaged four-wheel drive, which employed Ferguson technology, drove separate propeller shafts to the front and rear wheels. All the external body panels were made of plastic, with the exception of the doors which were steel although these were concealed by plastic airboxes.

Two versions produced

The 6R4, the name stood for six cylinder, rally car, four-wheel drive, was produced in two forms. There was the so-called Clubman model which developed some 250bhp – about 200 were made –

and a further 20 were built to International specifications which required a 380bhp engine.

At its launch in 1985 Rover announced that it would complete the necessary number of cars for homologation by November. This was undertaken at a special facility located within the Group's rambling Longbridge factory. So the car was ready in time to participate in the Lombard RAC rally of November 1985 and an example was placed a creditable third behind two Lancia Deltas. It was a good start.

In theory the prospects looked good for 1986. However, although the 6R4 was entered in the Monte Carlo, Sweden, Portugal, and Corsica events, none of the Metros completed the courses. Most of the problems were related to the V6 engine which suffered from more than its fair share of teething troubles which smacked of underdevelopment.

Then, halfway through the 1986 season, Group B competition was banned because of a calamitous series of crashes. And that, in truth, was the end of this mighty Metro's front-line competition career, although the cars were run with limited successes for the remainder of the year.

At this point Austin Rover withdrew from the rallying scene. But in 1987 all the parts and engines were sold to Tom Walkinshaw Racing whereupon the V6 engine reappeared under the hood of the Jaguar XJ220!

Above: The 6R4's wheels grew from 13in (330mm) to 16in (406mm), partly at the request of Michelin which supplied the tires.

Left: A standard Metro dash was fitted although the steering wheel and attendant stalks came courtesy of the larger Maestro EFi. Note the fly-off handbrake lever.

Specification	**MG** Metro 6R4
Engine location	Mid, in-line
Configuration	V6
Bore and stroke	92 x 75mm
Capacity	2991cc
Valve operation	Twin overhead camshafts per cylinder bank
Horsepower	250bhp @ 7000rpm
Transmission	Manual five-speed
Drive	Four-wheel
Chassis	Unitary
Suspension – front	MacPherson strut reverse bottom wishbone
Suspension – rear	Strut and reverse bottom wishbone
Brakes	Ventilated disc
Top speed	110mph (177km/h) limited
Acceleration	0-60mph (0-96km/h): 4.8 seconds

Toyota MR2

**Top speed
125mph**
201km/h

*Right: A 1985 MR2
revealing the efficiency of
its pop-up headlamps. This
Toyota did everything
expected of it, the only
apparent shortcoming
according to some drivers
being a lack of cockpit
space, a not uncommon
complaint of Japanese cars.*

*Below: The 1985 car in
profile. The air intake and
low nose indicate the
presence of the mid-located
engine with the front
airdam and rear wing
providing important
aerodynamic influence. The
MR-2 was only produced in
coupé form at this stage.*

An acclaimed mid-engined coupé, the
MR2 of 1984 represented a surprising
excursion for Toyota, which had hitherto
been best known for its popular sedans. But Japan's
largest car maker made a significant contribution to
the sports sector with this wedge-shaped coupé that
was able to attain 125mph (201km/h). A
supercharged version was capable of 135mph
(217km/h).

With Toyota dependent on the American market
for much of its sales, in the early 1980s it began to
manufacture a new generation of engines to
conform to the strict US emissions regulations.
This meant twin-overhead-camshaft/four-valve
cylinder heads and Toyota was soon to become a
world leader in the manufacture of such multi-valve
power units.

These engines also lent themselves to the
performance sector. In 1981 Toyota had established
links with Lotus and so it was able to draw on
Lotus' engineering expertise in the development of
its projected sports car. This was accorded the MR
prefix which stood for Midship Runabout.

It was produced in two forms. The mainstream
export version was powered by a 121bhp, 1.6 liter,
fuel-injected, twin-overhead-camshaft engine
courtesy of Toyota's Corolla GTi. There was also a
1.5 liter single-cam unit for the home market. In

both instances they were transversely mounted
behind the driver in a chunky aerodynamically
refined two-seater body with only a pair of air
intakes behind the doors to indicate the presence of
a mid-located power unit.

Supercharged for the USA

Sceptical pundits were confounded to find that the
MR2 possessed safe, predictable handling, together
with an excellent, flexible engine. And acceleration
– the 0-60mph (96km/h) time was 7.7 seconds –
was respectable for a car of this size. However, the

American market required some extra oomph and the result in 1986 was a 143bhp supercharged MR2 which increased the top speed by 10mph (16km/h) and shaved 0.7 seconds off the acceleration figure.

For the 1987 season a variation on the body style appeared in the form of the T-bar model with detachable transparent roof panels. The MR2 was destined to survive in this form until 1989, when it was replaced by a 2 liter car, instantly identifiable by softer body lines, but which retained the same mechanical layout and name. And the enlarged engine meant a 137mph (220km/h) top speed.

It was replaced for the 2000 season by the third generation MR2, an open two-seater with, for Toyota, wacky styling, a pop-up rear spoiler and projecting head rests for the occupants. A Turbo version is capable of speeds approaching the 150mph (241km/h) mark.

Above: The third generation MR2 appeared in 2000 – a convertible, but here with optional factory hardtop.

Below left: The 1985 MR2. Power-assisted steering was fitted as standard, along with electric windows.

Specification	Toyota MR2
Engine location	Mid, transverse
Configuration	Four-cylinder
Bore and stroke	81 x 77mm
Capacity	1587cc
Valve operation	Twin overhead camshafts
Horsepower	121bhp @ 6600rpm
Transmission	Manual, five-speed
Drive	Rear
Chassis	Unitary
Suspension – front	MacPherson strut, lower arm
Suspension – rear	MacPherson strut, parallel transverse links
Brakes	Disc
Top speed	125mph (201km/h)
Acceleration	0-60mph (96km/h): 7.7 seconds

Bentley Turbo R

**Top speed
145mph**
233km/h

Right: Bentley's winged B badge was designed by Frederick Gordon Crosby, The Autocar's accomplished artist who also designed the original radiator. This, however, was considerably reduced in depth from 1965 onward.

Below: A Bentley Turbo of 1984 with the radiator shell painted in the body color which indicated the presence of a turbocharged engine. At this stage no changes had been made to the suspension.

A significant milestone along the road of the Bentley revival, the Turbo R of 1985 represented a desirable refinement of a high-performance image that had first been crafted three years previously with the Mulsanne Turbo.

Although owned by Rolls-Royce, the Bentley marque had been in decline since the early 1960s. When the Rolls-Royce Spirit, which appeared in 1980, was being planned, incredibly there were serious thoughts about discontinuing the Bentley version. Fortunately, wiser counsels prevailed and the resulting model was given the Mulsanne name, after the straight on the Le Mans circuit; it evoked memories of Bentley's string of victories there during the inter-war years.

Powered by the corporate 6.7 liter V8 engine, this comfortable and luxuriously appointed four-door sedan was capable of 120mph (193km/h). However, perhaps inevitably the overwhelming majority of cars built bore the Rolls-Royce badge.

Then, against a background of the recession of the early 1980s, Rolls-Royce's marketing director, Peter Ward, sought to re-awaken memories of Bentley's racing heritage by turbocharging its

robust V8 engine. The resulting model, named the Mulsanne Turbo, appeared at the 1982 Geneva Motor Show. Outwardly distinguished by a radiator shell painted in the body color, rather than manufactured in the usual chrome, it was otherwise outwardly identical to the mainstream model, apart from discreet *Turbo* badges on the trunk lid and front fenders. Performance was transformed, however, with top speed increased by some 15mph (24km/h) to 135mph (217km/h).

All this was achieved with the minimum of modification. While the transmission was strengthened to cope with the increased power, the twin constraints of time and available funding meant that almost no obligatory changes were made to the suspension.

Appealing concept

The Mulsanne Turbo proved to be a great success because it appealed to a younger, more affluent generation of buyers and Rolls-Royce was sufficiently encouraged to take the concept one step further. The result, in 1985, was the Turbo R which addressed the suspension shortcomings of the original. Announced at that year's Geneva show, the Turbo R, the Mulsanne name was dropped, was the first Rolls-Royce product to be fitted with alloy wheels, in this instance wider, specially commissioned Ronal units.

The original model suffered from soft suspension which produced excessive body roll, but this problem was now redressed. The modifications principally involved increasing the stiffness of the front anti-roll bar by 100 per cent and the rear by 60 per cent. Greater resistance was also introduced to the power steering.

The output of the turbocharged engine was boosted and the Turbo R was some 10mph (16km/h) faster than its predecessor, being capable of 145mph (233km/h). It survived, in essence, for the next 12 years, the final example being completed in 1997.

Specification	Bentley Turbo R
Engine location	Front, in-line
Configuration	Turbocharged V8
Bore and stroke	104 x 99mm
Capacity	6750cc
Valve operation	Pushrod
Horsepower	298bhp @ 3800rpm
Transmission	Automatic three-speed
Drive	Rear
Chassis	Unitary
Suspension – front	Wishbones and coil spring
Suspension – rear	Semi trailing arms and coil spring, automatic self levelling
Brakes	Disc
Top speed	145mph (233km/h)
Acceleration	0-60mph (0-96km/h): 7.1 seconds

Left: The Turbo's dashboard was essentially that of the standard Mulsanne, apart from the presence of the word Turbo. No rev counter was fitted.

Below: An unturbocharged 1994 Brooklands. By this time the Turbo's painted radiator had been extended to all Bentleys.

Mazda RX-7 Turbo

**Top speed
148mph**
238km/h

 The Japanese Mazda company was for many years the only significant motor manufacturer to persevere with the Wankel rotary engine. In 1986 it launched a revised version of its successful RX-7 sports car and two years later came the Turbo version that was capable of speeds nudging the 150mph (241km/h) mark.

Its first Wankel-engined model, the two-seater 110S coupé of 1967, only sold 1176 examples in six years, although it was capable of 110mph (177km/h). By contrast, its RX-2 successor of 1970-78 found some quarter of a million buyers and the same engine was used in the simultaneously introduced RX-3 which shared its body with Mazda's conventionally powered 818. Like its RX-4 contemporary, it also ceased production in 1978.

Even more successful was the RX-7 coupé, a car capable of 125mph (201km/h) which was destined to remain in production until 1985. With over 570,000 produced, it proved to be a considerable success in America.

Turbine-like power

Its 1985 replacement retained the famous RX-7 name, and it was also a two-plus-two coupé with a 2254cc two-rotor Wankel engine mounted in a new chassis clothed in a body with rather Porsche-like lines. Able to attain 128mph (205km/h), its engine developed 150bhp. There was also a top-of-the-range 185bhp RX-7 Turbo which could hit 148mph (238km/h). This united the Wankel's smooth turbine-like power with the accelerative qualities of a turbocharger. The 60mph (96km/h) mark arrived in less than seven seconds, but on the debit side was an average fuel consumption of some 14 miles per gallon (16.6lit/100 km).

Originally produced, like the mainstream model, in coupé form, a convertible version aimed foursquare at Californian buyers was launched in 1987. A new version arrived for 1992 but European sales suffered because of the twin bugbears of high

Above: A cabriolet version of the RX-7. Dating from 1985, this body variant arrived two years later. Hard and soft tops followed in 1987, the latter being electrically activated.

Right: The revised RX-7 for the 1992 season was shorter, lighter, and narrower than its predecessor. More accelerative than the earlier version, thanks to its increased power (251bhp no less), there was a new injection system to ensure a near instantaneous response.

Left: The 1992 version, which, claimed Mazda, possessed better handling than the earlier car because of a lower center of gravity and passive rear-wheel steering built into the suspension. This helped to keep the car's handling neutral during fast cornering. The twin rear aerofoils were a distinctive feature. The interior styling reflected the curved lines of the exterior.

fuel costs and unfashionable emissions problems. These constraints led to the model being withdrawn from the European market in 1995, although it was reworked for American and Japan. This entailed creating a new tail, nose, and interior; power was increased to 280bhp and a four-wheel-drive RS version was offered.

A revised RX-7 coupé made its debut at the 1999 Tokyo Motor Show. This had developed from a RX-01 concept car that had appeared at the same event in 1995. Once again rotary powered and turbocharged, it is due to enter production in 2002. So against all expectations Mazda, since 1999 part-owned by Ford, has ensured that the Wankel engine has survived until the 21st century.

Specification	Mazda RX-7 Turbo
Engine location	Front, in-line
Configuration	Turbocharged twin-rotor Wankel
Bore and stroke	Not applicable
Capacity	2254cc
Valve operation	Not applicable
Horsepower	185bhp @ 6500rpm
Transmission	Manual five-speed
Drive	Rear
Chassis	Unitary
Suspension – front	MacPherson strut, lower wishbone
Suspension – rear	Semi trailing arms and coil springs
Brakes	Disc
Top speed	148mph (238km/h)
Acceleration	0-60mph (0-96km/h): 6.7 seconds

Left: Mazda RX-8, unveiled as a concept car at the 2001 Detroit Motor Show, is the RX-7's spiritual successor. Also powered by a twin-rotor Wankel engine, although unturbocharged, the unit develops 250bhp. Intended to enter production in 2002, Mazda claims a top speed of 150mph (241km/h).

Ford Sierra RS Cosworth

**Top speed
145mph**
233km/h

*Right: The Sapphire-bodied
RS Cosworth of 1988
boasted an excellent driving
position, thanks to Recaro
bucket seats that were
adjustable for height, reach,
and rake.*

*Below: The two-door RS
Cosworth was followed in
1988 by the four-door
Sapphire version. It was
based on the Sierra of the
same name, even if this did
not appear on the car!*

The public was stunned when in 1982 Ford unveiled the aerodynamically refined Sierra hatchback to replace its ultra-conventional best-selling Cortina. And just three years after its appearance the exclusive, potent RS Cosworth version hit the scene – this was able to attain no less than 145mph (233km/h).

While the mainstream Sierra was a family-sized five-door model, there was also a three-door version and this formed the basis of the Sierra XR4i of 1983-85, which was easily identifiable by its rear spoiler. It was powered by a 2.8 liter V6 overhead valve engine.

The RS Cosworth of 1986, however, was a far more potent offering, being tailored for a variety of motor sport activities. Outwardly it featured a large 'whale tail' spoiler, a mesh grille, and hood air vents, special spoked-type alloy wheels and side stripes. But the real difference was to be found under the hood.

Ford's association with the Northampton-based racing engine manufacturer Cosworth reached back

to 1960. Now Cosworth assessed the Sierra's 1982 engine line-up, which featured a quartet of four-cylinder single-overhead-camshaft power units, and proceeded to produce a twin-overhead-camshaft version of the 1993cc engine which was duly turbocharged and developed 204bhp in its basic YB form. But there was plenty of power in reserve – for rallying there was the YBB type with 300bhp available while the most powerful Group A racing version produced no less than 340bhp.

Superb handling

Production, exactly 5500 examples were built, was undertaken in the second half of 1986 at Ford's factory at Ghenk in Belgium, where the mainstream Sierra was manufactured. The RS's XR4i's predecessor had proved how well the Sierra could handle; now the second crucial ingredient of performance was added.

An even faster RS500 derivative was unveiled in 1987, the designation reflecting the fact that just 500 were built. This differed visually from the Cosworth in featuring an even larger spoiler and a wider radiator intake. This was to cool the more potent YBD version of the twin cam with fuel injection and a larger turbocharger. Developing 224bhp on the road, the competition units produced in excess of 500bhp.

The road cars were faster than the standard RS Cosworth, being capable of 154mph (248km/h), and the racing versions were highly successful in competition. They gained Ford the World Touring Car Championship in 1987, the 1988 European Touring Car competition and a host of related events the world over.

Above: The RS500 (left) with wide intakes below the bumper to cool the front discs. The huge rear spoiler was not retained on the Sapphire version next to it.

Below: The Sapphire Cosworth's turbocharged 2 liter twin-overhead-camshaft engine. Top speed was 145mph (233km/h).

Specification	Ford Sierra RS Cosworth
Engine location	Front, in-line
Configuration	Turbocharged four-cylinder
Bore and stroke	90 x 76mm
Capacity	1993cc
Valve operation	Twin overhead camshafts
Horsepower	204bhp @ 6000rpm
Transmission	Manual five-speed
Drive	Rear
Chassis	Unitary
Suspension – front	MacPherson strut
Suspension – rear	Wishbone, semi trailing arm and coil spring
Brakes	Disc, ventilated front
Top speed	145mph (233km/h)
Acceleration	0-60mph (96km/h): 6 seconds

Lancia Integrale

**Top speed
134mph**
216km/h

*Right: Only available in
left-hand-drive form, the
16-valve Integrale sported
an illuminated check panel
and a new revolution
counter. The steering wheel
was leather-rimmed.*

*Below: A 1990 Integrale
showing the distinctive
hood bulge demanded by
the 16-valve engine. A four-
wheel-drive model, there
was a 53/47 allocation to
rear and front wheels
respectively.*

A four-wheel-drive car that gave Lancia
the World Rally Championship for an
unprecedented six years between 1987
and 1992, the Integrale was an outwardly orthodox
four-door hatchback but with sophisticated
mechanicals. It could reach nearly 135mph
(217km/h). Paradoxically it attained its pre-eminent
position by accident rather than design.

In 1980 Fiat-owned Lancia had introduced the
front-wheel-drive Delta four-door hatchback styled
by Ital Design. It was available with a choice of 1.3
and 1.5 liter single overhead engines while the GT
version was powered by a 1.6 liter twin-cam unit.
Later, in 1984, came the HF Turbo with an
enhanced 130bhp engine which gained a further
10hp with the arrival, in 1986, of fuel injection.

Lancia had, in the meantime, produced the four-
wheel-drive S4 Delta rally car in 1984. Geared to
Group B competition, it was outwardly similar to
the roadgoing version but with a new mid-located,
1.7 liter, Abarth-designed, twin-cam four which
was both turbo- *and* supercharged.

Group A racer

The demise, in mid-1986, of Group B racing – the
result of one fatal accident too many (the final one
involved an S4) – saw Lancia rapidly respond by
replacing the S4 with the Delta HF 4WD, which
had been unveiled in prototype form at the 1982
Turin Motor Show. Tailored to Group A rules, it was
accordingly closely related to the Delta road car.

To qualify Lancia had to manufacture a minimum of 5000 examples in 1987. Such was its success that a further 500 examples of the HF Integrale, as it was known by late 1987, were also produced.

Usable road car

Unlike many homologation specials, this was a perfectly usable road car. It featured a transversely mounted, 185bhp, 2 liter, turbocharged twin-overhead-camshaft engine and a sophisticated four-wheel-drive system based, in part, on that used in the Delta S4. An epicyclic central differential produced a torque split of 56/44 from front to rear with a viscous coupling that locked when one pair of wheels began to spin. A Torsen rear differential apportioned torque at the rear end. Both suspension and brakes were uprated and wider wheels resulted in distinctive side pods being let into the wheel arches to accommodate them.

The rally cars, of course, were much more powerful. They won first time out at the 1987 Portugal event and went on to dominate the rally field for the next five years. The only significant change in specification was the arrival, in 1989, of a 16-valve cylinder head which duly appeared on the road cars.

The final Integrale of 1993 saw power upped to 215bhp and a smaller turbocharger was employed. When production ceased in 1994, Lancia ran down the curtains on its most successful rally car ever.

Above: This was the ultimate 'hot hatchback,' the hatch being what most other rally drivers saw. A light in Lancia's otherwise gloomy history. This is a 1992 Evolution model, no.0015.

Specification	**Lancia** HF Integrale
Engine location	Front, transverse
Configuration	Turbocharged four-cylinder
Bore and stroke	87 x 90mm
Capacity	1995cc
Valve operation	Twin overhead camshaft
Horsepower	185bhp @ 5300rpm
Transmission	Manual, five-speed
Drive	Four-wheel
Chassis	Unitary
Suspension – front	MacPherson strut and lower wishbone
Suspension – rear	MacPherson strut and transverse link
Brakes	Disc, ventilated at front
Top speed	134mph (216km/h)
Acceleration	0-62mph (0-100km/h): 6.6 seconds

Jaguar XJR-S

**Top speed
155mph**
249km/h

*Below: A 1988 XJR-S Le
Mans Celebration model,
launched in August and
named to commemorate
Jaguar's victory in the 24
hour classic just two
months earlier. The first
100 examples were all sold,
it was claimed, within four
days of the model's
announcement. In addition
to the external changes,
modifications were also
made to the suspension but
not the engine.*

Jaguar's long awaited E-Type replacement, the XJS coupé, arrived in 1975. It was a more refined and luxurious product than its famous forebear, but it was to be no less than 13 years before a sporting version arrived in the shape of the XJR-S.

Introduced amidst the gloom of the post-1973 oil crisis, the XJS was powered by the company's 5.3 liter V12 engine, first seen in the Series III E-Type of 1971. Able to accelerate to 60mph (96km/h) in a respectable 7.8 seconds, the XJS's Achilles' heel was its fuel consumption of some 11mpg (21.7lit/100km). Jaguar recognized the need to address the problem and the result, in mid-1981, was the more economical HE version.

In 1982 the corporate racing program was placed in the hands of Tom Walkinshaw's TWR group and this led to Jaguar winning Le Mans, after a 31-year absence, in 1988. TWR had been marketing Jaguar-approved performance accessories for the XJS since the mid-1980s and as a result JaguarSport was launched in May 1988, jointly owned by the company and Walkinshaw's highly successful business.

The idea was to produce up to 500 cars a year at TWR's premises at Kidlington, Oxfordshire. The first of these, the XJR-S, was launched in August 1988, 'as a tribute to the Le Mans-winning XJR-9' and it was based on the TWR XJS V12 that Walkinshaw had been marketing, with factory approval, since 1984. At this stage no changes were made to 290bhp V12 engine but the model was instantly identifiable by its body-colored bumpers, glass-fiber air dam, sill extensions, and rear spoiler.

Improved handling

Mechanical alterations were confined to stiffening the suspension, power steering, and new and wider alloy wheels. Handling therefore improved but performance remained essentially unchanged.

It was to be another year before the engine was uprated – the revised XJR-S of 1989 was the first recipient of a JaguarSport-enlarged 318bhp 6 liter engine that was extended to the production XJS in 1993. Further work was done to stiffen the suspension. While the new engine made little difference to the 155mph (249km/h) top speed, acceleration was improved with 1.2 seconds being shaved off the original 0-60mph (96km/h) figure of 7.5 seconds.

Yet a further version arrived for the 1992 season which incorporated structural changes made to the XJS in the spring of 1991. The engine now developed 338bhp and the model survived until 1993 when it was effectively replaced by the factory-built 6 liter XJS. During this six-year period some 500 examples were completed.

Specification	Jaguar XJR-S (6 liter)
Engine location	Front, in-line
Configuration	V12
Bore and stroke	90 x 78mm
Capacity	5343cc
Valve operation	Single overhead camshaft per cylinder bank
Horsepower	318bhp @ 5250rpm
Transmission	Automatic three-speed
Drive	Rear
Chassis	Unitary
Suspension – front	Wishbones and coil spring
Suspension – rear	Trailing arms and coil spring
Brakes	Disc
Top speed	155mph (249km/h)
Acceleration	0-60mph (0-96km/h): 6.3 seconds

Above and left: The distinguishing rear spoiler was mounted on the trunk lid. Inside there were JaguarSport logos, leather-bound steering wheel and gear knob, and piping trim on the leather seats. The first 100 cars were enhanced with special trim and paint and victory laurels engraved on the tread plates.

Ferrari F40

**Top speed
201mph**
323km/h

Right: Function rather than creature comfort is the keynote of the cockpit of a 1991 F40. Weight-saving was a consideration – note the drilled pedals.

Below: This is a pre-production Ferrari F40 of 1988. The sliding perspex windows are wholly in keeping with the model's racing pedigree although they were subsequently replaced by glass.

 Enzo Ferrari produced his first cars in 1947. In 1987 the F40 supercar was unveiled, so named in celebration of his 40 years as a car maker. This was no luxurious, refined model but a purposeful, no-frills coupé complete with a large rear wing and a top speed of 201mph (323km/h) making it, for a time, the world's fastest production car. It therefore decisively eclipsed the Porsche 959's speed of 197mph (317km/h).

Based on the floorpan of the 288 GTO of 1984, the F40 was powered by a related twin turbocharged V8 engine of a mere 3 liters capacity, although it developed a stupendous 478bhp. It was rear-mounted in a longitudinal position.

Weight-saving was an overriding consideration, and although a tubular space-frame chassis, which provided the outline of the cabin and tail sections, was retained, extensive use was made of Kevlar and carbon fiber. Both materials came courtesy of Ferrari's Formula 1 activities.

Kevlar and glass-fiber body panels also featured, and further kilograms were saved in the cockpit which was bereft of such niceties as carpeting and door trim. In consequence the F40 turned the scales at just 2425lb (1100kg). While Pininfarina had ultimate responsibility for the styling, the F40's body was produced at Maranello by Ferrari.

Three suspension settings

The all-independent suspension used the customary Ferrari wishbones and coil springs and there were no less than three settings – normal, high speed which involved lowering it by 0.75in (19 mm), and parking when it was raised by the same amount.

Although outwardly resembling a road car, the acceleration was phenomenal – this most exclusive of Ferraris was able to reach 200km/h (124mph) in a mere 12 seconds.

If for some reason you were not satisfied with this level of performance, for several million lire Ferrari would extract a further 200bhp from the trusty V8. Needless to say noise levels within the sparsely furnished cockpit made speech between driver and passenger virtually impossible. But then no one ever bought an F40 to hold conversations in!

Production began early in 1988. The F40 was priced in Britain at $270,600, some $112,000 more that its Testarossa stablemate. It remained in production until 1992; although it had been intended to restrict production to just 450 cars, worldwide demand for the model remained strong

Specification	Ferrari F40
Engine location	Rear, in-line
Configuration	Twin turbocharged V8
Bore and stroke	82 x 69mm
Capacity	2936cc
Valve operation	Twin overhead camshafts per bank
Horsepower	478bhp @ 7000rpm
Transmission	Manual five-speed
Drive	Four wheel
Chassis	Tubular steel, Kevlar and carbon fiber
Suspension – front	Wishbones and coil spring
Suspension – rear	Wishbones and coil spring
Brakes	Ventilated discs
Top speed	201mph (323km/h)
Acceleration	0-60mph (0-96 km/h): 4.7 seconds

and eventually nearly three times that number, 1311 F40s no less, had been completed before production ceased in 1992.

It had been an extraordinarily impressive car, daring and distinctive. Perversely, the even faster F50 appeared in 1995, two years *before* the marque celebrated its half century!

Above: The F40's unmistakable rear view; its body was made of race-proven fiberglass, Kevlar, and carbon fiber. This is a 1990 car with conventional side windows.

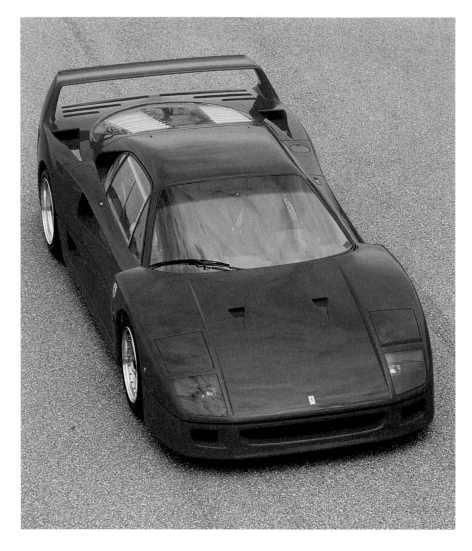

Above: The F40 in all its glory, utterly distinctive and sounding like a Formula 1 car when on the move.

Right: The engine of a 1991 F40, an all-alloy unit with twin water-cooled IHI turbochargers. Larger turbochargers were on offer for those owners who wished to race their F40s.

Opposite: The F40 was made from immensely strong Kevlar. Bonded to the chassis by adhesives, it was considerably lighter than steel and torsional rigidity was increased threefold.

It was wholly appropriate that the F40's launch at Maranello in July 1987 was attended by Enzo Ferrari himself, then a frail 89-year-old. The assembled multitude was treated to an insight from *Il Commendatore* regarding the thinking behind the F40's creation. 'It started in June last year when I suggested to the board a car which would be a reminder of the great days at Le Mans when you could drive a car on the streets or race it,' he revealed. There was consideration of naming the model after the 24 hour classic event which Ferrari had dominated for so many years, but the designation F40 was ultimately deemed more appropriate. And so it has proved to be.

The car can trace its ancestry back to the fabled GTO of 1962 described elsewhere in this book. Appropriately an example was on display at the unveiling to underline the association between the two. And while this celebrated sports racer reflected the model's spiritual origins, one element of its mechanical pedigree can be traced to the mid-

engined GTO road car that appeared at 1984 Geneva Motor Show.

The second branch of its family tree was provided by an one-off *Evoluzione* Ferrari of 1986, created for Group B competition which was killed off that year by the sport's organizing body. The aborted Group B was thus responsible for two of the world's fastest road cars of the 1980s, the Porsche 959 and the F40 which was some 4mph (6.4km/h) quicker.

Low drag coefficient

Pininfarina was responsible for the seductive bodywork, its brief being to produce a Ferrari that looked both backward to the marque's past glories as well as forward to the future. Great attention was paid to achieving as low an aerodynamic drag coefficient as possible and the result was a creditable Cd figure of 0.34. This was after experiments had been undertaken without the rear wing, which was eventually standardized, and the fitting of rear wheel spats, which were subsequently discarded.

A car capable of exceeding 200mph (322km/h) also required a wind-cheating underside. Pininfarina accordingly undertook pioneering experiments to ensure that the F40's wake, the spent air that was exhausted from behind the car, conformed to the most efficient 'shape' and also contributed to its stability.

The twin turbocharged V8 engine was essentially an enlarged version of the GTO unit and was created by a team headed by engineer Materazzi, who summed up the company's attitude to the F40. It represented, reported *Autocar*, 'the ideal tie between past and present.'

Enzo Ferrari died in August 1988 at the age of 90 in the first year of the F40's production. He could not have wished for a finer epitaph.

Lotus Elan

**Top speed
136mph**
219km/h

Right: The IHI turbocharged engine of a 1990 Elan SE, courtesy of Isuzu and enhanced by Lotus. Delco distributorless ignition and a Rochester fuel-injection system were fitted.

Below: An SE of 1990. Its body, created by Lotus's Vacuum Assisted Resin Injection process, was constructed of 54 pieces.

Lotus's original Elan of 1962 remained in production for no less than 12 years. However, its 136mph (219km/h) latter-day namesake of 1989 was destined for an all too short two-and-a-half year production run. Its manufacturing life was abruptly curtailed through a combination of the recession of the early 1990s and teething troubles that were then, alas, characteristic of the marque.

Lotus's founder, Colin Chapman, had taken the company upmarket in the mid-1970s with the Esprit/Eclat/Excel coupés, so a new open two-seater represented a return to the its sports car roots. But Lotus's ownership was thrown into doubt in 1982 following Chapman's sudden death from a heart attack. Four years later General Motors acquired the business.

Work on the project had begun in 1986 and the Elan retained, in essence, the backbone chassis of the original model. But there the resemblance ended. The first-generation Elan had employed a conventional front in-line engine and rear drive, but its successor was a front-wheel-drive car with the engine mounted in the transverse position.

Appropriately uprated by Lotus, it came courtesy of the GM-owned Japanese Isuzu concern and was a 1.6 liter, twin-cam, four-cylinder, 130bhp unit. However, the overwhelming majority of Elans were produced in 165bhp turbocharged SE form.

Left: The rear of the car opposite. The roof, which Lotus claimed could be lowered in less than 30 seconds, was neatly contained under the flush-fitting cover. Both the SE and basic Elan were fitted with electric windows and central door locking.

Below: Lotus racing driver and motoring journalist John Miles at the wheel of a 'Series 2' Elan, one of 800 SE examples built from spare parts in 1994. Identifiable by new wheels and a revised dashboard, purple and green metallic colors were added to the options list.

Distinctive body styling

Typically for a Lotus, suspension was all-independent with ingenious interactive wishbones at the front and wishbones and lower links at the rear. Roadholding was, as ever, outstanding. The mechanicals were cloaked in a distinctive open two-seater composite body styled by Peter Stevens, who is best remembered for having the lines of the superlative McLaren F1 to his credit.

However, when evaluated by the motoring press, doubts began to be expressed about the Elan's qualities. For while its performance more than came up to scratch, the whole experience did not perhaps match the pleasures of driving the no-frills front engine/rear drive Mazda MX-5 that cost some $10,000 less. And, paradoxically, this Japanese open two-seater had been inspired, in part, by the original Elan of the 1960s.

Despite carrying the clout of General Motors ownership, only 250 Elans were sold in America in 1991 and in June 1992 Lotus announced that it was to cease production. A total of 3857 had been completed and a further 800 'Series 2' cars were built from spare parts in 1994, by which time Lotus had changed hands, again.

But this was not quite the end of the story. The tooling had been acquired, in 1993, by the South Korean Kia concern which produced Elans re-engined with a 1.8 liter Mazda-based unit until 1998.

Specification	Lotus Elan SE
Engine location	Transverse
Configuration	Turbocharged four-cylinder
Bore and stroke	80 x 79mm
Capacity	1588cc
Valve operation	Twin overhead camshaft
Horsepower	165bhp @ 6600rpm
Transmission	Manual five-speed
Drive	Front
Chassis	Backbone
Suspension – front	Wishbones and coil spring
Suspension – rear	Wishbone, lower link and coil spring
Brakes	Disc, ventilated at front
Top speed	136mph (219km/h)
Acceleration	0-60mph (0-96km/h): 6.5 seconds

Mazda MX-5

**Top speed
128mph**
206km/h

*Right: Although the MX-5
was designed for fine
weather, the roof of this
1993 cars offers excellent
rear visibility thanks to the
large back window.*

*Below: The front of the
same car with,
characteristically, the roof
down. The body was steel
but the hood was made
of aluminum.*

Although there were faster cars around at
the same time as the Mazda MX-5, few
were more influential than this crisply
styled open two-seater inspired by British sports
cars of the 1960s. Although nominally a Japanese
car, it was created by Mazda's product planning
research facility located at Irvine, California. This
was because it was specifically tailored for the
large and lucrative American sports car market.

At this time practically all mainstream motor
manufacturers had turned their collective backs on
the low-cost open two-seater sports car. The
emphasis was on more expensive, better equipped
closed GTs. But for their inspiration the MX-5's
creators looked carefully at the sports models
which had been on sale in America in 1960s, most
significantly the Lotus Elan and Triumph Spitfire.
Both featured in-line engines, a twin cam in the
case of the Lotus, which drove the rear wheels.
Suspension in both cases was independent all-round.

Introduced early in 1989, the Mazda's full name
was the MX-5 Miata, and it cost a little less than
$13,000. Under the hood was a 1.6 liter twin-
overhead-camshaft four-cylinder engine, which
developed 116bhp, borrowed from Mazda's sedan
range where it had been transversely mounted. It

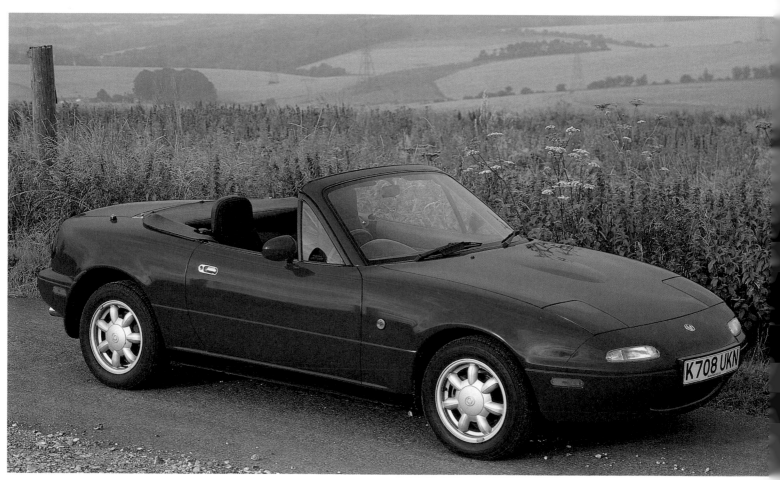

drove the rear wheels through a five-speed gearbox and torque tube.

Well-balanced sports car

Suspension was all independent and rack and pinion steering was employed, all of which combined to produce an assured, well-balanced sports car. The body, evidently influenced by the Lotus Elan, similarly featured pop-up headlamps. Top speed was 115mph (185km/h). Later, for 1994, an alternative 1.8 liter engine was introduced.

The MX-5 was updated for the 1998 season and while the new version superficially resembled the original, the pop-up headlamps were replaced by more conventional exposed units. Once again, there were 1.6 and 1.8 liter engine options and the latter's top speed was nudging the 130mph (209km/h) mark.

For 2001 a revised front end was introduced but, more significantly, the 1.8 liter engine now benefited from Mazda's S-VT sequential valve timing system, which boosted the unit's power by 16bhp, to 156bhp. Although top speed remained about the same, acceleration was improved.

The half-millionth MX-5 was completed in February 1999, which made it the most popular open two-seater sports car in the world. But in the meantime a host of manufacturers had followed in the MX-5's wheel tracks to revitalize and expand this previously neglected sector of the market.

Specification	**Mazda** MX-5 (1.8 liter)
Engine location	Front, in-line
Configuration	Four-cylinder
Bore and stroke	83 x 85mm
Capacity	1839cc
Valve operation	Twin overhead camshafts
Horsepower	140bhp @ 6500rpm
Transmission	Manual five-speed
Drive	Rear
Chassis	Unitary
Suspension – front	Wishbones and coil spring
Suspension – rear	Wishbones and coil spring
Brakes	Discs, ventilated at front
Top speed	128mph (206km/h)
Acceleration	0-60mph (0-96km/h): 7.9 seconds

Above: The 10th Anniversary Special Edition version of the MX-5 arrived in 1999 and boasted a unique dark blue finish, tweaked suspension, and, significantly, a six-speed gearbox. A total of 7500 were produced.

Left: The MX-5 was updated for 2000 with a new nose which featured enlarged air intakes and slimmer light clusters with clear lenses, along with projector lamps. The shell was also stiffer than its predecessor, engine output was boosted, and suspension tautened.

Lamborghini Diablo

**Top speed
202mph**
325km/h

Right: In 1993 Lamborghini announced the 30SE, built to commemorate the company's 30th anniversary in 1994. Power was upped to 525bhp but rear visibility was not its strongest point!

Below: The Diablo, this example dates from 1990, is clearly derived from its Countach predecessor, although perhaps it lacks the visual impact. It has endured for 11 years and has progressively improved during this production span.

With a top speed in excess of just over 202mph (325km/h), Lamborghini's Diablo just pipped the Ferrari F40 as the world's fastest car, that is until the Jaguar XJ220 came along in 1991.

The Miura and Countach had established Lamborghini's reputation for creating stunning flagship supercars and while the Diablo effectively inherited the latter's mechanics, the durable V12 was further enlarged, this time to 5.7 liters, with 485bhp on tap.

With a wheelbase 7.9in (200mm) longer than the Countach's, the coupé body was clearly derived from it. It was the work of Marcello Gandini, no longer with Bertone but now freelance, who was responsible for the styling of both the Diablo's illustrious predecessors. It did, however, lack some of the impact of his earlier work.

After some input from Chrysler, Lamborghini's owner in the years 1987 to 1994, the car was launched at Monte Carlo in January 1990. But in typical Lamborghini style, production did not begin until a year later, at the height of a world recession.

The world's fastest car

The company's claim of a top speed of 202mph (325km/h) and a 0 to 100km/h (62mph) figure of 4.9 seconds was subsequently confirmed by the American *Road & Track* magazine which attained 202.33mph (325.60mph), just 1.33mph (2.1km/h) quicker than Ferrari's F40. But its accolade as the world's fastest car proved to be short-lived with the launch, in October 1991, of the Jaguar XJ220 which could exceed 213mph (343km/h).

Left: A 1999 Diablo with its aluminum bodywork replaced by lighter, stronger carbon fiber. Arguably the best built model to date and a reflection of Volkswagen's ownership of Lamborghini.

Below left: The Diablo's instrument panel has much to commend it for functional appeal. The gear lever sits, Ferrari-like, in an open visible gate.

Improved aerodynamics

While the Diablo handled as you might expect a mid-engined car to do, its lack of power steering and anti-lock brakes were clear deficiencies. Four-wheel-drive was another but all these shortcomings were remedied in 1993 with the arrival of the Diablo VT, standing for Viscous Traction FWD. Then, for 1994, came the Diablo SE, for Special Edition, with a wildly optimistic claimed top speed of 220mph (354km/h), improved aerodynamics, and engine power boosted to 525bhp.

In 1996 came the lightweight SV, which stood for Sport Veloce, with 'only' 508bhp on tap. The same year saw the arrival of the long-awaited convertible version also with four-wheel drive. Much of the styling was reworked and the detachable Targa-style roof stored externally behind the driver.

Although Lamborghini has been owned by Volkswagen since 1998, the Diablo's replacement has enjoyed a typically lengthy gestation. In the meantime the fastest-ever Lamborghini, the Diablo GT, was unveiled in 2000 with a claimed top speed of 210mph (338km/h). The aluminum bodywork was replaced by carbon fiber which helped to reduce weight by 198lb (90kg). A 585bhp 6 liter engine arrived for 2001, which, after 11 years, was destined to be the final year of Diablo production.

Above: The long-heralded Diablo roadster appeared in 1996. Much of the bodywork was reworked, and the roof is carried outboard above the engine.

Specification	**Lamborghini** Diablo VT
Engine location	Mid, in-line
Configuration	V12
Bore and stroke	87 x 80mm
Capacity	5707cc
Valve operation	Twin overhead camshafts per bank
Horsepower	485bhp @ 7000rpm
Transmission	Manual five-speed
Drive	Four-wheel
Chassis	Tubular steel
Suspension – front	Wishbones and coil spring
Suspension – rear	Wishbones and coil spring
Brakes	Ventilated disc
Top speed	202mph (325km/h)
Acceleration	0-62mph (0-100km/h): 4.1 seconds

Enhanced power unit

The Diablo's V12 engine had not only been enlarged to 5992cc, its internal components also underwent revision. The bigger bored 87 x 84mm power unit had been enhanced by the fitting of a lighter crankshaft and stronger titanium connecting rods, the intention being to improve throttle response. Similarly each cylinder had its own coil to improve ignition, and changes were also made to the engine management system's microprocessors.

Fortunately none of these improvements did anything to detract from the unique sound being produced by this venerable alloy V12. Its keynote was explosions of pure power accompanied by a cacophony of gears, chains, and the attendant activities of four overhead camshafts.

An ingenious refinement, shared with Ferrari, was that the exhaust system had a throttle valve that remained shut at low engine speeds, but when the revs increased it was opened by the management system. This meant that the entire neighborhood would not be woken if the fortunate

Opposite: What the birds see – the Diablo roadster of 1995 with, unusually, the detachable carbon-fiber roof mounted outboard above the engine. The conversion was undertaken by Marcello Gandini, who was responsible for the lines of the mainstream Diablo coupé. With a claimed top speed of 170mph (274km/h), it was a little slower than the closed version.

Left: A 1997 SV-R. Lightened by 103lb (47kg), this track-ready, racing Sport Veloce model was immediately identifiable by its rear wing. Acceleration was better than the standard version because of its lower gearing. But the V12 engine was mildly detuned to develop 508bhp, so top speed fell to 183mph (295km/h).

Diablo owner started the 550bhp engine and floored the throttle. And, similarly, the resonance would not blast other road users off the highway.

Like the GT, the 2001 Diablo's aluminum body panels were replaced by carbon-fiber sections to keep the 10-year-old model's weight from getting out of hand. Their adoption also improved the build quality of the body because of the difficulty Lamborghini had previously experienced with hand finishing the large aluminum pressings of which it had been constructed.

Changes were also made to the interior where the seating position was improved for driver comfort. The lever in the handsome gated gearchange was also relocated so that it fell more readily to hand. Carbon fiber was also in much greater evidence in the cockpit than previously and there was a new air conditioning system. Less apparent was the fact that the front and rear track was increased by a modest 2.4in (60mm), the intention being to improve the Diablo's turning circle and its stability.

The ultimate expression of this famous line was only produced in VT form, while the open version was reserved for the sunnier climes of the American market. It was unquestionably the best-built Diablo in the model's history, thanks to Volkswagen's ownership, since 1998, of Lamborghini, the marque being allied to its Audi subsidiary.

Production ceased in 2001 to make way for the Murcielago – a new chapter in the history of this extraordinary car maker was about to unfold.

Left: The V12 engine that, in essence, has powered every Lamborghini since the marque's birth in 1963. Although originally front mounted, it has been longitudinally mid-located since the Countach appeared in 1974. This example, complete with carbon-fiber covers, is pictured in a 1997 Diablo. The engine survives in enlarged form in the current Murcielago.

TVR Griffith

**Top speed
155mph**
249km/h

*Right: A driver's eye view
of a left-hand-drive export
Griffith. The cabin was
acclaimed by commentators
for sympathetically echoing
the attractive external lines.*

*Below: One of the Griffith's
many virtues is that it looks
like nothing else on the
road, combining traditional
lines with assured
individuality. TVR's
subsequent models did not
disappoint either.*

Today TVR is renowned for combining
distinctive, eye-catching styling with
earth-shattering performance. The Griffith
can be regarded as the starting point for this
renaissance; it was unveiled at the 1990 British
Motor Show.

TVR dates from 1954 when Blackpool-based
Trevor (hence the TVR marque name) Wilkinson
began the production of glass-fiber-bodied specials
powered by a variety of Ford, Coventry Climax, or
BMC engines. However, the business experienced
many changes of ownership before it was acquired,
in 1982, by Peter Wheeler, a former oil industry
executive, who also possessed a formidable flair for
styling. A new era for TVR had dawned.

Unusually, Wheeler carves his shapes from
massive blocks of expanded polystyrene and the
open two-seater Griffith represented the first
outward expression of his talents. Its mechanical
origins are to be found in the model S of 1986
vintage, an open two-seater with a backbone space-
frame chassis and powered by a 2.8 liter Ford V6

engine. An S3 version was produced for the 1991
season. The other model in the TVR range was the
angular Rover V8-powered 420 convertible.

The Griffith represented a union of these two
concepts, being based on the S3 chassis and the
420's 3.9 liter V8 engine. However, its sleek open
two-seater body was unique to the car. It proved to
be as fast as it looked – TVR claimed a top speed
of 148mph (238km/h) with 60mph (96km/h)
arriving in a shattering 4.9 seconds.

Improved specification

The new model generated considerable interest on its announcement but there was to be an 18-month hiatus before the Griffith entered production early in 1992. TVR had spent this interval in improving its specification – the original S3-derived chassis was replaced by a stronger frame with all-round independent suspension, courtesy of the company's Tuscan racing car. And the Rover V8 was now produced in 4.2 liter form.

While the body lines, which had received many plaudits on its 1990 launch, remained essentially the same, the finish of the car was carefully refined. Concealed door catches were introduced, a backlit

number plate was fitted and the rear lights were now flush-fitting.

TVR claimed a top speed of 155mph (249km/h) for the production version. The model was upgunned from mid-1993 with the arrival of the outwardly identical Griffith 500 powered by a TVR-enhanced 5 liter version of the seemingly indestructible and robust Rover V8.

This endowed the car with what its makers called, to the delight of its owners, a 'howling boom' exhaust note. Still in production at the time of writing (2002), the Griffith is now powered by TVR's own AJP V8 engine and is capable of speeds in excess of 160mph (257km/h).

Above: A Griffith with its solid detachable roof panel in place. When not in use, it filled the otherwise reasonably sized trunk.

Below left: The 4.3 liter alloy V8 was a Rover-based unit which provided stunning performance and a magnificent exhaust note.

Specification	TVR Griffith 500
Engine location	Front, in-line
Configuration	V8
Bore and stroke	94 x 90mm
Capacity	4988cc
Valve operation	Pushrod
Horsepower	325bhp @ 5500rpm
Transmission	Manual five-speed
Drive	Rear
Chassis	Tubular
Suspension – front	Wishbones and coil spring
Suspension – rear	Wishbones and coil spring
Brakes	Disc
Top speed	155mph (249km/h)
Acceleration	0-60mph (0-96km/h): 4.1 seconds

Mitsubishi 3000GT

**Top speed
155mph**
249km/h

*Below: This hi-tech
Mitsubishi with its Chrysler-
designed body changed
little outwardly between its
1990 launch and 1993 when
this example was built. Less
apparent is the four-wheel
steering and computer-
controlled suspension.*

At the time of its announcement in 1990,
the four-wheel-drive 155mph (249km/h)
Mitsubishi 3000GT was a state-of-the-art
model, crammed with electronic gizmos and an
abundance of mechanical refinements. It is still in
production and survives as a reminder of Japanese
prowess in the fields of automobile technology and
increasingly integrated electronics.

The 3000GT coupé is the product of a mixed
parentage, its sophisticated mechanicals having
appeared in Mitsubishi's experimental HSX sports
coupé displayed at the 1989 Tokyo Motor Show. It
featured both four-wheel drive and also four-wheel
steering which operating in conjunction with
computer-controlled suspension and brakes.

These were then transferred to what was
originally named the Mitsubishi Starion GTO, but
the body, complete with aerodynamically refined
pop-up headlamps, was courtesy of Chrysler with
whom the Japanese car company had, in 1971,
formed an association. It was sold on the American
market as the Dodge Stealth.

Twin turbochargers
The complex mechanicals and electronics were
optional fitments on Mitsubishi's luxurious Sigma
sedan. Power came from the same source but the
transversely mounted 281bhp V6 engine with twin
overhead camshafts per bank was twin turbocharged
in the 3000GT.

The suspension was designed to tailor its responses automatically to the type of terrain the car was covering. There were two settings: 'tour' was the norm while 'sport' resulted in a stiffer setting.

Inside the driver was presented with a battery of electronically displayed information, although whether he or she really required a TV screen which indicated whether the air from the air conditioning system had reached the farthest reaches of the interior is open to question!

At 3792lb (1720kg), the 3000GT was a heavy car and, despite its advanced specifications, the consensus among commentators was that the engine was outstanding, but that the model behaved better in a straight line than when it was going around corners…

Visual and mechanical updates arrived for the 1994 season. The rather dated pop-up headlamps were replaced by integrated units and engine power was boosted to 320bhp. A six-speed close-ratio gearbox replaced the original five-cog unit.

Up until the 1996 model year, this Mitsubishi was only available in coupé form but for that season it was joined by a convertible version which was marketed under the Spyder name. It was only available in the American market.

Currently the 3000GT is still produced and a non-turbo 224bhp version is also available, the latter car being capable of a still respectable 143mph (230km/h).

Specification	Mitsubishi 3000GT
Engine location	Transverse
Configuration	Twin-turbocharged V6
Bore and stroke	91 x 76mm
Capacity	2972cc
Valve operation	Twin overhead camshafts per cylinder bank
Horsepower	281bhp @ 6000rpm
Transmission	Manual five-speed
Drive	Four-wheel
Chassis	Unitary
Suspension – front	MacPherson strut
Suspension – rear	Wishbones, trailing arms and coil spring
Brakes	Ventilated disc
Top speed	155mph (249km/h)
Acceleration	0-60mph (96km/h): 5.8 seconds

Left: Interior of a 1995 car with six-speed gearbox that arrived for 1994 along with a passenger airbag.

Below: A 3000GT of 1995. The design had been revised in the previous year with flush headlamps replacing the pop-up variety. Mitsubishi also tidied up the strakes along the car's flanks.

Vauxhall Lotus Carlton

**Top speed
176mph**
283km/h

*Right: The Lotus Carlton's
rear spoiler was far from
just decorative – it helped
to keep the rear wheels
firmly on the road.*

*Below: The front spoiler
with its substantial air
intakes, widened wheel
arches, and Ronal alloy
wheels distinguished this
model. The drag coefficient
was a creditable 0.31.*

Apart from a rear spoiler and a couple of
air intakes let into the hood, there was
little outwardly to signal the difference
between a Lotus Carlton and the mainstream five-
seater family model on which it was based. But
with a claimed top speed of 176mph (283km/h) it
was, in 1990, the world's fastest sedan car.

Introduced in 1986, the Carlton was the
Vauxhall version of the German-built and designed
Opel Rekord, both makes having been owned since
the 1920s by the American General Motors
Corporation. More recently, in 1986, GM had
acquired British sports car manufacturer and
engineering consultant Lotus, and this concern was
responsible not only for effecting the important
modifications but also for completing the model's
assembly. Announced at the 1989 Geneva Motor
Show, this BMW-beater did not enter production
until late in 1990 and it was also badged as the
Opel Lotus Omega in Europe.

Developing no less than 377bhp, the engine
was based on the 3 liter unit used in Vauxhall's
flagship Carlton GSi. Possessing unique 95 x
85mm internal dimensions, which gave 3615cc, it
was fitted with an aluminum twin-overhead-
camshaft four-valve cylinder head. The
turbochargers were twin Garrett T25 units, each
with its own water-cooled intercooler. There was a
phenomenal 419lb/ft of torque.

Left: The interior was another departure from the norm with leather upholstered seats supplying plenty of side support, although the rears were bucket-style. The steering wheel was adjustable for rake and the speedometer read to 180mph (290km/h).

Below: A hoodful of engine! The great virtue of this twin turbocharged 3.6 liter V6 was its flexibility with a broad power band and no less than 377bhp on tap. Lotus had done its work well.

Drive was taken via a six-speed ZF gearbox, similar to that used on the in-house Chevrolet Corvette, to a strengthened differential. Further departures from standard were modestly uprated suspension, substantial 12.5in (317mm) ventilated all-round disc brakes with racing calipers and massive Ronal alloy wheels.

Connolly leather interior

The interior was also peculiar to the model, being trimmed throughout in Connolly leather hide with fully supportive sports front seats, each of which contained an electronic 'memory.' Electric windows and sunroof also featured.

In total nine pre-production cars were built and testing was undertaken at the Nardo high-speed circuit in southern Italy where speeds of 176mph (283km/h) were achieved. Vauxhall optimistically spoke of 180mph (290km/h) being possible. However, this prompted controversy and corporate advertisements made no mention of its potential top speed, only its impressive 0-60mph (0-96km/h) figure of 5.2 seconds.

GM envisaged making 1100 cars over three years. While it sold for a competitive $67,000, the model, alas, ran into the recession of the early 1990s. While Lotus completed them at an initial rate of 13 a week, production was curtailed a year early in December 1992. In all 950 were completed, 150 short of the original figure, with the Carlton accounting for 320 and the balance of 630 given over to the Opel version.

Specification	Vauxhall Lotus Carlton
Engine location	Front, in-line
Configuration	Twin turbocharged six-cylinder
Bore and stroke	95 x 85mm
Capacity	3615cc
Valve operation	Twin overhead camshafts
Horsepower	377bhp @ 5200rpm
Transmission	Manual six-speed
Drive	Rear
Chassis	Unitary
Suspension – front	MacPherson strut and coil spring
Suspension – rear	Multi link, semi trailing arm and coil spring
Brakes	Ventilated disc
Top speed	176mph (283km/h)
Acceleration	0-60mph (0-96km/h: 5.2 seconds

1991–2000
McLaren to the Fore

Britain returned to the fast car fray with a vengeance in the 1990s with McLaren's spectacular F1 supercar. It is still, at the time of writing (2002), the world's fastest roadgoing model, being capable of 240mph (386km/h). Like its Bugatti EB110 and Ferrari F50 contemporaries, the race-bred coupé from Woking, Surrey made extensive use of light and immensely strong carbon fiber in its construction.

It is no accident that the car's creator, Gordon Murray, pioneered the use of this aircraft industry material when working, in 1978, for racing car constructor Brabham. First extended to road models in the 1980s, it seems destined to relegate the tubular space-frame chassis to oblivion.

Honda NSX

**Top speed
161mph**
259km/h

*Right: Interior of a 3.2 liter
NSX. Like the exterior, this
has been criticized for a
lack of flair. Roadholding
is, however, outstanding.*

*Below: Honda's flagship
has remained essentially
unchanged over the years
although the 3.2 liter
version of 1997 had a
revised front spoiler.*

A significant challenge by Honda designed to take on the best of Europe's supercars, the mid-engined NSX of 1990 was applauded for its excellent engine and faultless road manners. It was this latter virtue which attracted the customers rather than the anonymous styling, for this Honda is one of the best-handling cars of its generation and it remains in production at the time of writing (2002).

The Japanese company's reputation was based on its preeminent position as the world's largest manufacturer of motorcycles, and a string of two-wheeled racing successes helped to cement its status. So when, in 1962, Honda decided to extend its range to motor cars, it went without saying that their engineering would be assured and innovative. Two years later, in 1964, Honda became the first Japanese car maker to compete in Formula 1. There were teething troubles but it began a racing connection that continues to this day.

Honda drew on its competition experience when it came to develop the NSX, and, because this was a prestigious model to take on the likes of Ferrari and Porsche, the company lavished considerable time on the NSX's development. Work began on the concept in 1984, a respectable six years before it entered production.

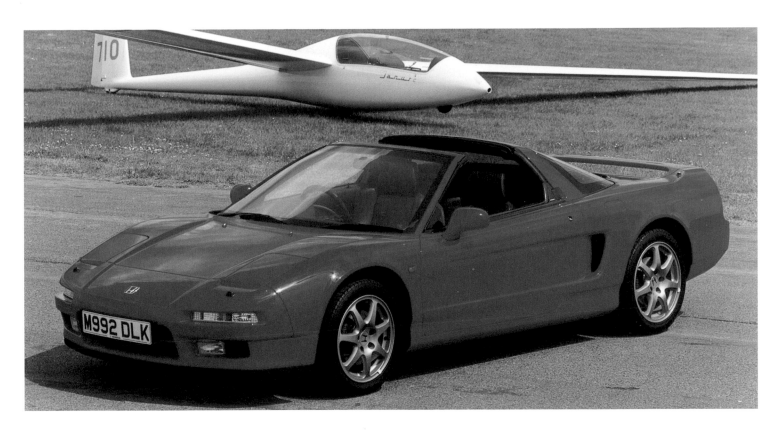

Mixed development

A mid-engined design, the first to be attempted by Honda, was chosen from the outset. Development work was undertaken using an enhanced experimental City model, a mini car sold in Europe as the Jazz. Further work was undertaken on a similarly modified Civic CRX coupé. A European ingredient to the mix was contributed by the HP-X, a Pininfarina-styled coupé with power courtesy of a V6 engine from the Formula 2 Honda race car. Further initiatives were undertaken with V8 engines, some of which were turbocharged.

With America targeted as the new car's principal market, it was appropriate that the NSX was launched in Chicago in 1989. But even then Honda's engineers were still not satisfied and further modifications were made to the model's bodywork while the wheelbase was extended by 1.5in (38mm).

By the time that the car entered production in 1990 with its definitive NSX designation, it was widely acclaimed for the quality of its mechanicals. Nowhere was this more apparent that in the mid-located, transversely positioned 270bhp 3 liter V6 engine. An alloy twin-overhead-camshaft unit with four valves per cylinder, it was designed to rev to no less than 8300rpm, thanks to the race-proven titanium connecting rods. Two innovative devices helped to distribute power evenly throughout the rev range. One was variable valve timing, or VTEC, which Honda had first used in its CRX of 1984, and the other was a variable volume induction system which was intended to improve breathing and produce more power at high revs.

Drive was taken to the rear wheels via a five-speed manual gearbox, although an alternative automatic version was also available. A traction-control system, which reduced power to the rear wheels as soon as the brakes were applied, was fitted. Honda's racing heritage was also reflected in wishbone suspension which used aluminum components rather than the usual steel.

Above: The NSX was enhanced with a Targa-style roof in 1995 which proved particularly popular in America, although this is a UK-registered right-hand-drive version. A six-speed semi-automatic gearbox arrived at the same time. Otherwise the mixture was as before with Honda's formidable engineering displayed to excellent effect.

Specification	Honda NSX
Engine location	Mid, transverse
Configuration	V6
Bore and stroke	90 x 78mm
Capacity	2977cc
Valve operation	Twin overhead camshafts per cylinder bank
Horsepower	270bhp @ 7100rpm
Transmission	Manual five-speed
Drive	Rear
Chassis	Unitary
Suspension – front	Wishbones and coil spring
Suspension – rear	Wishbones and coil spring
Brakes	Ventilated disc
Top speed	161mph (259km/h)
Acceleration	0-60mph (96km/h): 5.9 seconds

Aluminum body

The coupé body was also to have been made of steel but by the time of the Chicago launch it had also been changed to aluminum. While its lines were competently executed, the roof being finished in a contrasting black, the car perhaps lacked the design flair associated with its European competition.

Above: The 1997 updates are not apparent from the rear. The suspension was essentially unchanged but Honda revised the steering, which was a sophisticated electric power-assisted rack-and-pinion system. Changes were also made to the brakes – Honda claimed that, in addition to their increased effectiveness, their balance was also improved.

Right: The bigger bored 3.2 liter V6 engine which developed 276bhp was actually 5.2lb (2.4kg) lighter than its predecessor because of its carbon and alloy cylinder liners. A driver-friendly dual mass flywheel had been fitted from the outset to keep clutch pressure as light as possible.

However, any doubts regarding the quality of Honda's flagship were immediately dispelled once drivers got behind the black-finished wheel. The NSX's chassis was outstanding and the model exhibited predictable, safe handling, even on the tightest corners. It was fast as well – on the open road the Honda's top speed just exceeded the 160mph (257km/h) mark.

Unfortunately for Honda, the appearance of the NSX coincided with the world recession of the early 1990s. Honda responded by beginning work on a faster, lighter version which only appeared on the home market for the 1993 season. This featured carbon-fiber body panels with a reworked front end, revised suspension, and wider, larger tires. The V6 engine was enlarged to 3.2 liters and it was tuned by Mugen, a company which specialized in enhancing Formula 1 power units. It was owned by the son of the company's founder, Soichiro Honda. All these ministrations increased top speed to 170mph (273km/h) with the 0-60mph (96km/h) figure reduced by 0.8 second to 5.1 seconds.

The challenge thrown down by Toyota's newly introduced Supra of 1993 resulted in Honda uprating the model for 1994 with larger 17in wheels. Power-assisted steering, which had previously only been a feature of the automatic NSX, was also made standard. The manual gearbox was also refined to reduce the already muted transmission noise.

Targa top

A revised NSX with detachable Targa-type top was launched in the 1995 season in response to the success of Fcrarri's F335. Slightly heavier than the coupé, on account of the extra reinforcement, there were further unseen improvements including a new drive-by-wire throttle and changes to the traction-control system. In consequence Honda claimed a 62mph (100km/h) figure of 5.9 seconds and a top speed of 167mph (269km/h).

An engine enlargement to 3.2 liters, foreshadowed in 1993, followed in 1997; power

was up to 290bhp. Honda also took the opportunity of lightening the car, which by this time had acquired a six-speed manual transmission. However, the automatic version, a favorite with Americans, retained the 3 liter unit.

With time running out for the NSX, a replacement must be in the offing. Honda has set itself an extremely high standard to follow.

Above: A sporting concept, the NSX-R was displayed at the 2001 Tokyo Motor Show with conventional faired-in, rather than pop-up, headlights that prefaced their appearance on the latest version of this mid-engined Honda. Carbon fiber is used for the hood, engine cover, and the rear spoiler, hence the contrasting color.

Left: The NSX-R's enhanced interior. Its competition heritage is underlined by the Recaro carbon-fiber Aramid bucket seats. The steering wheel is a leather-bound Momo component. Honda's publicity enthuses that the interior wraps 'the driver in an ambience tailor-made for spirited driving.'

Dodge Viper

**Top speed
172mph**
277km/h

*Right: Simplicity is the
essential theme of the Viper
and this is no more
apparent than in the no-
frills cockpit. The seats are
supportive and boast
inflatable lumbar control.
Legroom is also good.*

*Below: Although only
produced in left-hand-drive
form, the car is sold in
Europe as the Chrysler
Viper because the Dodge
name is used on a French
truck. It has the virtue of
looking good when viewed
from any angle.*

500/500/500. These figures alluringly
stand for brake horsepower, pounds/feet
of torque, and (in truth) approximate
cubic inches, and they are being used as a
marketing formula to promote the second
generation Dodge Viper that is due to hit the streets
of its native America in August 2002.

It has been a remarkable success story for the
hunky no-frills two-seater that began life as a
concept car back at the 1989 Detroit Motor Show.
Created for Dodge's Chrysler parent by Carroll
Shelby, who was responsible for the 1960s AC
Cobra (hence the related Viper name), this
unashamedly 'back to basics' concept of an open
two-seater was powered by an overhead-valve V10
engine intended for the next generation of Chrysler
trucks and sports utilities.

Such was its reception at the show, Chrysler
decided to put this unconventional Dodge into
production. The body, with its steel center section
and glass-fiber nose and tail and replete with
Ferrari, Jaguar, and Cobra echoes, was retained
essentially intact, but the power unit did require
some modification.

Aluminum engine block

Revamped by in-house Lamborghini, the original
cast-iron block was replaced by an aluminum one;
changes to the combustion chamber and valve gear
produced a unit that developed 400bhp, a 100bhp
improvement on the original. The red rocker boxes
were Ferrari-inspired. The exhaust outlet of
drainpipe-like proportions emerged from an
exposed muffler just below the passenger's door.

Above left: Inside the Viper's V10 engine that began life as a truck unit and was reworked by in-house Lamborghini in aluminum. A big, low-revving 8 liter, overhead valve actuation was via hydraulic tappets and pushrods.

Above right: The way forward. Chrysler's GTS/R concept Viper of 2000 forms the basis of the next generation of cars. It is longer, wider, and lower than the original.

Left: Although the Viper began life as an open two-seater, a coupé version was inevitable, the GTS being unveiled in 1993. This profile underlines the success of the conversion which looks like a new model in its own right.

Entering production in 1992, Chrysler claimed a top speed of 165mph (266km/h) with 60mph (96km/h) arriving in a raucous and exceedingly rapid 4.5 seconds.

The 1993 Los Angeles Motor Show witnessed the appearance of a coupé version – the GTS, at it was titled, used a more powerful 450bhp engine. Lighter than the open car and more aerodynamically efficient, it was also noticeably faster and able to attain over 170mph (274km/h). As with the roadster, there was a gap, in this instance three years, before the first production version GTS reached its customers during 1996.

In the meantime the roadster was being up-gunned and the 550bhp Venom was followed in 1997 by the Venom 600 with no less than 635bhp on tap.

Chrysler sprung another surprise at the 2000 Detroit show when it unveiled the Viper GTS/R concept coupé and it in turn inspired the '03 season version that made its surprise debut at the 2001 Detroit event. The RT-10 Convertible is an open car like the original, and most noticeably it inherited the concept's distinctive sculptured side panels.

Specification	**Dodge** Viper GTS
Engine location	Front, in-line
Configuration	V10
Bore and stroke	4 x 3.85in (101 x 98mm)
Capacity	487cid (7990cc)
Valve operation	Pushrod
Horsepower	378bhp @ 5100rpm
Transmission	Manual six-speed
Drive	Rear
Chassis	Tubular
Suspension – front	Wishbones and coil spring
Suspension – rear	Wishbones and coil spring
Brakes	Disc
Top speed	172mph (277km/h)
Acceleration	0-60mph (0-96km/h): 5.3 seconds

It is 0.7in (18mm) shorter and lighter than the present version but with a 2.5in (66mm) longer wheelbase. The V10's capacity has been increased to 8.3 liters, actually 505cid, and Chrysler is hoping that the recurring 500 theme will prove irresistible to potential customers, and is aiming the car at an even wider public than the original.

Above: The GTS/R Viper concept that was unveiled at the 2000 Detroit Motor Show. However, practicality will override visual exuberance for the production Viper which will have a simpler front spoiler than this example. It will also sit somewhat higher off the ground than this car and be a roadster!

Right: The familiar 8 liter V10 engine which is exposed by opening a smaller hood on the present production Viper. The engine has been converted to dry sump lubrication which has allowed the Chrysler engineering team to extract a further 50bhp, to give 500bhp. Otherwise the pushrod unit is essentially the same as that used in the production Viper.

A concept car was the starting point for the original Viper, so it is wholly appropriate that the next generation model is also based on such a vehicle. The GTS/R, unveiled at the 2000 Detroit Motor Show, sprang in essence from the sport coupés that Chrysler had raced since 1994 at Le Mans when, for the first time, GT cars were able to compete with Group C sports prototypes. For the record its best position came in 1999 when a Viper GTS/R was placed 10th. And in the three years between 1997 and 1999 the model was also ruling champion in GT2 events.

So this concept had pedigree aplenty. Designer Osamu Shikado, who had joined Chrysler from Toyota in 1994, recognized that although the car would have to be evidently different, it should also be visually related to the first generation Viper. But it is a larger car, having a 3in (76mm) longer wheelbase and a 2in (50mm) wider track. It also sits some 3.5in (90mm) closer to the road although the wheels are larger, 19in at the front and 20in diameter at the rear which compares with the 17in of the production version.

The original Viper had large hot air outlets located just behind each front wheel arch and these were perpetuated in the GTS/R but were accentuated and sculpted into the doors. Although

the car was lower in overall terms, the tail was actually taller than the original and it was used as a platform for a large rear wing to help keep the 500bhp developed by the 8 liter V10 engine firmly on the road. In a break with tradition, the power unit was converted to dry-sump lubrication and it produced 50bhp more than the production Viper.

The chassis and all-round wishbone and coil suspension were essentially unchanged but the larger diameter wheels meant uprated brakes with 13.9in (355mm) discs.

Left: The dashboard is a visually pleasing combination of brushed aluminum, carbon fiber and leather. Although these materials will not reach the production line, the layout of the instruments will.

Below left: The GTSR legend appears behind the front wheel arches. Yet, despite the R suffix, this is a road car.

Below: While the rear spoiler played an important visual and practical role, it will not be a feature of the RT-10 Viper that is scheduled for 2003.

Stylish cockpit

There was a completely new interior which featured a combination of carbon-fiber, leather, and brushed aluminum with the rev counter located right in the middle of the dash. The cockpit was suffused with echoes of Le Mans, even the headlining being made of carbon-fiber! However, such niceties as the beautifully crafted aluminum door hinges, front spoiler supports, and substantial rear wing are, alas, being sacrificed to the realities of the production line.

With the new RT-10 roadster not due until 2003, the GTS/R will, in the meantime, provide an accurate pointer to the future and it suggests that a coupé version cannot be following far behind.

Light Car Company Rocket

**Top speed
145mph**
233km/h

*Below: Head-on view of the
Rocket which can be
nothing else but a racer for
the road. The front double
wishbones ingeniously use
spherical bearing joints in
conjunction with anti-
vibration bushes which are
allied to high geared rack-
and-pinion steering. Double
wishbones are also
employed at the rear.*

Unconventional, light, and potent, the
mid-engined Rocket provides seat-of-the-
pants performance and is able to hit
145mph (233km/h) although it feels like twice that
figure to the lucky driver! Make no mistake, the
Rocket is no whim of a garden-shed amateur. It is a
deadly serious exercise, the work of respected
racing car designer, Gordon Murray, better known
as the creator of the McLaren F1.

Although the Rocket has been around since
1992, Murray had been mulling over the project a
good 20 years before that. It was then that he and
his racing driver friend, Chris Craft, using Colin
Chapman's evergreen Lotus Seven as their starting
point, conceived a road car which embodied some
echoes of the Formula 3 motorcycle-engined 500cc
racers that enjoyed popularity in Britain in the early
post-war years.

The 1002cc Yamaha four chosen for the Rocket,
a 143bhp engine with twin overhead camshafts and
no less than five valves per cylinder, was
accordingly mid-located. This was the only
proprietary component to be bought in.

The gearbox was a five-speed sequential unit
but the transaxle was a bespoke component, the
work of Peter Weismann's US-based Traction
Products, which specialized in the manufacture of
transmission systems for Indianapolis cars. A
feature of this unit was two alternative ratios which
produced no less than 15 forward speeds and five
reverse. In 1998 *Autocar's* Colin Goodwin attained
a mind-boggling 101mph (162km/h) in reverse gear
hurtling down the runway of a Gloucestershire
airfield. A brave man!

To keep the weight as low as possible, every
part was purpose-designed, from the stove-

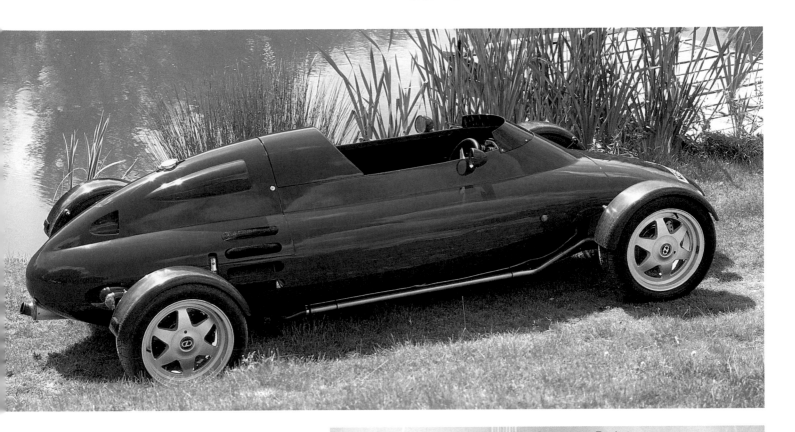

enameled space-frame chassis to the suspension components. This meant that the Rocket turned the scales at just 775lb (352kg). If Murray had used off-the-shelf parts, it would have added a further 325lb (147kg) to the finished product.

Pillion passenger option

Manufacture was assigned to Craft's Light Car Company with Bob Curl having the task of bringing the concept to production. He was also responsible for the design of the glass-fiber racing car-inspired body that is based on a Formula 1 Vanwall of 1957 vintage. The dashboard is made of carbon fiber, along with the cycle-type fenders. While this, by its nature, is a single-seater, there is room for a second seat if the owner requires one with the passenger riding 'pillion.'

As a consequence of such a design the Rocket's weather equipment is virtually non-existent. It is devoid of such creature comforts as a roof and doors and sports only the briefest of windshields to keep the elements at bay.

Once behind the wheel (or should that be the stick?) of the Rocket, you're never far away from the cacophony produced by the Yahama's four situated just behind the seat. The Light Car Company is currently based in Stanford in the Vale, Oxfordshire from where it continues to produce a trickle of these unusually potent roadgoing racers.

Specification	Light Car Company Rocket
Engine location	Mid, transverse
Configuration	Four-cylinder
Bore and stroke	76 x 56mm
Capacity	1002cc
Valve operation	Twin overhead camshafts
Horsepower	143bhp @ 10,500rpm
Transmission	Manual five-speed
Drive	Rear
Chassis	Space-frame
Suspension – front	Wishbones and coil spring
Suspension – rear	Wishbones and coil spring
Brakes	Ventilated disc
Top speed	145mph (233 km/h)
Acceleration	0-60mph (96km/h): 4.4 seconds

Above: The Rocket has a body made of a glass-reinforced sandwich which, happily, lacks any superfluous additions. The headrest is removable.

Left: The driver sits in a figure-hugging Tillet adjustable seat which is trimmed in leather.

Jaguar XJ220

**Top speed
213mph**
343km/h

*Right: The XJ220's lines
are stunning and it also has
the virtue of being easy to
drive at high speed. Unlike
the 1988 show car, this
model has conventional
doors rather than the
memorable upward-opening
variety. The rear wing is
barely noticeable.*

*Below: If the XJ220's
mechanical specification
was a simplified version of
that of the original show
car, the body lines were
stunning and bore no
resemblance to any other
roadgoing model. This
example is finished in
Silverstone Silver. Five
metallic finishes were
available to customers,
mostly in darker hues.*

 Between the fall of 1991 and the end of
1993, the Jaguar XJ220, with a top speed
of 213mph (343km/h), was the world's
fastest production car. That was until the arrival of
the McLaren F1…

The starting point of what was really a very un-
Jaguar-like project came in December 1984 when
the company's director of engineering, Jim Randle,
inspired by Porsche's 959, began thinking in terms
of a 500bhp Jaguar supercar. This would be
powered by a non-standard version of the corporate
V12, a 6.2 liter unit with twin overhead camshafts
and four-valve cylinder heads, rather than the usual
5.3 liter single cam/two-valve ones.

With engineers volunteering their labor and
working on Saturday mornings, it took nearly four
years to bring the project to fruition. The completed
mid-engined silver coupé was unveiled at the 1988
Birmingham Motor Show. Clad in a stunning body
styled by Jaguar's Keith Helfet, complete with
scissor doors and with a host of refinements, it had
a theoretical top speed of over 200mph (321km/h).

Decision to proceed

Although Jaguar was acquired by Ford in 1989, the
new management decided to proceed with the
project and announced that 350 examples of a
simplified XJ220 would be built at a cost of
$505,400 each, which was about twice the price of
a Ferrari F40. The new version was unveiled in
October 1991 at the Tokyo Motor Show but the
world was by then in a deepening recession.

Eight inches (203mm) shorter than the
Birmingham Show car and shorn of its V12 engine,
scissor doors, four-wheel drive, adaptive
suspension, and anti-lock brakes, the coupé
nevertheless outwardly resembled the original.

Under the rear decking was a stubbier (but no
less potent) twin turbocharged 3.5 liter V6 engine
which developed an astounding 524bhp. The top
speed was a world-beating 213mph (343km/h) and
100mph (161km/h) arriving in an eye-blinking
eight seconds.

Far left: The 220's interior was not over-elaborate but was commended for its excellent driving position and body-hugging seats. The door-mounted dials were a novel feature.

Left: Around half the length of the original show car's V12, the deceptively small V6 packed a considerable punch, although critics were disappointed by its exhaust note.

12 per cent price rise

Unfortunately the 220's price had risen by some 12 per cent, to $564,000, and a number of prospective customers who had paid a $70,000 deposit found in the chill of 1991 that they were unable to complete the order.

There was also a lightened version, the XJ220-C of 1993. A trio of these cars entered that year's Le Mans 24 hour race and one example won the GT class, although it was subsequently disqualified on a technicality.

But the project continued to be overshadowed by controversy and in the event the projected production figure of 350 was cut to 275. The last car was completed in the spring of 1994.

Specification	Jaguar XJ220
Engine location	Mid, in-line
Configuration	Twin turbocharged V6
Bore and stroke	94 x 84mm
Capacity	3498cc
Valve operation	Twin overhead camshafts per bank
Horsepower	542bhp @ 7200rpm
Transmission	Manual five-speed
Drive	Rear
Chassis	Bonded aluminum honeycomb
Suspension – front	Wishbones and coil spring
Suspension – rear	Wishbones and coil spring
Brakes	Ventilated disc
Top speed	213mph (343km/h)
Acceleration	0-60mph (0-96km/h): 4 seconds

Above: The 220S was a GT racer based on the XJ220Cs that ran at Le Mans in 1993. It was not given the Jaguar name. It was a joint venture between TWR Motorsport and the Coventry-based Jaguar restorer XK Engineering. Launched in 1995, it was some 772lb (350kg) lighter than the XJ220 and 140bhp more powerful, the V6 engine being boosted to 680bhp.

Right: The 220S interior differed from the mainstream XJ220 in having leather-trimmed racing seats and a full safety harness. There was air conditioning but no CD stereo unit. While most of the body was made of composite materials, the original doors were retained.

Le Mans racers

The XJ220-C cars that TWR entered at the 1993 Le Mans event were closely related to the production versions. They differed principally in having their aluminum panels replaced with carbon-fiber sections which saved some 440lb (200kg) of weight. Changes were also made to the suspension geometry and brakes.

To conform to GT rules the cars were fitted with 1.2in (32mm) air restrictors to limit the V6's output to 500bhp, perversely some 42bhp less than it produced in the road car.

A trio of British racing green 220s entered the GT class in the 24 hour event. The fact that one car had won a GT event at Silverstone in May, the month before Le Mans, augured well for the race proper. With Porsche's 911 Turbo SLM regarded as the prime challenger, in June the 220-C's lapped Silverstone five seconds faster than the speeds they achieved on the circuit in the previous month.

Le Mans was dominated by a trio of Peugeot's 905s, and two of the TWR Racing's 220-Cs withdrew suffering from overheating, one of the cars having suffered a 'cooked' engine after the driver had switched off. However, the surviving Jaguar, driven by David Coulthard, David Brabham, and John Nielson, managed to pull off the GT class victory, their task having been made easier by the Porsche crashing during the night. But they did not have an easy run and this success was achieved despite a 73-minute pit stop to replace a leaking fuel tank. In 23 hours 56 minutes the 220-C covered 306 laps which compared with the winning Peugeot's 375 circuits.

But there was to be a sting in the tail. All three cars had been declared illegal on the preparatory qualifying laps. The decision was challenged by

Left: On the 220S the original aluminum body panels were replaced, front and rear, by carbon-fiber units. It turned the scales at 2425lb (1100kg) and just 2205lb (1000kg) when the luxury refinements were removed. Note the number plate – this is TWR's Tom Walkinshaw's own car.

Below left: While the front of the 220S resembled the production XJ220, the rear of the body differed in being integral with the roof line, rather than detachable, and incorporated fender pillars to support an adjustable aerofoil. BBS wheels replaced the Speedline originals while the brake system was uprated with six-piston Brembo front calipers and AP rear ones.

TWR boss Tom Walkinshaw and they were allowed to race pending an appeal. The objection arose because the Jaguars were not fitted with catalytic converters. But the 220-C was prepared for IMSA rules to race in America and, as a road car, it was fitted with a catalyst as standard. The Le Mans authorities maintained that it should also feature on the racing version.

Unfortunately the Jaguar was stripped of its class victory on the grounds that its entrant had failed to appeal after qualifying. And that, alas, was the end of this supercar's Le Mans career.

Below: Priced at $350,000, you could have bought two for the price of just one McLaren F1. It was intended to be a drive-to-the-circuit GT racer although the 220S was seldom used in competition. Most found their ways into private collections the world over, most notably to Japan.

Toyota Supra

**Top speed
155mph**
249km/h

*Right: The Supra's low-key
interior was deliberate.
Toyota designers eschewed
the gizmos of the Mitsubishi
3000's cockpit. These seats
are finished in tan leather.*

*Below: A British-registered
1996 Supra. The car is
stable at high speeds with
handling aided by excellent
steering. The air intake
located ahead of the back
wheels helps to cool the
rear discs.*

This is a model that progressively
improved as each generation appeared –
the best of the breed was the final version
introduced in 1993. Its top speed was limited to
155mph (249km/h), but it was capable of much,
much more.

The Supra name first appeared as a variant of
Toyota's two-plus-two Celica coupé of 1982. Then
in 1986 the Supra emerged as a model in its own
right in the form of a purpose-designed hatchback
coupé which retained its predecessor's front
engine/rear drive configuration. The engine was a
fuel-injected 210bhp 3 liter single-overhead-
camshaft unit which gave the model a top speed of
135mph (217km/h). The Turbo version of 1989 was
even quicker, able to exceed 140mph (225km/h),
but commentators deemed the handling inferior to
that of Honda's acclaimed NSX.

Like its rival, the new Supra of 1993 had
experienced a lengthy gestation period, in this
instance one of no less than eight years. But unlike

the mid-engined Honda, the new Toyota retained a
conventional mechanical layout. However,
weightsaving was an absolute prerequisite and as a
result it was 310lb (141kg) lighter than its
predecessor. This was no mean feat as model lines,
like the humans that create them, tend to get
heavier as they get older. This explained the
inclusion of such features as plastic gas tanks,

N501 PPJ

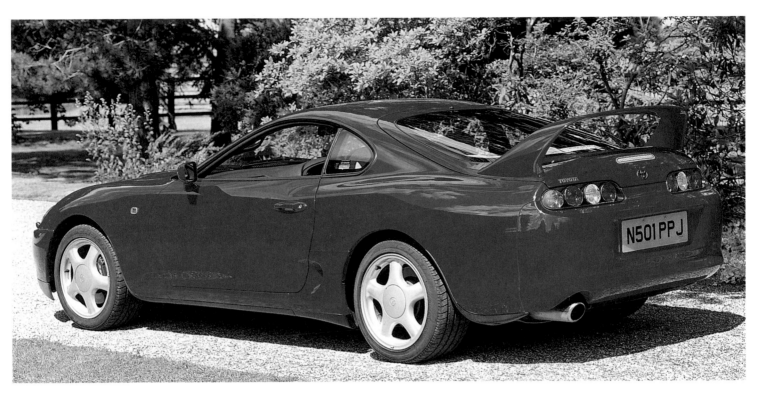

aluminum suspension, a single (rather than twin) exhaust pipe and a much publicized carpet made of hollow-fibered threads!

Six-cylinder engine

Although a V8 engine was considered, a six-cylinder unit was finally employed because it was lighter and its narrower dimensions made it easier to package the turbochargers. The production version was a 320bhp twin turbocharged twin-overhead-camshaft 24-valve unit of 2997cc capacity. This was sold on the European market but there was an unblown 220bhp Supra for US customers, the engine being shared with the Lexus coupé.

Unusually for the day a manual six-speed gearbox was employed and, like its predecessor, suspension was by all-round wishbones and coil springs. Bodily the lines of the 1993 Supra's coupé had evolved from the previous generation's car, and it was again a three-door hatchback. The profile could be enhanced on the turbo model by the fitment of a rear spoiler.

Handling was an improvement and acceleration was similarly bettered, the turbocharged Supra being able to attain 60mph (96km/h) in a shade over five seconds. Top speed was limited to 155mph (249km/h), even if experimental versions had been capable of 181mph (291km/h)! Production ceased in 1997 and, for the time being at least, there were to be no more Supras.

Specification	**Toyota** Supra
Engine location	Front, in-line
Configuration	Twin turbocharged six-cylinder
Bore and stroke	86 x 86mm
Capacity	2997cc
Valve operation	Twin overhead camshafts
Horsepower	320bhp @ 5600rpm
Transmission	Manual six-speed
Drive	Rear
Chassis	Unitary
Suspension – front	Wishbones and coil spring
Suspension – rear	Wishbones and coil spring
Brakes	Ventilated disc
Top speed	155mph (249km/h)
Acceleration	0-60mph (96km/h): 5.1 seconds

Above: The rear spoiler was an optional fitting but the car looked rather tail heavy without it. However, it pushed the body's drag coefficient up a point to 0.33.

Left: What many other drivers saw as the Supra sped past. The single, rather than twin, exhaust pipes were adopted as a weight-saving measure.

Bugatti EB110

**Top speed
212mph**
344km/h

*Right: The Bugatti's
understated interior was
functional but still had
some wood trim in evidence.
The car was only available
in left-hand-drive form.*

*Below: Open wide! The
scissor doors reflect the
influence of former
Lamborghini designer
Marcello Gandini, who was
responsible for the first
version of the EB110's body.*

 During the interwar years the French
Bugatti company produced some of the
world's most famous racing and sports
cars. This mid-engined four-wheel-drive
descendant, christened the Bugatti EB110, entered
production in 1993 and its SS variant was, briefly,
the world's fastest car. Capable of 217mph
(349km/h), this was just 4mph (6.4km/h) more than
the Jaguar XJ220.

The Italian-born, French-domiciled Ettore
Bugatti was an immensely talented artist-engineer
who in 1910 began building cars under his own
name at Molsheim in Alsace. His Type 35 of 1924
is still regarded as the most beautiful racing car of
all time and it was also one of the most successful.
Bugatti died in 1947 at the age of 66 and the
company built its last car in 1952, although it
continued in business mostly undertaking sub-
contract work for the aviation industry. In 1968 it
was taken over by SNECMA, France's nationalized
aircraft company.

Revival of Bugatti

However, the first the public knew of a revival of
the marque occurred in October 1987 when
Romano Artioli, who held the Ferrari franchise for
northern Italy and southern Germany, registered
Bugatti Automobili in Luxembourg. He then
appointed Paolo Stanzani, who had been
responsible for engineering Lamborghini's

Left: The Bugatti's lines were distinctive but considered uninspiring by many. The linear intakes on the sides of the body were introduced to duct air to the rear disc brakes.

Below: The EB110's rear spoiler rose at speeds over 75mph (120km/h) and retracted when it dropped to below the 50mph (80km/h) mark. The rectangular ventilation slots were introduced to assist engine cooling.

celebrated Countach, as his technical director. Stanzani began work immediately on a purpose-designed 3.5 liter V12 engine which employed the obligatory twin overhead camshafts and no less than five valves per cylinder.

The new power unit was enhanced by the addition of no less than four tiny IHI water-cooled turbochargers and it developed a formidable 700bhp. This was some 150bhp more than what was required!

Stanzani's Lamborghini associations were reflected in the choice of Marcello Gandini, who had the lines of the Miura and Countach to his credit, to style the new Bugatti. He produced a competent, if rather dated, design which lacked the visual flair for which he was usually renowned. But then Stanzani fell out with Artioli who in July 1990 sacked him.

In the meantime work was underway on a lavishly equipped purpose-designed factory at Campogalliano on the outskirts of the town of Modena – better known as the home of Ferrari. Its designer was Giampaolo Benedeni and Artioli, dissatisfied with Gandini's styling, appointed the architect to head an in-house team which re-worked the design.

However, when the car was unveiled in Paris on September 14 1991, the eve of what would have been Ettore Bugatti's 110th birthday (hence the EB110 name), there were collective reservations about the coupé's appearance. A few changes were effected when the model was displayed at the 1992 Geneva Motor Show although production did not begin until early in 1993.

Specification	Bugatti EB110 GT
Engine location	Mid, longitudinal
Configuration	V12
Bore and stroke	81 x 57mm
Capacity	3500cc
Valve operation	Twin overhead camshafts per cylinder bank
Horsepower	553bhp @ 8000rpm
Transmission	Manual six-speed
Drive	Four-wheel
Chassis	Unitary
Suspension – front	Wishbones and coil springs
Suspension – rear	Wishbones and coil springs
Brakes	Ventilated discs
Top speed	212mph (344km/h)
Acceleration	0-60mph (96km/h): 4.6 seconds

Right: A detail of the rear deck with a corner of the purpose-designed V12 engine revealed. In fact it was possible to view the top of the power unit through the transparent engine cover. The EB monogram on the right dates from 1910 and stands for Ettore Bugatti, creator of the legendary marque.

Below: The timidly executed radiator echoed that of the original Bugattis. The main air intake was for the mid-located engine fan-assisted radiator with the secondary one for brake cooling, essential on a high performance car. The side mirrors were positioned to facilitate rear visibility.

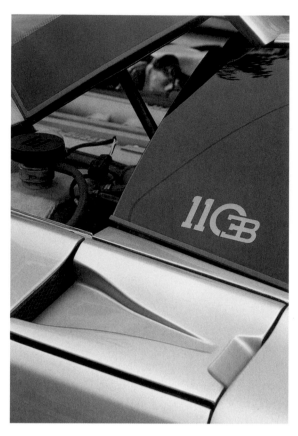

Technically superb

The car was a technical *tour de force* with a light, strong but costly carbon-fiber sub-structure, appropriately the work of Aérospatiale Bugatti, so securing a bond between the marque's past and present history. With the V12 engine mounted longitudinally behind the driver, the six-speed gearbox was located within the crankcase although it was separately lubricated.

Drive to all four wheels was permanently engaged with 72 per cent of power being allocated to the rear and the 28 per cent balance conveyed to the front via a centrally located differential. Suspension was by wishbones, coil springs and pullrods at the front and double coils at the rear. The tires were specially developed for the EB110 by Michelin

Disappointingly the aluminum body looked visually uninspiring when set alongside its Ferrari and Lamborghini rivals, although it featured upward-opening doors in the Countach/Diablo traditions.

An uncompromising two-seater, the Bugatti was a remarkably easy car to drive with power-assisted steering, clutch, and brakes. While the engine was

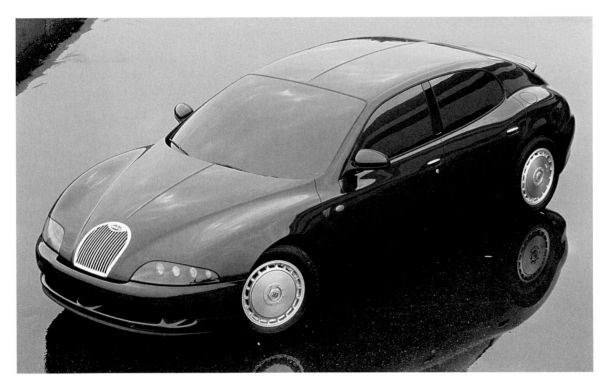

Left: Although it never reached production, Ital Design's EB112 four-door sedan concept, displayed at the 1993 Geneva show, is of interest because it relocated the 3.5 liter engine from the middle to the front of the car. Also note that the rendering of the Bugatti radiator is far bolder, and visually more successful, than that of the EB110.

not particularly noisy, it emitted an agreeable and distinctive rumble at low revs. Roadholding was deemed outstanding, thanks to the permanently engaged four-wheel drive.

On the debit side was a rather cramped cockpit, a shortcoming that was compounded by a lack of trunk space. On the plus side of the equation, the seats were very comfortable and the air conditioning excellent. Ride was outstanding; only left-hand-drive examples were built.

Its claimed top speed of 212mph (341km/h) was a mere 1mph (1.6km/h) slower than Jaguar's supercar, and Bugatti was keen to obtain the accolade of the world's fastest production car. To achieve this the V12 was boosted from 553bhp to 600 and a new model, the EB110 SS, for Sport Stradale or Road Racer, arrived in mid 1993. Unlike its predecessor, this was also produced in right-hand-drive form.

By stripping out many of its sophisticated accoutrements, the SS was some 440lb (200kg) lighter than the original version which was renamed the EB110 GT. The outcome was a claimed top speed of 217mph (349km/h) with 60mph (96km/h) arriving in just 3.4 seconds. However, the SS was soon overtaken by the McLaren F1 which entered production early in 1994.

Unfortunately Artioli was now overreaching himself. He had exhibited a projected EB112 four-door sedan with Ital Design-styled body at the 1993

Geneva Motor Show and later in the year acquired Lotus from General Motors. Yet in September 1995, a mere four years to the month after the EB110's launch, the Campogiallano factory closed with corporate debts of $60 million. A mere 139 cars had been built.

Just three years after that, in September 1998, the Bugatti name was acquired by Volkswagen. Its sensational Veyron prototype, which is described later in this book, possesses all the stunning individuality and sensational performance that was absent from Artioli's EB110.

Below: This stillborn coupé variant on the sedan theme shown above was also the work of Ital Design and was designated EB118. It was also front-engined – note the hot air outlet on the front fender. However, the work was not wasted because both concepts represented the starting point for Volkswagen's revival of the marque which began in 1998.

McLaren F1

**Top speed
240mph**
386km/h

*Right: A unique seating
position for a special type
of road car. In the F1 the
driver sits forward of the
two passenger seats which
are located either side of
him, or her.*

*Below: A hidden refinement
was fan-assisted underfloor
aerodynamics intended to
extract the maximum
performance from the F1.
Even the electric mirrors
were wind-tunnel tested!*

Although it appeared back in 1993, the fabulous McLaren F1 with a top speed of 240mph (386km/h) still bears the mantle of the world's fastest production car.

McLaren is, of course, better known as the manufacturer of Formula 1 single-seaters. It was in the early 1990s that its chief designer, Gordon Murray, who had long harbored the desire to produce 'the ultimate road car,' was given the corporate green light to proceed. Murray was in the enviable position of being able to design what could only be named the F1 from a clean sheet of paper. There would be no components carried over from any other models and racing car technology would feature prominently in its specification.

Aerodynamic styling

McLaren was also fortunate to secure the services of stylist Peter Stevens, and his aerodynamically efficient rakish coupé with its two distinctive scissor doors perfectly complemented Murray's mid-engined mechanics.

The power unit was a longitudinally mounted purpose-designed 6 liter BMW V12 with twin-cam cylinder heads. Drive went to the rear wheels (rather than all four which was the fashion) via a six-speed gearbox. With 550bhp on tap the brakes were four-caliper racing-type Brembo units.

The V12/gearbox unit was attached directly to a central monocoque tub and here Formula 1 input was immediately apparent as it was built up from no less than 94 sections of carbon fiber, aluminum and honeycomb which were then oven-baked in McLaren's own facility.

When the F1 was unveiled on the night prior to the 1993 Monaco Grand Prix, which was appropriately won by McLaren, the company announced that just 300 F1s would be built priced at $756,000 apiece. This worked out at $252,000 per occupant because the McLaren was not a two-but a three seater. Unusually the driver sat centrally, the red upholstered seat being set forward of the others. Once so ensconced, the lucky individual would be in charge of one of the fastest, and safest, cars on the road.

With such a pedigree it was natural that the F1 would soon gravitate to the racetrack. The competition GTR version of 1994 was lighter, and with its power upped to a restricted 630bhp it won the 1995 and 1996 GT Championships. It also triumphed at Le Mans in 1995 when these extraordinary McLarens took first, third, fourth, fifth, and thirteenth places. In celebration a handful of 668bhp LM F1s were built. The ultimate GT of 1997 was longer and wider than the original but only eight were produced.

Despite the mouth-watering specifications, demand for the F1 never reached the expected levels and only 100 had been completed by the time production ceased at the end of 1997.

Specification	McLaren F1
Engine location	Mid, in-line
Configuration	V12
Bore and stroke	86 x 87mm
Capacity	6064cc
Valve operation	Twin overhead camshafts per bank
Horsepower	627bhp @ 7400rpm
Transmission	Manual six-speed
Drive	Rear
Chassis	Carbon-fiber monocoque
Suspension – front	Wishbones and coil spring
Suspension – rear	Wishbones and coil spring
Brakes	Ventilated discs
Top speed	240mph (386km/h)
Acceleration	0-60mph (0-96km/h): 3.2 seconds

Left: A bespoke 6 liter BMW V12 even if the covers, that conceal twin overhead camshafts, are marked McLaren. The exhaust system incorporates four catalytic converters.

Below: Open wide! The efficiency of the brakes can be taken as read, the discs being arrested by light alloy four-piston calipers.

Above: Still bearing the dust from its triumph at the 1995 Le Mans event, the winning McLaren was displayed at that year's Goodwood Festival of Speed, which took place only days after the F1's triumph. when Yannick Dalmas, J Lehto, and Masanori Sekiya averaged 104.98mph (168.99km/h) for the 24 hours.

Right: Unusually the F1 driver sits in the middle of the car so the right seat of the 1995 Le Mans-winning car was filled with electronic aids, an indication of the space age technology that now assists drivers of long-distance races.

Roadgoing racer

McLaren's 1995 Le Mans victory underlined the versatility of this extraordinary car. It was the first occasion since the 1940s that a roadgoing model had won the 24 hour event.

An increase in F1 production, coupled with pressure from customers, meant that the car could be homologated for a newly instituted GT racing series. The resulting GTR version was created for the 1995 International GT Endurance Series of races, which began in February of that year. What was effectively a lightened version of the road car was created and it dominated the season to take that year's GT championship, an achievement that the McLaren repeated in 1996.

The 668bhp developed by the BMW V12 was 41bhp more than the original power unit, but the emphasis was placed on reliability rather than flat-out performance. Modifications were confined to stripping out the interior and changes were also made to the suspension with the original compliant mountings replaced by solid anchorage, competition springs, an anti-roll bar, and slick tires.

Outwardly similar, the GTR was, however, immediately identifiable by the presence of a rear wing. Ambitiously, no less than six examples were entered in the GT class for the 1995 Le Mans event. McLaren clearly meant business.

To the collective surprise of commentators and the crowd, pundits opined that the McLarens were too slow. However, GTRs dominated the race and one car, driven by Dalmas, Lehto, and Sekiya, led for all but 11 of the 298 laps. Strong opposition came from a Porsche-engined Courage that was beaten into second place. However, one GTR succumbed to gearbox trouble.

McLaren responded to this triumph by producing the commemorative LM version that was finished in a distinctive orange hue which echoed the team's Formula 1 livery of the 1960s. It sold for nearly $1,119,000, some $230,000 more than the mainstream model. Just five examples were built. Outwardly resembling the standard F1, it featured extra front-brake cooling inlets and a polished

carbon-fiber rear aerofoil courtesy of the GTR. There was also an enlarged central hood duct to feed a rather basic cockpit ventilation system and holes in the top of each rear side window.

The LM weighed in at 2341lb (1062kg), 132lb (60kg) lighter than the GTR and 168lb (76kg) less than the standard F1 for the millionaire-in-the-street. Paradoxically, it was slightly slower than the standard F1, although designer Gordon Murray claimed that it was more fun to drive because it was quicker through the six gears…

Above: The extended tail of the longer and wider GT version of 1997.

Below: A 1996 car, chassis 068. The F1 was a costly coupé with impeccable race-bred credentials – in 1998 an example was timed at 240mph (386km/h).

Ferrari F50

**Top speed
202mph**
325km/h

*Opposite top: The F50 body
is built entirely of race-
proven carbon fiber and the
material also features in the
central monocoque tub
around which the car is
built up. Like the McLaren,
the rear wheels are wider
than the fronts.*

*Below: The view as one
overtakes you! The Ferrari
badge on the front fender
leaves you in no doubt as to
this car's pedigree. Note the
break in the rear wing line,
the rear section of the body
hinges at this point.*

Although Ferrari celebrated its 50th
anniversary in 1997, the commemorative
F50 arrived prematurely in 1995. While
outwardly resembling a 1970s sports racer, at its
heart was one of the company's successful Formula
1 racing cars re-vamped for the road.

The fastest and most powerful Ferrari of its day,
it was based on the 641 series single-seater in
which Alain Prost won six races during the 1990
season. Like so many of its contemporaries, the
F50 was built up around a central tub with a
Nomex honeycomb core skinned in epoxy resin-
bonded carbon fiber. Most of this was concealed by
the bodywork, but the material was also outwardly
apparent, being used for the body panels, seats, and
even the gearlever knob.

Strong retro styling

The Pininfarina-styled body, that was produced in
coupé (with and without a detachable roof) and
open forms, displayed strong retro influences while
the big fixed rear wing was an obligatory fitment.

Both turbocharging and four-wheel drive were
eschewed. Unlike the F40 which had used a blown
V8 engine, the F50 was powered by a mid-located,
longitudinally mounted, 4.7 liter V12 that evolved
from the racer's 3.5 liter unit. Developing 513bhp,

the 109.2bhp per liter made the F50 the most
powerful normally aspirated supercar of its day. In
consequence it was able to reach 60mph (96km/h)
in a blistering 3.7 seconds and could attain 202mph
(325km/h), just 1mph (1.6km/h) faster than its no-
frills F40 predecessor.

Drive was taken by a new six-speed gearbox, although a conventional gate, rather than the usual steering wheel-mounted push button changes, was used. The combined unit was bolted directly to the rear bulkhead.

Instrumentation consisted, in essence, of just a rev counter and speedometer. In line with Formula 1 practice, the blue-hued dials were liquid crystal displays on which the needles only appeared when the ignition was switched on.

Suspension was a compliant system which rapidly responded to road conditions via an electronic control unit. The car's construction was very weight-conscious, and the complete vehicle turned the scales at a respectable 2712lb (1230kg). But relating a road car so closely to Formula 1 technology produced its own problems because noise – the result of shackling the V12, gearbox, and rear suspension directly to the cockpit – proved to be an insuperable obstacle.

Ferrari engineers therefore recognized that customers would have to live with the concept of a racer only mildly tamed for the highways of the world. Production was set at 349 cars and exactly that number was completed by the time the last example appeared on July 30 1997, the year in which Ferrari celebrated its half centenary.

Left: This could be a shot of the engine of a Formula 1 Ferrari, and the F50's is similarly a dry-sump unit. The twin cam heads are made of aluminum although the V12 block is of cast iron. There are no less than five valves per cylinder, three inlet and two exhaust.

Specification	Ferrari F50
Engine location	Mid, in-line
Configuration	V12
Bore and stroke	85 x 69mm
Capacity	4698cc
Valve operation	Twin overhead camshafts per bank
Horsepower	513bhp @ 8000rpm
Transmission	Manual six-speed
Drive	Rear
Chassis	Carbon-fiber composite monocoque
Suspension – front	Wishbones, pushrod and coil spring
Suspension – rear	Wishbones, pushrod and coil spring
Brakes	Ventilated disc
Top speed	202mph (325km/h)
Acceleration	0-60mph (0-96km/h): 3.7 seconds

TVR Cerbera

**Top speed
185mph**
298km/h

TVR, having wooed the public with its Griffith open two-seater of 1990, followed up with another visually stunning model in the form of the two-plus-two Cerbera coupé for the 1994 model year. And the provision, from 1995, of a corporate V8 engine transformed it into a 185mph (298km/h) car.

In its original manifestation, the Cerbera was, in effect, a lengthened version of the Rover V8-engined Chimaera open two-seater of 1993. Low and lithe, the new model, pronounced 'cher-berra,' was offered with a 4 liter Rover V8 engine. Acceleration was brisk, 60mph (96km/h) came up in a little over five seconds and the car possessed a 158mph (254km/h) top speed. However, it did not enter series production and the definitive Cerbera, in the best traditions of the marque, took a little more time to evolve.

A 5 liter Rover-based V8, courtesy of the Griffith 500, was offered as an option, but a much improved Cerbera appeared at the 1994 British Motor Show. It differed mechanically from the original and also benefited from body refinements.

The Cerbera was the first recipient of a TVR-initiated Al Melling-designed 4.2 liter V8 engine which replaced the Rover units from the 1995 season. This remarkable engine developed 350bhp without the usual accompaniment of twin overhead camshafts and four valves per cylinder.

In addition TVR stylists subtly revised the coupé's lines with an extra 3in (76mm) being added to the model's wheelbase. The original low look

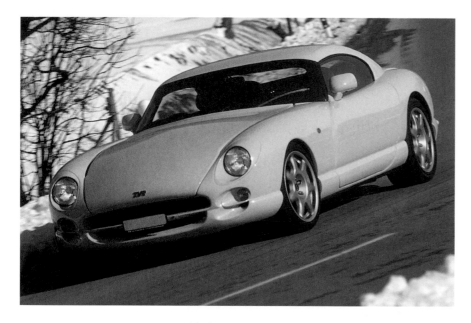

Above: The Cerbera is really a 'two-plus-one' coupé; there isn't much room for rear passengers. Handling is excellent and novel features abound. The electric door releases, for instance, are to be found beneath the side mirrors!

Right: This head-on view of the Cerbera emphasizes its utterly individual, yet strong and functional, shape. As a performance car this TVR could outaccelerate many of its more expensive contemporaries. The model's definitive lines were refined by TVR designers Damian McTaggert and Nick Coughlan.

Left: The view as a Cerbera accelerates away from you. Unlike the Rover V8-based power unit which emitted a disappointingly non-urgent waffle, TVR's own unit sounds rather more purposeful as a distinctive howl emanates from the twin exhaust pipes.

Below: TVR lived up to its reputation for distinctive interiors with this unusual design in which the gauges are mounted on the steering column and viewed through the lower segment of the steering wheel. The asymmetric dashboard is similarly unorthodox.

was maintained but the roof line was modestly raised to permit more headroom for the rear passengers. The headlamps now had smoked fairings.

There were more radical changes inside the car in the form of a symmetrical dashboard with, unusually, some of the instruments attached to the steering column. They could be easily seen through the lower segment of the steering wheel.

Potent speedster

This Cerbera proved itself a potent and exceptionally fast car with some 27mph (43km/h) being added to the top speed and 60mph (96km/h) arriving in a mere four seconds. Not only this. Ride and handling were superior to any previous TVR. This was due to a combination of the lengthened chassis and the additional rigidity imparted by the roof, modifications that were coupled with an ongoing development program.

The quality of the interior, always a bugbear with makers of specialist sports cars, was similarly light years ahead of what TVR had been producing even a few years previously.

Alternative engine options arrived with a 4.5 liter version being offered for 1998. A 4 liter six-cylinder-engined model, the Cerbera Speed Six, followed for 2000. Still being manufactured at the time of writing (2002), the Cerbera continues to delight and inspire a new generation of owners.

Specification	TVR Cerbera
Engine location	Front, in-line
Configuration	V8
Bore and stroke	88 x 86mm
Capacity	4185cc
Valve operation	Single overhead camshaft per cylinder bank
Horsepower	350bhp @ 6500rpm
Transmission	Manual five-speed
Drive	Rear
Chassis	Tubular backbone
Suspension – front	Wishbones and coil spring
Suspension – rear	Wishbones and coil spring
Brakes	Ventilated disc
Top speed	185mph (298km/h)
Acceleration	0-60mph (96km/h): 4 seconds

Bentley Continental T

**Top speed
170mph**
274km/h

*Right: The T's special
interior with engine-turned
aluminum dashboard and
center console. Bentley's
Personal Commission
service enhances interiors
to suit an individual buyer's
own requirements.*

*Below: A Monaco Yellow
Continental T for 2000. The
model has a noticeably
shorter wheelbase than the
original. Great care is taken
with the door furniture, the
interiors of the handles
being carefully knurled.*

The Continental coupé of 1991 had the
distinction of being the first Bentley for
32 years to have its own purpose-designed
bodywork. Hitherto, the magnificently appointed
and refined sedans had been based on the products
of its Rolls-Royce parent company. When this
potent and luxurious grand tourer appeared, it
signalled the emergence of Bentley as the dominant
of the two marques after it had faced near
extinction in the 1970s.

In 1982 the Bentley Mulsanne Turbo sedan had
been unveiled. This was based on its Rolls-Royce
Silver Spirit stablemate with the 6.7 liter V8 engine
turbocharged to produce a 135mph (217km/h) car.
It was followed, in 1985, by the better-handling
Turbo R. Both models had the virtue of
immediately attracting a new, affluent and, above
all, youthful clientele which responded positively to
a revival of Bentley's long dormant performance
profile. In consequence, in 1990 Bentley
production outnumbered Rolls-Royce output for the
first time since the 1950s.

Bespoke body styling

The next step was a bespoke body which was the
work of consulting stylists, John Heffernan and
Ken Greenly. Their Project 90 concept coupé was
displayed at the 1985 Geneva Motor Show and the
public response was sufficiently encouraging for
the company to proceed with the venture. The
Continental R duly appeared six years later at the
1991 Geneva event.

Based on the Turbo R's mechanicals, the model's name was a tribute to Bentley's legendary Continental of the 1951-59 era. The blown V8's output was boosted to 328bhp and this, along with the coupé's better aerodynamics, ensured that the model was able to carry a potential four passengers in considerable comfort at speeds of up to 150mph (241km/h). Bentley had been reborn.

Subsequently, at the 1996 Geneva show, the Crewe-based company unleashed the Continental T which it billed as the fastest Bentley yet. Wider, with a 4in (100mm) shorter wheelbase and lighter than the R on which it was based, engine output was increased to 400bhp. Capable of 170mph (274km/h) and able to reach 60mph (96km/h) in a mere 5.8 seconds, the T was also enhanced by a special interior with mottled aluminum dashboard, red starter button, micro-alloy disc brakes, revised suspension, and electric traction control.

An even faster-accelerating variation on the theme appeared in 2000 with the Special Commission T, identifiable by its aerodynamically refined body lines. A further 20bhp was extracted from the venerable V8 by blueprinting the engine and adjusting the management system.

The seats were upholstered in quilted Connolly leather but there were only two of them. The rear ones were removed to leave space for bespoke matching leather luggage, fittings that were very reminiscent of the sporting Bentleys of the 1920s!

Specification	Bentley Continental T
Engine location	Front, in-line
Configuration	Turbocharged V8
Bore and stroke	104 x 91mm
Capacity	6750cc
Valve operation	Pushrod
Horsepower	400bhp @ 4000rpm
Transmission	Automatic four-speed
Drive	Rear
Chassis	Unitary
Suspension – front	Wishbones and coil spring
Suspension – rear	Semi-trailing arm and coil spring
Brakes	Ventilated disc
Top speed	170mph (274km/h)
Acceleration	0-60mph (0-96km/h): 5.8 seconds

Left: The visually enhanced appearance of the Bentley Continental T's venerable aluminum V8 engine, which dates back in essence to 1959. Less apparent is the presence of the Garrett turbocharger, Bosch Jetronic fuel injection and Zytek engine management system. An electronic traction system momentarily cuts back the engine if the wheels slip or spin.

Left: When a Continental T is on the move, and during spirited acceleration and cornering, the car's viscous control differential transfers power from a spinning wheel to one with traction. This is because of the substantial amount of power and torque, to the tune of 645lb/ft at 2100rpm, developed by the big V8.

Subaru Impreza WRX STi

**Top speed
150mph**
241km/h

*Below: One of the 424
Impreza replicas that
Subaru produced in 1998 to
commemorate the fact that
it had won the World Rally
Championship for the three
successive years between
1995 and 1997. Powered by
a 2.2 'flat' four engine, it
developed some 250bhp.*

 Like Lancia's Integrale, the Impreza is a deceptive car. Introduced in 1993, outwardly it looked an unexciting model but it combined outstanding handling with formidable reliability, particularly when let loose on the rally field. In consequence Subaru won the World Rally Championship for three successive years between 1995 and 1997.

Subaru has come a long way since its first model, the diminutive rear-engined glass-fiber-bodied 360 of 1958, was described in an American consumer report as 'the most unsafe car on the market.' This one-time motor scooter manufacturer learned quickly. In 1966 it introduced an unfashionable four-cylinder horizontally opposed 'flat' engine in its FF-1 sedan. Then it offered a four-wheel-drive version of its Leone model in 1973 and became more ambitious when it extended turbocharging to its engines in 1981.

The company moved upmarket with its Legacy sedan of 1989 and the cheaper Impreza followed in 1993. This employed four-wheel drive that could be either permanently or optionally engaged. Produced in sedan form or as a five-door hatchback, the Impreza was powered by Subaru's usual horizontally opposed four-cylinder engine that was available in 1.5, 1.6, and 1.8 liter guises. Single overhead camshafts were fitted to each cylinder bank with four valves per cylinder.

While on the debit side this meant poor accessibility, certainly compared with an in-line or transverse engine, nevertheless the 'flat' four, with

Left: Richard Burns, England's first World Rally champion, shows how it's done during his triumphant 2001 season at the wheel of his Subaru which came fourth in a series which was won by Peugeot.

Below: For 2002 the Subaru Impreza Sti will be available to British customers in two forms. There is the standard model (left), able to attain 148mph (238km/h). Its deeply spoilered Sti Prodrive neighbor is named after the company which prepares the rally cars.

its low center of gravity, made a positive contribution to the model's superlative handling.

Commitment to competition

Subaru had rallied a Legacy RS Turbo with some success and it renewed its commitment to competition with the Impreza WRX. The turbocharged and reworked 2 liter engine with twin cam heads produced no less than 240bhp. For homologation purposes, 2500 examples of a road car were built. It was outwardly identifiable by the presence of a large hood scoop, wide alloy wheels, a deep front air dam, and twin fog lights.

A coupé version of the Impreza arrived in 1994 and this formed the basis of the 22B rally version which was specially constructed by the corporate motorsport division, Tecnica International, and prepared by Prodrive of Banbury, Oxfordshire.

The WRX was soon proving its worth, although in 1993-94 international rallying was dominated by Toyota. However, in 1995 the Impeza gave Subaru its first ever World Rally Championship win and its star performer, Colin McRae, won the driver's title – the first Briton to attain that accolade. Subaru was to repeat the triumph in the next two years, although in 1998 it lost out to Mitsubishi.

This first generation Impreza was replaced in 2000 by a new version which retained its proven, successful and unusual mechanicals. After all, if ain't broke, don't fix it!

Specification	**Subaru** Impreza WRX STi
Engine location	Front, in-line
Configuration	Horizontally opposed four-cylinder
Bore and stroke	92 x 75mm
Capacity	1994cc
Valve operation	Twin overhead camshafts per cylinder bank
Horsepower	280bhp @ 6500rpm
Transmission	Manual five-speed
Drive	Four-wheel
Chassis	Unitary
Suspension – front	MacPherson strut
Suspension – rear	MacPherson strut dual link, anti-roll bar
Brakes	Ventilated disc
Top speed	150mph (241km/h)
Acceleration	0-60mph (96km/h): 4.7 seconds

Jaguar XKR

**Top speed
155mph***
249km/h
*limited

*Right: Although the XK8 on
which the R is based can be
regarded as the E-Type's
successor, it is a much more
refined product and is only
available with automatic
transmission.*

*Below: The Jaguar XKR is
distinguished by its meshed
radiator grille that is
similar to that on the XJR
sedan which shares the
same 4 liter supercharged
engine. Note the absence
of bumpers.*

The XKR, which Jaguar claims is its
fastest-accelerating car, can reach 60mph
(96km/h) in just 5.2 seconds. It made its
debut at the 1998 Geneva Motor Show. That was
two years after the XK8, on which it is based,
appeared at the same venue.

Available in coupé and convertible forms which
revealed plenty of visual reminders of its famous E-
Type forebear, the XK8 of 1996 was an all-new car
powered by a 4 liter, 290bhp, V8 twin-cam engine
that was making its debut in the model. However,
refinement was the order of the day because it was
only available with five-speed automatic
transmission courtesy of Mercedes-Benz.

The engine was subsequently extended to the
existing XJ6 sedan which was accordingly
transformed into the XJ8 for the 1998 season. A
new XJR supercharged version, in which the V8
was enhanced by the fitment of a Eaton M112
blower boosting output to 370bhp, was capable of a
limited 155mph (249km/h) top speed and was able
to hit 60mph (96km/h) figure in 5.3 seconds.

50th anniversary

The similarly upgunned XKR followed at the 1998
Geneva event, which was also the 50th anniversary
of the introduction of Jaguar's legendary XK120
sports car. The XKR shaved a second off the blown
sedan's time to 60mph (96km/h), attaining this
figure in the aforesaid 5.2 seconds, while the top
speed remained the same.

Left: The XKR 100 of 2001 is a limited edition model created to commemorate the centenary of the birth of Jaguar's founder, William Lyons. Enhancements include matt black finish, '100' badges, and alloy wheels in the manner of the impending F-Type sports car. Some XJR sedans are similarly enhanced.

Below: The model also gets a black leather interior, sports steering wheel, Momo gearknob, DVD satellite navigation system, reverse park control, and automatic windshield wipers. Production is limited to 1000 examples of all three cars.

Although outwardly resembling the XK8, the R, which is available in both open and closed forms, was easily identifiable by its bright mesh radiator grille. This provided a visual link with the XJR sedan that sports a similar feature.

When the blown 4 liter V8 engine was transferred to the sports car, adequate cooling became a major factor, so two louvered panels were set into the hood to let the hot air out. A red background to the Jaguar radiator badge, alloy wheels, and a discreet rear lip were the only other identifying features.

The XKR is also enhanced by the presence of CATS, which stands for Computer Active Technology Suspension. As its name suggests, this provides electronically controlled adaptive damping, but the damper settings were also altered to make the car's handling even firmer.

Limited edition

To celebrate Jaguar's entry to Formula 1 in 2000, the company produced the limited edition XKR Silverstone with uprated suspension, enhanced interior and silver, rather than the usual gold, alloy wheels. The engine was unchanged; just as in the mainstream model, you might think that you were in a standard XK8, that is until you pressed hard on the accelerator…

Specification	Jaguar XKR
Engine location	Front, in-line
Configuration	Supercharged V8
Bore and stroke	86 x 86mm
Capacity	3996cc
Valve operation	Twin overhead camshafts per bank
Horsepower	370bhp @ 6150rpm
Transmission	Automatic five-speed
Drive	Rear
Chassis	Unitary
Suspension – front	Wishbones and coil spring
Suspension – rear	Wishbones and coil spring
Brakes	Ventilated disc
Top speed	Limited to 155mph (249km/h)
Acceleration	0-60mph (96km/h): 5.2 seconds

Mercedes-Benz CLK-GTR

**Top speed
199mph**
320km/h

*Below: Awesome and
purposeful, the radiator and
headlamp treatment of the
CLK-GTR was shared with
the CLK coupé; this road-
tamed racer even
incorporates Mercedes-
Benz's famous tri-star
mascot. Although often
regarded as a successor to
the 300SL coupé of the
1950s, the doors are not
of the gullwing variety
although the car does
possess a similarly high
sill line.*

 With a price tag of $1.5 million, the CLK-GTR Mercedes-Benz of 1998 is not only the most expensive car in this book, it is still, at the time of writing, the company's fastest road car, being capable of 199mph (320km/h).

It is a spiritual successor to the fabled 300SL gullwing coupé of 1954-57, although it does not possess such memorable doors, using front-mounted scissor ones instead of gullwings. It was conceived as a roadgoing version of the company's racer which won the 1997 and 1998 GT championships. Homologation required that just one road car should be made, but Mercedes-Benz, which approved the project in March 1997, decided to build a 'small quantity' for private customers. The first of the strictly two-seater coupés was delivered in November 1998 with the last of 25 examples being finished in the summer of 1999.

Built in batches of three, each taking four to six weeks to complete, the work was undertaken by AMG at its factory at Ludwigsburg near Stuttgart. Since 1998 AMG had been Mercedes-Benz's in-house performance arm. The car only differed in detail from the track-ready GTRs. The Kevlar bodyshell was reinforced, the suspension retuned to increase the ride height, and 18in (457mm) wheels were fitted. Inside there were sports seats, three-point safety belts, twin air bags, and an integrated roll cage.

There were visual reminders of the newly introduced CLK coupé although these were confined to the radiator grille, the four headlamps, and instrumentation.

Racer tamed for the road

Built up around a carbon-fiber monocoque, the car's occupants could be in little doubt that this was a racer tamed for the road. Mounted longitudinally and directly attached to the rear bulkhead in the manner of the Ferrari F50, the 6.8 liter unit was based on the 5.9 liter V12 used in the S600 passenger models but developed by the UK-based Ilmor Engineering. Developing 612bhp with a massive 572lb/ft of torque, it raucously drove the rear wheels through a six-speed manual gearbox which was operated by twin paddles located behind the steering wheel. Unlike the similar unit used by Ferrari, the CLK-GTR was fitted with a clutch. Acceleration was astounding with 62mph (100km/h) arriving in just 3.8 seconds.

Interestingly, this latter day 'silver arrow' was diametrically opposed in concept to McLaren's celebrated F1 which featured racing technology in a car that was specifically designed for road use. This awesome Mercedes-Benz coupé was, by contrast, a racer tamed for the highway. In consequence, it was fitted with power steering, power brakes, and traction control, all refinements that were noticeably absent from the F1.

Specification	Mercedes-Benz CLK-GTR
Engine location	Mid, in-line
Configuration	V12
Bore and stroke	89 x 92mm
Capacity	6898cc
Valve operation	Twin overhead camshafts per bank
Horsepower	612bhp @ 6800rpm
Transmission	Manual six-speed
Drive	Rear
Chassis	Carbon-fiber monocoque
Suspension – front	Wishbones, pullrod and coil spring
Suspension – rear	Wishbones, pullrod and coil spring
Brakes	Ventilated disc
Top speed	199mph (320km/h)
Acceleration	0-62mph (0-100km/h): 3.8 seconds

Above: Although it is not a particularly practical road car, the 'Silver Arrow' could not be anything but a Mercedes-Benz. The body panels are made of Kevlar and the rear spoiler is an essential aid to produce stability and downforce.

Left: The cockpit is a little congested although safety features abound with the presence of an integrated roll-over cage, and airbags for driver and passenger.

Maserati 3200GT

**Top speed
174mph**
280km/h

*Right: The long-awaited
Spyder convertible which
arrived for the 2002 season
is powered by a new
Ferrari-developed 4.2 liter
V8 engine. The Ital Design-
styled open car is
distinguished by its
conventional rear lights
which differ from the
coupé's distinctive 'hockey
stick'-shaped lenses.*

*Below: Hot Maserati: the
Asetto Corsa 3200 of 2001
with a special handling
pack that includes variable
suspension settings and
tauter springs. It marks the
end of the line for Maserati's
long-running 3.2 liter
V8 engine.*

n 1993 Maserati, after suffering decades
of corporate uncertainty, was acquired by
Fiat. The first outward fruits of this
change of ownership was the arrival, in 1998, of
the 3200GT coupé, a car capable of over 170mph
(274km/h). The omens looked good.

Work on the project began following the 1993
take-over and a coupé concept was commissioned
from Ital Design. The new model was to be
powered by Maserati's proven 3.2 liter V8 engine
but it was extensively revised to the extent that no
less than 90 per cent of the component parts were
new. In 1997 management of the company was
assigned to in-house Ferrari, with the Maserati
range being priced some 25 per cent below the
products of its erstwhile rival.

Announced at the 1998 Paris Motor Show, the
3200 represented a clean break for a company that
had previously been starved of investment to the
extent that build quality had been compromised.
Not only was the worth of the new coupé, a
genuine two-plus-two, apparent for all to see, its
lines were soberly executed so as not to clash with
the more visually extravagant Pininfarina-styled
Ferraris. The 3200 was evidently aimed at Aston
Martin DB7 and Jaguar XK8 territory.

With a claimed top speed of 174mph (280km/h)
and a credited 0-62mph (100km/h) figure of 5.1

seconds, in the main the 3200 lived up to
expectations. It also boasted traction control and
adaptive damping. Its impressive performance and
high speed stability reflected the results of many
hours of wind-tunnel testing.

Automatic option

It was originally fitted with a manual six-speed
Getrag gearbox, but some commentators found this
heavy in operation until the oil warmed up, and the
clutch less than smooth A welcome automatic
option arrived in 1999. Its top speed of 168mph
(270km/h) and acceleration rate were, inevitably,
slightly down on the manual version. But it had the
virtue of being easier to drive than the original.

Also new for 2001 was the more potent Assetto Corsa (Racing Order) version with uprated anti-roll bar, tauter springs, and unique 15 spoke alloy wheels. Just 350 were produced which marked the end of Maserati's twin turbocharged V8 engine.

A long heralded Spyder (open) version of the 3200 entered production for 2002, it having been preceded by the Barchetta, a no-frills sports racer developed specially for the 2001 Geneva show. Built on a shortened version of the coupé's platform, with 8.7in (220mm) removed from the wheelbase, the Spyder was powered by a new 4 liter V8 engine that, more significantly, was also extended to the coupé. This is lighter than the original and potentially higher revving. Its arrival will herald Maserati's return to the all-important American market.

Above: Nice lines – the 3200GT with the classic outline of the Ital Design-styled coupé body shown to advantage.

Left: The Spyder of 2002. The wheelbase of this open car is 8.7in (220mm) shorter than the coupé's and it boasts computer-controlled suspension.

Below left: The Spyder's well-appointed cockpit is upholstered in leather and features hi-tech navigational aids.

Specification	Maserati 3200
Engine location	Front, in-line
Configuration	V8
Bore and stroke	80 x 80mm
Capacity	3217cc
Valve operation	Twin overhead camshafts per cylinder bank
Horsepower	370bhp @ 6250rpm
Transmission	Manual six-speed
Drive	Rear
Chassis	Unitary
Suspension – front	Wishbones and coil spring
Suspension – rear	Wishbones and coil spring
Brakes	Ventilated disc
Top speed	174mph (280km/h)
Acceleration	0-62mph (100km/h): 5.1 seconds

Audi TT

**Top speed
145mph**
233km/h

*Right: Audi's stylistically
adventurous TT. This is the
more powerful 225bhp
version in which four-wheel
drive is a compulsory
fitting. Sure-footed and
rapid, this turbocharged
model has sold well.*

*Below: A TT roadster of
2000. Unlike the coupé
version, this is strictly a
two-seater with obligatory
roll-over bars for driver
and passenger protection.
The distinctive wheels
echoed those of the Bugatti
marque of the 1920s.*

Outwardly unconventional, stylistically distinctive and capable in its most potent form of 145mph (233km/h), Audi's TT is a skilful combination of old and new themes. It comes courtesy of the hi-tech arm of Volkswagen's growing family of marques.

Like Porsche's Boxster and the Dodge Viper, the TT sprang from a concept car. It was conceived at Audi's California-based design center and from the outset its stylist, Freeman Thomas, drew inspiration from German Bauhaus design themes of the 1930s.

Appearing in coupé form at the 1995 Frankfurt Motor Show, the TT was based on the floorpan of Audi's impending A3 hatchback of 1996, and thus by extension the new generation VW Golf. It was powered by the transversely mounted 1.7 liter twin-overhead-camshaft four-cylinder engine used in the corporate A4 sedan line.

Such was the enthusiastic reception accorded to the TT that Audi decided to put it into production, first as a coupé and then in open form, the latter concept having been revealed at the 1995 Tokyo show. Outwardly almost identical to the original

concept car, apart from the addition of rear quarterlights and an enlarged air intake, the TT coupé was launched at the 1998 Paris Motor Show.

With 3.5in (89mm) removed from the A3/Golf platform, the stubby TT was offered with a choice of power units. Both used essentially the same turbocharged, 1.7 liter, four-cylinder, twin-overhead-camshaft/five valves per cylinder engine which powered the Audi A3 and A4 and Volkswagen's Golf GTi.

Plenty of choice

However, turbo pressure was boosted so that the entry level TT unit developed 180bhp. This produced a top speed of 140mph (225km/h) with 60mph (96km/h) arriving in 7.1 seconds. Four-wheel drive came with a Haldex electronically controlled clutch as its heart, but the car was also offered with the option of front-wheel drive. There was a choice of five- or six-speed gearboxes.

However, the top-line 225bhp version was only specified with four driven wheels. Increased power meant that it could attain 145mph (233km/h) and it was about one second quicker to 60mph (96km/h). This coupé is, in truth, just a two-plus-two.

The roadster version made its public debut at the 1999 Geneva Motor Show and, like its closed counterpart, it bore a close visual similarity to the TT concept car although every panel was subtly altered and it was 1.5in (38mm) longer. But, unlike the coupé, it is a strictly a two-seater.

Built in Hungary, in 2000 Audi celebrated the production of the 100,000th TT and there is an even faster version in the offing with a rumored 265bhp on tap.

Below left: The cockpit of the TT coupé is replete with echoes of Bauhaus design themes from the 1930s.

Below: A TT coupé of 2000 with a rear spoiler introduced, along with suspension modifications, to address safety scares (now resolved) that surfaced soon after its unveiling.

Specification	Audi TT
Engine location	Front, transverse
Configuration	Turbocharged four-cylinder
Bore and stroke	81 x 86mm
Capacity	1781cc
Valve operation	Twin overhead camshafts
Horsepower	225bhp @ 5900rpm
Transmission	Manual six-speed
Drive	Four wheel
Chassis	Unitary
Suspension – front	MacPherson strut and wishbone
Suspension – rear	Wishbones and coil spring
Brakes	Ventilated disc
Top speed	145mph (233km/h)
Acceleration	0-60mph (96km/h): 6.2 seconds

Aston Martin DB7 Vantage

**Top speed
185mph**
298km/h

*Below: The Vantage coupé
and Volante versions of the
DB7, a line that dates from
1993 and which was
enhanced in 1999 by the
arrival of V12 power.*

 In 1999 Aston Martin uprated its
superlative DB7 coupé with essentially the
same 5.9 V12 engine that was later used
in the Vanquish. As a result the enhanced model
has been transformed into a 185mph (298km/h) car.

The DB7 owes its origins to the fact that Aston
Martin and Jaguar are both owned by Ford, which
acquired the businesses in 1987 and 1989
respectively. Jaguar had been working on the so-
called F-Type, a spiritual successor to the legendary
E, and this was re-thought soon after Ford took
control. In the event the concept was sidelined but

the work was not wasted because it formed the
basis of the DB7.

Walter Hayes, who took over as Aston Martin's
chairman during the trough of the world economic
depression in 1991, needed little prompting to
recognize that the company urgently needed a
second, cheaper line to sell in higher volumes than
its $186,000 Virage which, in any event, had failed
to fire the public's imagination.

In 1992 an agreement was forged with Tom
Walkinshaw's TWR Racing based at Bloxham,
Oxfordshire which was where Jaguar's XJ220

Left: The Volante version of the DB7 was introduced in 1996. Its Vantage V12-engined equivalent arrived, like the coupé, in 1999. The open model is a beautifully refined car and is also produced at Aston Martin's Oxfordshire factory.

Below: The 5.9 V12 engine which powers the DB7 Vantage and, in essence, the Vanquish began life as two Ford Duratec V6 engines mounted end to end. It was magnificently refined by in-house Cosworth.

supercar was being produced. The outcome, in 1993, was the visually stunning 165mph (265km/h) DB7 which made its sensational debut at the Geneva Motor Show. A two-plus-two coupé and a triumph for its stylist, Ian Callum, it revealed echoes of the fabled DB4/6 series of cars.

Six-cylinder supercharged engine

It was six-cylinder-powered and the engine was a TWR-developed supercharged 3.2 liter version of Jaguar's AJ6 unit, courtesy of the XJ6 sedan. The DB7's Jaguar origins were also reflected by the fact it used a modified XJS floorpan.

Priced at $110,000, a significant $76,000 less than the Virage, production did not begin until 1994. The DB7 was found to live up to its looks with good roadholding and outstanding ride. It was able to attain 60mph (96km/h) in a little over its claimed 5.5 seconds.

Six years after the model's debut, the 1999 Geneva event played host to what was named the DB7 Vantage, the six-cylinder engine having been replaced by a Ford-based 5.9 liter V12 unit developed by in-house Cosworth Engineering. It added some 20mph (32km/h) to the model's top speed and shaved 0.5 second from the 0-60mph (96km/h) figure.

Outwardly identifiable by its larger frontal air intake and changes to its sills, although the six remained in production for a time, the DB7 is, at the time of writing (2002), exclusively 12-cylinder-powered. Together with the acclaimed Vanquish of 2001, Aston Martin is now really motoring!

Specification	Aston Martin DB7 Vantage
Engine location	Front, in-line
Configuration	Supercharged V12
Bore and stroke	89 x 79mm
Capacity	5935cc
Valve operation	Twin overhead camshaft per cylinder bank
Horsepower	420bhp @ 6000rpm
Transmission	Manual six-speed
Drive	Rear
Chassis	Unitary
Suspension – front	Wishbones and coil spring
Suspension – rear	Wishbones and coil spring
Brakes	Disc, ventilated at front
Top speed	185mph (298km/h)
Acceleration	0-60mph (96km/h): 5 seconds

Panoz AIV

**Top speed
130mph**
209km/h

Below: There isn't a lot of room in the AIV's cockpit. The instruments are courtesy of Mustang Cobra and easy to read. However, you sit high and the tops of the doors are low, so you're exposed to plenty of buffeting!

Below right: The body, like the space-frame it conceals, is made from aluminum and defies description while the windshield comes courtesy of the Volkswagen Super Beetle. The badge on the hood incorporates the Irish shamrock, a pointer to the origins of the Panoz marque.

 It's rare, raucous, and rapid. For this V8-engined open two-seater, which rather resembles a beached whale on wheels, is perfect transport for the enthusiast who wants something a little different (gulp) from the norm.

Panoz Auto Developments, based in Georgia, USA, sold its first cars in 1992 with a chassis based on the Irish-built TMC kit car of 1983-88 vintage. This unlikely liaison occurred because Donald Panoz, whose father emigrated to America from Italy in the early 1900s, established Elan Pharmaceuticals in Ireland. In 1988 his 26-year-old son, Daniel, applied for a job with the Thompson Motor Company, only to find that it was in the process of being liquidated.

He duly acquired the rights to the space-frame that had been designed by Frank Costin, a man whose distinguished engineering career embraced the design of the Vanwall, Lotus Mark 8, and Marcos chassis. In 1989 Panoz established a factory at Hoschton, some 50 miles (80km) from Atlanta, and in 1997 he entered a GT at Le Mans, initiating a commitment to the event that continues to this day.

As far as its road cars were concerned, Panoz engineers replaced the TMC's original four-cylinder Ford units with a 5 liter V8 engine, courtesy of the Ford Mustang, and this evolved into the AIV open two-seater of 1996. The services of stylist Freeman Thomas, who had essayed the lines of the Audi TT, were retained and he came up with the distinctive open two-seater cycle-winged aluminum body that, it should be said, looks like nothing else on the road.

Aluminum intensive

The original space-frame was replaced by a modern and considerably lighter aluminum backbone chassis and this metallic theme was extended to the engine which was a new Ford alloy 4.6 liter V8 with twin-cam heads and 32 valves. Now the reason for the AIV name, it stands for Aluminum Intensive Vehicle, becomes apparent.

If the styling is controversial, there is no argument about this Panoz's performance, notwithstanding the provision of a five-speed

Specification	**Panoz** AIV
Engine location	Front, in-line
Configuration	V8
Bore and stroke	90.2 x 90mm
Capacity	4601cc
Valve operation	Twin overhead camshafts per cylinder bank
Horsepower	305bhp @ 5800rpm
Transmission	Automatic five-speed
Drive	Rear
Chassis	Backbone
Suspension – front	Wishbones and coil spring
Suspension – rear	Wishbones and coil spring
Brakes	Disc, ventilated at front
Top speed	130mph (209km/h)
Acceleration	0-60 mph (96 km/h): 4.5 seconds

energy-absorbing automatic gearbox. With its excellent power-to-weight ratio, the AIV can sprint to 60mph (96km/h) in 4.5 seconds, reach the ton in 13.5 and it has a top speed of 130mph (209km/h).

Behind the wheel you can feel the full effects of this performance which is accompanied by buffeting aplenty. The robust chassis, coupled with all-round wishbones suspension, means that the AIV corners like a racer. Perhaps it's not everyone's cup of tea, but how boring the motor industry would be without such imaginative excursions into unorthodoxy.

Above left: Panoz's Esperante of 2000 is, in effect, a conventionally bodied AIV, which has now ceased production. It has a Ford Mustang engine.

BMW M5

**Top speed
160mph**
257km/h

*Below: A picture is worth a
thousand words: an M5 at
speed. The understated
5-series modifications
include twin scoops in the
front bumper which feed the
engine's induction system
while the fog lights are oval
and headlights xeon. Less
discernible is the radiator
chrome surround that is
wider than usual.*

 The M5 is a car that refused to die. When
in 1996 BMW launched its current 5
series, it did not include its acclaimed and
potent M5 version in it, maintaining that its top-of-
the-range 540i would do double duty as such. But
its competitors thought otherwise so BMW revived
the M5 concept for the 1999 season to beat off the
competition. The outcome is a sports sedan with
outstanding handling that is capable of exceeding
160mph (257km/h).

M stands for Motorsport – the Munich company
established this division in 1972. One of its roles
was to produce specially modified versions of
BMW's already impressively engineered sports
sedans. The first M5 appeared in 1980 but it
differed from its successors in being powered by
the 3.5 liter six-cylinder engine used in BMW's
sports racing M1. However, the M5 which set the

benchmark for future models of the same name
arrived in 1985, and the second-generation version
following in 1990. This survived until 1996.

Significantly more power

Then there was a hiatus until the third-generation
M5 broke cover for 1999. Like its predecessors,
external modifications were kept to a minimum. Its
starting point was the already outstanding 4.3 liter
V8-powered 540i. At its heart was a 4.9 liter V8
which BMW claimed was 95 per cent new. With an
output of 400bhp, a significant 114bhp more than
that developed by the 540 unit on which it was
based, almost every component was different and
engine efficiency was enhanced by a Vanor variable
valve timing system.

A drive-by-wire throttle was fitted and flicking
a *Sport* button on the dashboard produced a more

Specification	**BMW** M5
Engine location	Front, in-line
Configuration	V8
Bore and stroke	94 x 89mm
Capacity	4941cc
Valve operation	Twin overhead camshafts per cylinder bank
Horsepower	400bhp @ 6600rpm
Transmission	Manual six-speed
Drive	Rear
Chassis	Unitary
Suspension – front	MacPherson strut
Suspension – rear	Multi link and coil spring
Brakes	Ventilated disc
Top speed	160mph (257km/h)
Acceleration	0-60mph (96km/h): 5.4 seconds

rapid response from the car than the normal setting allowed. Adjustments were also made to the steering to provide the driver with easier parking and straight line precision.

Important modifications were made to the suspension which was lowered by 0.6in (15mm) at the front and 0.4in (10mm) at the rear with the springs and dampers uprated accordingly. With gunmetal alloy wheels peculiar to the model, the M5 was also distinguished by the presence of four – rather than the usual two – exhaust pipes.

Aimed foursquare at the enthusiast, the M5's interior features bespoke seats for four which provides greater comfort and support than those fitted to the rest of the 5 series models. In short the M5 does everything expected of it. BMW is not likely to let such a desirable variant lapse again!

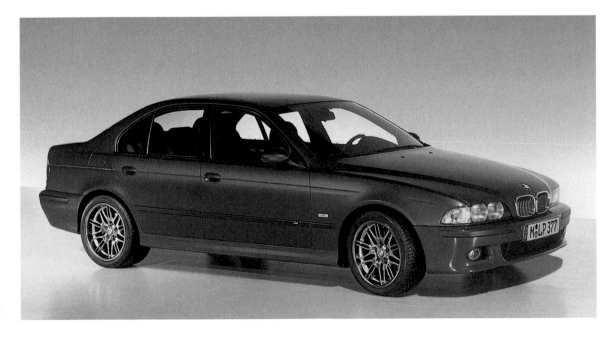

Above left: The alloy 4.9 liter 400bhp V8. Note the precision twin induction pipes uppermost on the left and the outer banks of cam boxes just visible.

Above: The alloy wheels have a satin finish and the famous M5 badge is mounted low on the right of the trunk lid.

Left: The M5's bespoke streamlined side mirrors fold up out of the way to improve aerodynamics.

Shelby Series 1

**Top speed
170mph***
274km/h
*Claimed by
manufacturer

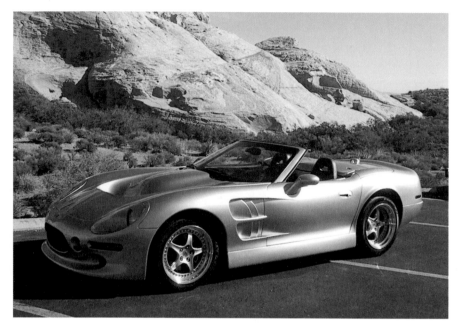

Spiritual successor to the legendary AC Cobra of the 1960s, Carroll Shelby's Series 1 is a potent 170mph (274km/h) open two-seater from the American master of performance motoring. Unlike his previous projects which were based on other manufacturers' cars, this car is purpose-designed, although it does employ a proprietary engine.

Announced at the 1997 Detroit Motor Show, the Series 1 was based on a square-section tubular steel chassis enhanced with a carbon-fiber and glass-fiber body replete with Ferrari and Cobra themes. However, after some 50 years of being associated with Ford projects, the Series 1 is powered by a 4 liter General Motors V8, courtesy of Oldsmobile's Aurora sedan.

In a bid to reduce weight, the original chassis was dispensed with and replaced by an aluminum space-frame. The all-round coil and wishbone suspension was also aluminum-based. A modification was also made to the gearbox which in the 1997 show car was mounted in unit with the engine. Production versions have a ZF transaxle with power being delivered by a torque tube which also has a structural role.

The Detroit event also provided Shelby with the opportunity of gauging public reaction to the interior which originally reflected a stark, no-frills specification. By contrast, the production Series 1 is far better equipped and has air conditioning, electric windows, and a CD player.

Most of the interior fittings come from the GM parts bin but the leather upholstered seats are peculiar to the car and are the work of Shelby, a one-time racing driver, himself.

Above: The Shelby's body, made from carbon and glass fiber, which is replete with European and American retro themes. The hood bulge has a practical function and conceals a duct to expel hot air away from the radiator.

Right: The distinctive spoilered tail is readily apparent as are the vents on the front fenders. Apart from having a decorative function, they permit heated air generated by the front disc brakes to escape. The car is only produced in left-hand-drive form.

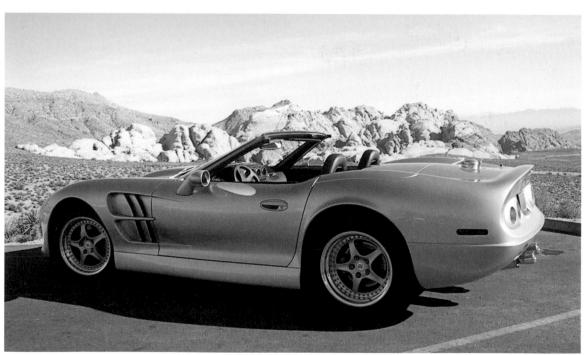

Speedway tuition

The extensive use of lightweight materials means that the Shelby turns the scale at 2597lb (1178kg), and it can reach 60mph (96km/h) in well below five seconds. On the road, in addition to its accelerative qualities, the Shelby has been praised for its predictable roadholding and excellent steering. Production is based at Shelby's new factory located alongside the Las Vegas Speedway and included in the car's price is a day's tuition around the circuit.

The Shelby experienced a protracted birth and production did not begin until 2000. And the original price, a very reasonable $88,200, has risen to a more viable $113,000, because Venture Industries, an American engineering concern, has taken a 75 per cent stake in the business. This has meant increased production and an improvement in build quality.

Above: The well-equipped cockpit is in contrast to the first version of the car.

Left: The Shelby's strictly two-seater styling should stand the test of time.

Below left: The console which is faced with carbon fiber contains both a radio and a CD player.

Specification	Shelby Series 1
Engine location	Front in-line
Configuration	V8
Bore and stroke	87 x 84mm
Capacity	3995cc
Valve operation	Twin overhead camshafts per cylinder bank
Horsepower	320bhp @ 6500rpm
Transmission	Manual six-speed
Drive	Rear
Chassis	Space-frame
Suspension – front	Wishbones and coil spring
Suspension – rear	Wishbones and coil spring
Brakes	Ventilated disc
Top speed	170mph (274km/h)*
Acceleration	0-60mph (96km/h): 4.4 seconds*

*Manufacturer's claim

Pagani Zonda C12

**Top speed
200mph***
322km/h
*Claimed by
manufacturer

*Right: The Mercedes-Benz
6 liter V12 engine has been
enhanced by AMG, the
company's in-house tuner
and engine enhancer.
Having initially powered
the discontinued S-type
sedan, it has been easily
adapted to its new
mid-location.*

*Above: Other drivers will
be in no mistake that they
have a Pagani in front of
them. The inspiration for
this cluster of quadruple
exhaust pipes is the
American space program.
NASA has got a lot to
answer for!*

*Right: The Zonda S with its
distinctive split rear spoiler
uses a more powerful 7 liter
engine. Other outward
changes have been made to
the distinctive carbon-fiber
body which amply reflects
the car's impressive
performance.*

One of the latest recruits to the supercar
league, the Pagani is a sensationally
styled mid-engined coupé with a claimed
top speed of 200mph (322km/h). It is the brainchild
of Argentinian-born Horacio Pagani, who as a
young man became friends with his fellow
countryman, five times world motor racing
champion Juan Fangio. The latter's letter of
introduction to Maserati's former chief engineer,
Giulio Alfieri, then at Lamborghini, resulted in
Pagani obtaining a job there.

Concentrating on styling and recognizing the
potential of light and immensely strong carbon-
fiber structures, Pagani was responsible for the
lines of the Countach Anniversary model of 1988.
However, soon afterwards he left Lamborghini to
set up Modena Engineering to concentrate on
design and carbon-fiber technology, and he soon
built up an international clientele of customers.

Then he decided to produce his own car which
he originally intended to name Fangio, after his
mentor. Although he eventually settled for Zonda,
which means wind from the Andes, the former
champion's influence is apparent in Pagani's use of
a Mercedes engine. Mechanically inspired by the
Sauber-Mercedes sports racers, he claims that the
body lines were influenced by the voluptuous
contours of his wife Cristina's figure!

Sensational debut

The Zonda made a sensational debut at the 1999
Geneva Motor Show. The chassis was a
combination of a carbon-fiber backbone and steel
space-frames at either end. It was powered by a
V12 Mercedes-Benz 6 liter engine, courtesy of its
recently discontinued S series cars. Longitudinally
located, it drives the rear wheels via a five-speed
ZF gearbox. Weighing just 2756lb (1250kg), its
makers claimed, optimistically as it turned out, a
0-60mph (96km/h) figure of under four seconds.

Left: The Zonda's lines take visual inspiration from Pagani's wife Cristina and the wind tunnel. The front of the Zonda S (below) has a more clearly defined nose and repositioned headlights.

Below left: The current Zonda is fitted with a factory developed six-speed gearbox which replaces the original five-cog ZF unit. Early owners will be able to upgrade to the later gearbox.

Following the Geneva debut, Pagani announced that it would also be offering an even faster version with the engine enlarged to 7 liters and enhanced by Mercedes-Benz's in-house tuner AMG. Appearing at the 2000 Geneva event, this version was designated the Zonda S and it differed outwardly from the base model in having a more clearly defined nose with the aerofoil, that had been a feature of the 1999 car, now divided – a modification which also makes a contribution to the car's extraordinary visual impact.

It also differed mechanically in possessing a Pagani-developed six-speed gearbox which replaced the five-cog ZF original. Although longer by 1.9in (50mm) than the standard C12, its makers say that weight remains the same, so enhancing acceleration and top speed.

By the time of the Geneva show, Pagani claimed that he had built nine cars, a total which included pre-production versions, and had orders for another five. His aim is to build 25 cars a year.

Specification	**Pagani** Zonda C12
Engine location	Mid, longitudinal
Configuration	V12
Bore and stroke	89 x 80mm
Capacity	5987cc
Valve operation	Twin overhead camshafts per cylinder bank
Horsepower	394bhp @ 5200rpm
Transmission	Manual six-speed
Drive	Rear
Chassis	Monocoque
Suspension – front	Wishbones and coil spring
Suspension – rear	Wishbones and coil spring
Brakes	Ventilated disc
Top speed	200mph (322km/h)*
Acceleration	0-62mph (96km/h): 4.5 seconds*

*Manufacturer's claim

Lotus Exige

**Top speed
124mph**
200km/h

Below: A racer for the road, an Exige on the move. Note that in addition to the mid-located engine air intakes, a secondary roof-mounted duct also directs air to the power unit. The roof line is higher than might be expected because it has to accommodate an owner's helmeted head! The wheels are shod with specially developed Yokohama tires.

The Exige coupé is the latest manifestation of Lotus's successful Elise mid-engined roadster. Based on the Sport Elise racer, the closed car underlines the versatility of a concept that first appeared in 1995. Conceived during the era when Bugatti owned Lotus, the model was named Elise after the granddaughter of its chairman Romano Artioli. But his business collapsed in 1995 and in the following year Lotus was acquired by the Malaysian Proton concern.

The Elise, spiritual successor to the no-frills Lotus Seven of the 1950s, was powered by a 118bhp version of Rover's 1.8 liter K-series engine, and featured an advanced extruded aluminum epoxy-bonded chassis which weighed a mere 154lb (70kg). All-round aluminum composite brakes represented another significant first. A glass-fiber body was also synonymous with the marque.

Able to attain 124mph (200km/h) and reach 60mph (96km/h) in 5.9 seconds, the Elise possessed the roadholding and distinctive character

on which Lotus had built its reputation. However, on the debit side was undue engine noise and a fabric roof that could be difficult to erect.

Of greater significance as far as the future Exige was concerned was the 150mph (241km/h) 200bhp Sport Elise coupé conceived for a one-make race series run in 2000 by Lotus Motorsport. Announced in April 2000, the Exige is effectively a mildly detuned version of the Sport powered by a 177bhp version of the Rover four, although a more potent 190bhp version is also available.

This performance is assisted by the lines of the coupé body that possesses about the same drag coefficient as the roadster although it exerts more downforce. And, like the racer, it is fitted with a rear wing.

Based on the Sport Elise chassis, in the interests of practicality the Exige dispensed with the racer's central driving position. It reverted to two-abreast seating although only the driver's seat can be adjusted fore and aft.

Respectable performance

While Lotus claimed a 0-100mph (161km/h) figure of a respectable 12.3 seconds and a top speed of 136mph (219km/h), in reality these claims appeared somewhat optimistic, the actual figures being 13.7 seconds and 124mph (200km/h) respectively. Nevertheless, the Exige, like its parent, possesses oodles of noisy character, to which is coupled outstanding steering and handling.

Left: An Exige on the Lotus stand, which the company claimed to be its largest ever, at the 2000 British Motor Show. The hot air outlets can be seen on either side of the twin exhaust pipes.

Specification	Lotus Exige
Engine location	Mid, transverse
Configuration	Four-cylinder
Bore and stroke	80 x 89mm
Capacity	1796cc
Valve operation	Twin overhead camshafts
Horsepower	190bhp @ 7800rpm
Transmission	Manual five-speed
Drive	Rear
Chassis	Extruded aluminum
Suspension – front	Wishbones and coil spring
Suspension – rear	Wishbones and coil spring
Brakes	Ventilated disc
Top speed	124mph (200km/h)
Acceleration	0-60mph (96km/h): 5.5 seconds

Above left: The rear wing of the Sport Elise was replaced by this rather smaller version which Lotus maintained produced aerodynamic characteristics that were more appropriate for the road user. It generates 99lb (45kg) of downforce at 100mph (161km/h) and it thus considerably assists the Exige's roadholding.

Left: The no-frills philosophy of the Exige is underlined by the cockpit – while the driver's seat is adjustable, the passenger's is fixed. The belts are a full four-point mounting. Perversely, it is possible to have an in-car entertainment facility indicated by the radio aerial and speaker mounts.

Morgan Aero 8

**Top speed
160mph**
257km/h

By any standards it is a sensational car, but for an old established company like Morgan it is positively light years removed from its other products. The 160mph (257km/h) Aero 8 made its sensational debut at the 2000 Geneva Motor Show and it combines the traditional looks for which the marque is justifiably famous with state-of-the-art mechanicals.

The model, which revives a name previously associated with its formative three-wheeler line, sprang from a racing car that Charles Morgan, the company's present managing director, campaigned during the 1997 season. The work of Jaguar's former engineering director, Jim Randle, and created for that year's GT championship, its chassis was constructed from laser-cut aluminum sections. These were then glued and bonded together in much the same way in which the Lotus Elise frame is constructed.

Hitherto every Morgan since the marque's foundation in 1910 featured sliding pillar independent front suspension. But the GT2 racer used an unrelated and distinctive all-independent system which has been inherited by the Aero 8. This uses long cantilever upper arms with lower wishbones at the front with long transverse rear wishbones and coil springs as the suspension medium. While the racer's chassis came up to scratch, its Rover V8 engine, based on the unit used to power the Plus 8, was beginning to show its years and rendered the car uncompetitive.

Morgan has made no such mistakes with its new road car and it is powered by BMW's current 286bhp 4.4 V8, as used in the 5-Series sedan, but of a unique specification to Morgan. The gearbox is also German and is a six-speed Getrag unit.

Controversial bodywork

Perhaps the most controversial aspect of the new car is its bodywork with the front headlight treatment producing raised eyebrows in some quarters. But at least this new Morgan cannot be mistaken for anything else! The lines of the open

Above: The aerodynamically refined front end gives the Aero 8 a personality all of its own. Power is courtesy of BMW and, unlike previous examples of the marque, all-independent suspension is employed.

Right: Benefiting from low weight and a combination of old and new themes, the Aero's alloy wheels are individually etched with the Morgan badge. They allow plenty of air to reach the all-round discs.

two-seater evoke some of the spirit of the traditional Morgans, but the Aero 8 only uses about a dozen parts, namely the hinges, hood latches and doors, in common with its contemporaries. However, it does retain the time-honored ash frame used with an aluminum monocoque.

It may come as a surprise to discover that the Aero was wind tunnel-tested. The drag coefficient figure of 0.39 is not outstanding but it is a revelation in Morgan terms, and is 40 per cent lower than that achieved by the Plus 8 whose body lines are firmly rooted in the 1930s.

With a selling price of just under $70,000, some $23,000 more than the Plus 8, the Aero 8 represents a considerable gamble by Morgan which is one of Britain's few remaining indigenous car companies.

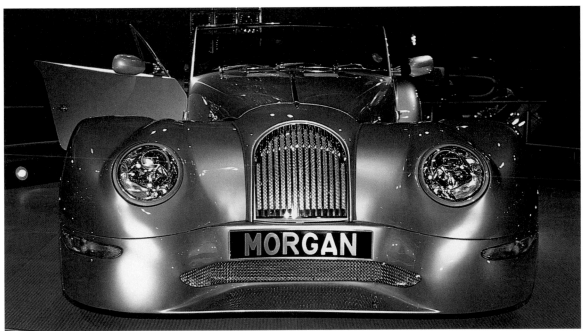

Above: The Aero's handling and performance have been praised, this being aided by the car's light weight.

Left: The new Morgan as it appeared at the 2000 British Motor Show. Access to the car is good, thanks to the long doors.

Below left: The interior similarly echoes old and new themes. The windshield is electrically heated and the ash frame, rather than being concealed by trim, is exposed.

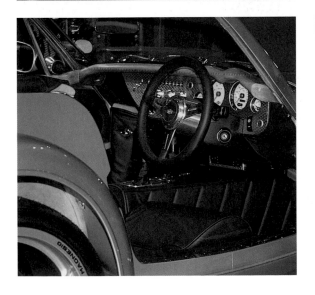

Specification	**Morgan** Aero 8
Engine location	Front, in-line
Configuration	V8
Bore and stroke	82 x 92mm
Capacity	4398cc
Valve operation	Twin overhead camshafts per bank
Horsepower	286bhp @ 5500rpm
Transmission	Manual six-speed
Drive	Rear
Chassis	Aluminum monocoque
Suspension – front	Cantilever, wishbones and coil spring
Suspension – rear	Wishbones and coil spring
Brakes	Ventilated disc
Top speed	160mph (257km/h)
Acceleration	0-60mph (0-96km/h): 4.7 seconds

BMW Z8

**Top speed
155mph***
249km/h
*limited

*Right: The Z8's instrument
panel contains retro
elements. Moving the
instruments to the center of
the dash means that the
driver has an uninterrupted
view down the hood.*

*Below: Inspired by BMW's
507 of the 1950s, with the
fender-mounted side vents
echoing that model, the Z8's
structure makes extensive
use of aluminum and is
essentially a hand-made
product.*

The latest recruit to BMW's fabled Z
series sports car line, the Z8 clearly draws
its visual inspiration from the company's
classic 507 model of the 1950s. Produced between
1957 and 1959, the 507 was powered by a 3.2 liter
V8 engine and could be wound up to 135mph
(217km/h). But it was expensive for its day and
only 250 were produced. Now in demand by
collectors, it fired the imagination of BMW's
chairman and old car fan Bernd Pischetsreider and
his fellow board member and classic car enthusiast
Wolfgang Rietzle.

The result, the work of Henrik Fisker, the
Danish head of BMW's California studio, was the
Z8 concept car. It was unveiled at the 1997 Tokyo
Motor Show. While some features of the concept
car were sacrificed for the production line, the Z8,
which appeared for the 2000 season, closely
resembled the show version. But this was no
pastiche of the original, it also incorporated a raft
of 1960s features, courtesy of Austin-Healey,
Jaguar, and Aston Martin. However, the most

significant difference between the two cars is that
the production version has been shorn of its D-
Type-inspired rear fin. It has been replaced by more
production-friendly twin roll-over hoops.

Aluminum space-frame

Aluminum featured extensively in the construction
of the Z8, most significantly the space-frame that
was welded and glued together, while the
suspension components were made of the same

metal. It therefore comes as no surprise to find that the body panels are also aluminum with the bumpers and trunk lining made from strong and ultra-light carbon fiber. The Z8 weighs a very respectable 3494lb (1585kg).

It also perpetuated the spirit of the 507 in having a V8 engine, although this is a 5 liter unit developing an awesome 400bhp and comes courtesy of BMW's formidable M5 sedan. Under-hood warm air escapes through distinctive 507-style vents positioned on each side of the front fenders.

Retro styling

There was a choice of a six-speed manual gearbox and an SMG sequential version of the same unit. Inside the retro themes were continued with a chrome plate and leather-bound steering wheel. These went hand in hand with the latest gizmos, such as satellite navigation, a ten-speaker stereo, and a hands-free cell phone.

Although the Z8's top speed was limited to 155mph (249km/h), without this restriction it could probably attain 180mph (289km/h) and it can sprint to 62mph (100km/h) in just 4.7 seconds.

Unlike its much cheaper Z3 relative which is produced in America, the Z8 is assembled by hand in Germany. This is no mass-produced car; just ten a week are being built so this BMW will only be available for the fortunate few.

Above: The rear lights are distinctive and the twin exhaust pipes indicate a V8 engine. The back tires are wider than the front ones.

Left: The model's 4.9 liter V8 engine is inherited essentially intact from BMW's potent M5 sedan. The Z8 is fitted with electronic stability and traction control.

Specification	BMW Z8
Engine location	Front, in-line
Configuration	V8
Bore and stroke	94 x 89mm
Capacity	4941cc
Valve operation	Twin overhead camshafts per bank
Horsepower	394bhp @ 6600rpm
Transmission	Manual six-speed
Drive	Rear
Chassis	Tubular aluminum
Suspension – front	MacPherson strut and coil spring
Suspension – rear	Multi link and coil spring
Brakes	Ventilated disc
Top speed	Limited to 155mph (249km/h)
Acceleration	0-62mph (0-100km/h): 4.7 seconds

Aston Martin Le Mans Vantage

**Top speed
200mph+**
322km/h

*Right: Aston Martin
banished the usual wood
veneer in the Le Mans for
titanium, a theme that
echoed the Project Vantage
concept car of 1998.*

*Below: The front of the Le
Mans is noticeably different
from the Vantage on which
it was based. The nose and
the hood and fender air
intakes are all peculiar to
the model.*

 Unashamedly purposeful and with a top speed in excess of 200mph (322km/h), this potent Aston Martin was able to hit 100mph (161km/h) in under 10 seconds. Little wonder that the supercharged V8 engine developed no less than 600bhp.

It represented the final expression of a line that began with the lackluster Virage coupé of 1989. Since 1950 Aston Martin has applied the Vantage name to the most powerful model of its day and this Virage-based car was the flag-bearer developed for 1993.

The output of its 5.3 V8 engine was boosted from 310 to 550bhp, principally by the fitment of two Eaton superchargers. With a top speed approaching 190mph (306km/h), its brakes needed to be good and the 14in (356mm) diameter discs, courtesy of the corporate Group C racer, were the largest then fitted to a production car.

Three years on, in August 1995, a Mark II version of the model appeared that could be easily identified by a distinctive crackle-finished radiator grille. Beneath the surface no less than 700 modifications had been effected to refine handling, improve the gear change and reduce noise levels.

Then for 1998 came the top-of-the-range Vantage 600, the output of the venerable but robust V8 having been boosted to 600bhp, each blower now boasting its own intercooler. There was a new five-speed gearbox, actually a Chevrolet Corvette ZR1 unit but with the top gear blanked off. Speeds in excess of 200mph (322km/h) were attainable.

Outward changes were minimal and discreet; for instance, the shape of the radiator grille was accentuated by a thin chrome surround. There was also a small but significant badge which declared *Works Prepared* and *Newport Pagnell* which is where this Aston Martin was built.

Anniversary of Le Mans victory

The 1999 Geneva Motor Show witnessed the arrival of the ultimate version, the Le Mans Vantage, which celebrated the 40th anniversary of Aston Martin winning the 1959 24 hour classic

event and the World Sports Car Championship. Available in 550 and 600bhp guises, the Le Mans was instantly identifiable by its reworked nose with enlarged radiator ducts in a new grille panel. It also incorporated an extended spoiler to aid downforce.

The range of color schemes included the almond green paint of a hue used by the 1959 works team. Inside, the Le Mans revealed the influence of the interior of the Project Vantage concept car of the previous year. Just 40 cars, one for each year, were produced.

The last Le Mans off the line appeared at Aston Martin's stand at the 2000 British Motor Show, so allowing the V12-engined Vanquish to take center stage in 2001.

Below: The license plate says it all! The Le Mans is based on the Vantage 600 which appeared in 1998. The thin chrome surround was a distinctive feature.

Bottom left: The Vantage engine. The output of the two Eaton superchargers, introduced in 1993, was boosted so that the V8 developed 600bhp. Each unit has its own intercooler and water pump.

Specification	Aston Martin Le Mans Vantage
Engine location	Front, in-line
Configuration	Twin supercharged V8
Bore and stroke	85 x 100mm
Capacity	5340cc
Valve operation	Twin overhead camshafts per bank
Horsepower	600bhp @ 6750rpm
Transmission	Manual six-speed
Drive	Rear
Chassis	Unitary
Suspension – front	Wishbones and coil spring
Suspension – rear	Wishbones and coil spring
Brakes	Ventilated disc
Top speed	Over 200mph (322km/h)
Acceleration	0-60mph (96km/h): 3.9 seconds

Grinnall Scorpion S-IV

**Top speed
150mph***
241km/h
*Claimed by
manufacturer

This racing car for the road has evolved from a potent BMW motorcycle-engined three-wheeler that its creator Mark Grinnall named the Scorpion III. The IV suffix stands for four wheels and this light and exceedingly lively open two-seater with its retro racing body is capable of a blustery but hugely enjoyable 150mph (241km/h).

Grinnall made his name uprating the lackluster Triumph TR7 with V8 power, converting some 300 examples in this way between 1981 and 1995. But it would not be until 1993 that he began producing vehicles under his own name. The Scorpion was a rapid three-wheeler that was powered by a choice of BMW K-series motorcycle engines which ranged from 75 to 120bhp in output.

The open glass-fiber two-seater body in which the occupants were only protected from the elements by a rudimentary windshield was styled by Steve Harper of MGA Developments, a company which specializes in the production of prototype cars for the motor industry.

By early 2000 some 200 Scorpions had been sold by which time Grinnall and his team, who are based in Bewdley, Worcestershire, were at work on a four-wheel derivative. Announced at the 2000 British Motor Show, the Scorpion IV is, stylistically, also the work of Harper who is now a Volvo designer. Clearly derived from the three-wheeler, it is, inevitably, both wider and longer. It maintains the no-frills functional doorless concept, complete with the obligatory cycle fenders.

Above: It hasn't just landed, it's the four-wheel version of Grinnall's Scorpion, and the minimalist approach is readily apparent. The composite doorless body conceals a robust space-frame chassis and the cockpit is, contrary to appearances, remarkably roomy.

Right: Head-on view of the Scorpion S-IV with its race-bred unequal length wishbone suspension exposed to the elements. The front brakes would not look out of place on a Ferrari and are 12in (305mm) Brembo discs. The function of the protective roll-over bars is clear to see.

Fiat engine as standard

The mid-located in-line engine comes from Fiat, the 2 liter five-cylinder turbocharged 220bhp unit being better known for powering its potent and attractive Coupé. More powerful versions are available on request. Its comes with a six-speed gearbox with drive conveyed to the rear wheels via a power-lock differential.

The chassis is made from oval-contoured steel tubing and incorporates no less than four bulkheads making it extremely rigid. Suspension is all-independent and braking the responsibility of powerful Brembo calipers.

As might be expected, the two-seater cockpit is essentially minimalist. The seats are fixed and orthopaedically contoured with the driver's dimensions being accommodated by adjustable pedals. There is a shallow windshield that does not require a windshield wiper. Weighing no more than 1433lb (650kg), the Scorpion is remarkably agile with sparkling performance and predictable roadholding. It is available in right- or left-hand-drive forms.

Specification	**Grinnall** Scorpion S-IV
Engine location	Mid, in-line
Configuration	Turbocharged five-cylinder
Bore and stroke	82 x 75mm
Capacity	1998cc
Valve operation	Twin overhead camshafts
Horsepower	220bhp @ 5750rpm
Transmission	Manual six-speed
Drive	Rear
Chassis	Space-frame
Suspension – front	Wishbones and coil spring
Suspension – rear	Trailing arm and coil spring
Brakes	Ventilated disc
Top speed	150mph (241km/h)*
Acceleration	0-62mph (100km/h): 4 seconds*

*Manufacturer's claim

If it gives you a taste for a Grinnall product, you might like to sample another model line: a BMW-engined tricycle that also seems to have captured the public's imagination…

Above left: The seats are fixed, instrumentation basic and the windshield is low enough to obviate the need for a windshield wiper.

Above: The rear brakes are smaller than the front ones while, perhaps surprisingly, the wheels are 17in (432mm) at the front and 18in (457mm) at the rear.

Left: Recessed lights, hot air outlets and twin chromed mufflers characterize the Scorpion IV's unmistakable rear. The outline of the seats are imaginatively echoed in the tail.

Noble M12 GTO

Top speed 155mph*
249km/h
*Claimed by manufacturer

Right: The instrumentation is functional with analog dials set in a dashboard that matches their contours. The rest of the cockpit echoes this basic approach.

Below: The Noble doing what it does best, on the move and offering owners a ride that is both pliant and controlled.

Superlative roadholding coupled with impressive performance are the hallmarks of the mid-engined Noble M12 GTO coupé announced in 2000. Capable of 155mph (249km/h), this car firmly occupies Lotus territory and, it is whispered, it is in some respects superior to the acclaimed Elise.

Engineer Lee Noble has been a significant player in the precarious world of specialist sports car manufacture since 1985. He originally created a Group C-inspired coupé with a finely engineered space-frame chassis, and this appeared in revised and more curvaceous Rover V8-powered Mark 3 form in 1987. It survived until 1990 but was revived as the Ultima sports car in 1992. Noble was also responsible for the design of the 200mph (322km/h) Ascari coupé of 1995.

Currently located at Cosby, Leicestershire, in 1998 Noble's reconstituted company produced the M10 roadster. Based on a space-frame chassis, it was available with a choice of two mid-located Ford engines: a 1.8 liter four-cylinder Zetec unit or a 2.5 liter V6. But while it was a highly competent mechanical confection, commentators deemed that the glass-fiber body lacked flair.

The M12 coupé that appeared two years after the M10 in 2000 is an ingenious derivative. The glass-fiber body is both distinctive, agreeably executed and possesses a rear wing. Power comes courtesy of a Ford V6 engine. Unlike the roadster, it develops no less than 310bhp, thanks to its twin Garrett turbochargers. Combined with a remapped engine management system, this provides a flexible, responsive engine with all the bite expected from a blown power unit. Significantly the M12 is an extremely light car and turns the scales at a mere 2160lb (980kg).

Minimalist design approach

Lee Noble's particular area of expertise is chassis design and the frame is essentially the same as that of its roadster predecessor. However, there are detail differences in the design of the wishbone suspension, this being used at the rear in place of the M10's radius arms. The driving compartment contains no-frills light padded bucket seats reflecting a minimalist design approach adopted to keep weight down.

Hand-built to its customers' specifications by manufacturers Noble Moy Automotive, ride and roadholding are, by all accounts, outstanding. This is, in truth, a track car that has been tamed for road use and the M12 looks destined to compete for survival in one of the most precarious market sectors. Let's hope for the best – the first year's production has, apparently, already been sold.

Above: The Noble manages to combine a distinctive, thoroughly professionally executed body with an outstanding chassis.

Left: Bucket seats with a minimum of padding are fitted together with two racing harnesses. However, conventional seat belts are available as well.

Specification	**Noble** M12 GTO
Engine location	Mid, transverse
Configuration	Twin turbocharged V6
Bore and stroke	82 x 79mm
Capacity	2595cc
Valve operation	Twin overhead camshafts per cylinder bank
Horsepower	310bhp @ 6000rpm
Transmission	Manual five-speed
Drive	Rear
Chassis	Space-frame
Suspension – front	Wishbones and coil spring
Suspension – rear	Wishbones and coil spring
Brakes	Ventilated disc
Top speed	155mph (249km/h)*
Acceleration	0-60mph (96km/h): 3.9 seconds*

* Manufacturer's claim

Chevrolet Corvette Z06

**Top speed
171mph**
275km/h

*Right: The Z06 name is
inspired by a special
Corvette Sting Ray of the
1960s although the hp
figure refers to the higher
American SAE rating.*

*Below: Based on the
Corvette Hardtop, the Z06's
styling changes include new
10-spoke alloy wheels, air
vents behind the front
wheels, and mesh-covered
frontal air intakes.*

One hundred miles an hour (161km/h)
from standstill in less than a tire-
scorching 10 seconds is just one of the
attributes of the Z06, the latest version of the
legendary Corvette, which was unveiled in 2000.

It was named in memory of the 1962 racing
Sting Ray coupé, of which only 199 examples were
built. But this latter-day version is rather more
plentiful and will account for about 20 per cent of
Corvette production. With annual output running at
some 33,000 cars, that's the equivalent of about
6500 examples per year.

The current Corvette shape appeared in 1997
and it is the fifth generation of a line that began
back in 1953. It had a glass-fiber body, just like the
original, and a full length perimeter seamless
tubular chassis lurked beneath those distinctive and
aerodynamically refined contours, which accounted
for an impressive 0.29 drag coefficient. A notable
feature was the fact that the all-independent
suspension was available with an active option.

Coupé and convertible models

Power was provided by a new LS1 all-alloy 345cid
(5.7 liter) V8 which developed 345bhp and drove
through a six-speed manual gearbox. Produced in
coupé and convertible forms, these were joined for
the 1999 season by a hardtop with detachable lift-
out roof panels. It is this latter version, which is
lighter than the coupé, that forms the basis of the
Z06. Outwardly similar to the mainstream 'Vette, it
can be identified by new ten-spoked alloy wheels
and discreet air intakes introduced in the front
spoiler and ahead of the rear wheels.

Left: This Corvette's lines are not interrupted by bumpers. The air vents in the rear apron are another feature peculiar to the Z06. The Eagle F1 tires are specially developed by Goodyear, the wheels being one inch (25mm) wider than the originals.

Below: The new wheels with their forged alloy rims display the all-round ventilated discs to good effect; brakes are activated by a Bosch anti-lock system. The Corvette's gas tank can hold 18 gallons (68lit) of fuel.

However, the real changes were to be found beneath the hood with the revised LS6 V8 now producing 385bhp. Improvements to harness the extra horses included high compression cylinder heads, redesigned inlet manifolding for better breathing, a 'hotter' camshaft, and less restrictive titanium exhaust system.

Active-handling system

The already rigid suspension was also uprated with a new tauter rear springs; transverse front and rear, they are made from a composite material. The real secret of the Z06's roadholding is General Motors' second-generation active-handling system. Subtle and ingenious, its most significant feature is that it senses possible trouble ahead and the fuel supply and Bosch anti-lock disc brakes are unobtrusively trimmed accordingly. The driver, benefiting from supportive and distinctive red and black seats, will probably be unaware of its intervention!

Sure-footed, fast – it's capable of 171mph (275km/h) – and an uncompromising sports car, the Z06 is the latest manifestation of a line which, nearly 50 years on, shows itself to be as vibrant as ever.

Specification	Chevrolet Corvette Z06
Engine location	Front, in-line
Configuration	V8
Bore and stroke	3.9 x 3.6in (99 x 92mm)
Capacity	345cid (5654cc)
Valve operation	Pushrod
Horsepower	385bhp @ 6000rpm
Transmission	Manual six-speed
Drive	Rear
Chassis	Tubular steel
Suspension – front	Wishbones and transverse leaf spring
Suspension – rear	Wishbones and transverse leaf spring
Brakes	Ventilated discs
Top speed	171mph (275km/h)
Acceleration	0-60mph (0-96km/h): 4 seconds

Renault sport Clio V6

**Top speed
145mph**
233km/h

*Right: Perhaps surprisingly,
the interior is standard Clio
although air conditioning
and a CD changer are
available at extra cost. It is,
of course, only a two-seater.*

*Below: Not only does the
deep front spoiler with its
enlarged air intakes
indicate something special,
the mid-located air intakes
reveal the presence of a
V6 engine.*

The Clio supermini of 1990 was Renault's
big seller of the decade – the sport is a
low-production second-generation
145mph (233km/h) car for the discriminating
enthusiast who craves impressive performance and
outstanding handling. In truth Renault has revived
the concept of the 5 Turbo of 1983 and, like its
predecessor, this hot Clio's V6 engine occupies the
space usually reserved for the rear passengers!

This is a project that originated as a concept car
which Renault unveiled at the 1998 Paris Motor
Show. It took some two years to bring it to
production, the model appearing at the start of the
2001 season. The build process is, however,
somewhat protracted. In France Renault sport (the
lower-case 's' is Renault's choice) takes delivery of
the 3 liter V6 used in the top-line version of the
Laguna sedan. It proceeds to rework it and extract a
further 20bhp in the process. New pistons, a raised
compression ratio, improvements to the inlet ports
and a new exhaust are added which results in
engine output being upped to 230bhp. Mounted

transversely behind the front seats, it drives the rear
wheels via a bespoke six-speed gearbox. Its
presence involves replacing the original torsion
beam rear suspension with a multi-link layout.

Lengthened and lowered

With the track widened by 4.3in (110mm) at the
front and 5.4in (138mm) at the rear, the wheelbase
has been lengthened by 1.2in (30mm) and the sport
sits 2.6in (66mm) lower to the ground.

The standard body and mechanicals are dispatched to Sweden where the British TWR company, which is also responsible for fine-tuning the chassis, assembles them at its Uddevalla factory. There the necessary modifications are made to the three-door hatchback hull and the car is assembled at the rate of 12 per day. On its announcement the finished product was competitively priced at $36,400.

On the road the sport is a potent, flexible car with the Clio's performance transformed by the new engine – 60mph (96km/h) arrives in under seven seconds and 100mph (160km/h) in a shade over 17.

The chassis engineering has been deemed excellent and the driver gets plenty of warning of any troubles ahead. Roadholding is impressive, thanks to that mid-located engine, and handling only becomes unpredictable when the car is pushed to the limit. In short this is a driver's car with comfortable, supportive seats although, remember, there's only room for two!

Above: A sport Clio really proves its worth on well-maintained straight roads rather than unmade, twisting ones.

Below left: The badging says it all and this is the world's only mid-engined hatchback. There's even a little luggage space.

Specification	Renault sport Clio V6
Engine location	Mid, transverse
Configuration	V6
Bore and stroke	87 x 82mm
Capacity	2946cc
Valve operation	Twin overhead camshaft per cylinder bank
Horsepower	230bhp @ 6000rpm
Transmission	Manual six-speed
Drive	Rear
Chassis	Unitary
Suspension – front	MacPherson strut
Suspension – rear	Multi link and coil spring
Brakes	Ventilated disc
Top speed	145mph (233km/h)
Acceleration	0-60mph (96km/h): 6.7 seconds

TVR Cerbera Speed 12

**Top speed
240mph+**
386km/h

Right: The Speed 12 readily betrays its racing origins, with the cabin featuring a minimalist approach – the emphasis is firmly on weight-saving.

Below: The Cerbera's body is made of carbon fiber. The twin exhaust pipes emerge ahead of the rear wheels on both sides.

 Some members of the exclusive 200mph-plus (322+km/h) club rely on subtlety to achieve their ends. No one could accuse TVR of adopting this approach with the Speed 12. With an anticipated 800bhp under its massive hood, it is attempting to wrest the mantle of the world's fastest car away from the McLaren F1.

This big Cerbera's starting point was the sports-racing Speed 12 that TVR exhibited at the 1996 British Motor Show. It was sidelined late in 1999 when the GT1 class for which it had been designed was discontinued. However, it was revamped for GT2 competition in 2000 and is also destined for road use as 'a race car with number plates.' Unveiled at the Croft circuit, near Newcastle, in April 2000, the mighty 7.7 liter V12 engine was displayed in a detuned format and developed a mere 800bhp. It is hoped to have this version in production by late in 2002.

The Speed 12 power unit

TVR has been producing its own engines since 1996 and the Speed 12 power unit consists of two twin-cam 24-valve cylinder blocks from the company's Tuscan Speed Six model mounted at 90 degrees to one another on a common crankcase. A 60 degree angle is far more common for Vee

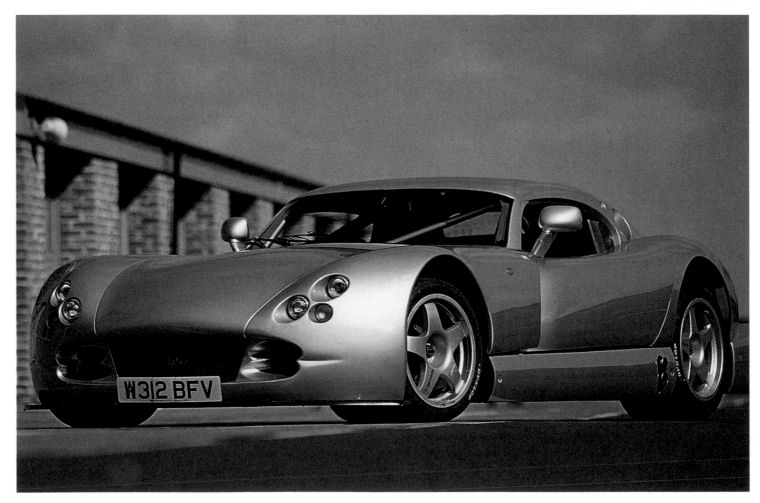

engines so the resulting power unit is much wider than the norm and is mounted lower in the chassis.

Drive is taken through a six-speed Hollinger sequential gearbox and while the competition Speed 12 uses an automatic clutch, its roadgoing half brother has a conventional manual one.

Double wishbone suspension is employed all round and incorporates coil springs and pushrod-operated dampers. The brakes are massive AP racing ventilated discs at the front, arrested by no less than six piston calipers, with slightly smaller units at the rear. The stupendous horsepower developed by the V12 means that the massive 18in (457mm) diameter Speedline alloy wheels are wider at the rear than at the front.

With a chassis made of tubular steel and an aluminum honeycomb, the massive, audacious coupé body of the TVR flagship is made from carbon fiber with a large spoiler fitted at the rear to provide downforce and stability. The interior is austere with the accent on weight-saving; the instruments are grouped in a semi-circle around the steering column.

McLaren beater?

Only time will tell whether TVR's chairman, Peter Wheeler, will achieve his ambition of toppling the hi-tech McLaren from its perch. But bearing in mind TVR's extraordinary renaissance in recent years, the Blackpool-based company's bid deserves serious consideration.

Below: The TVR flagship on the move. The car, says its maker, is for 'racing drivers, not rich kids' who will drive to the circuit, compete in a race and then return home in it.

Specification	**TVR** Cerbera Speed 12
Engine location	Front, in-line
Configuration	V12
Bore and stroke	96 x 89mm
Capacity	7736cc
Valve operation	Twin overhead camshafts per bank
Horsepower	800bhp @ 7250rpm
Transmission	Sequential six-speed
Drive	Rear
Chassis	Tubular steel and aluminum honeycomb
Suspension – front	Wishbones, pushrod and coil spring
Suspension – rear	Wishbones, pushrod and coil spring
Brakes	Ventilated disc
Top speed	240mph (386km/h) (projected)
Acceleration	N/A

Ferrari 550 Barchetta Pininfarina

**Top speed
186mph**
299km/h

Right: While the instrument panel is related to the 550 Maranello, the Barchetta's seats are new and are leather-trimmed carbon fiber. Competition-inclined owners can have a racing harness fitted.

Below: The Barchetta's nose is also 550-based, and the presence of an air intake is a reminder that this is a front-engined V12 Ferrari. The wheels are split-rim alloys.

Ferrari built a mere 448 examples of the 550 Barchetta Pininfarina, the open version of its 550 flagship coupé unveiled at the 2000 Paris Motor Show. Produced to commemorate the 70th anniversary of the creation of the famous Turin-based styling and coachbuilding establishment, it was priced at $241,000; wealthy collectors were said to be offering $42,000 above this asking price, even for second-hand examples.

After 23 years of producing mid-engined supercars, in 1996 Ferrari unveiled the 550 Maranello coupé with a front-located 485bhp 5.4 liter V12 engine. Capable of 199mph (320km/h), it is no surprise to find that it consumed gas at a rate of 6.6mpg (35.5 liters/100km) for town driving, a figure that soared to around 15mpg (15.6 liters/100km) on long runs!

Originally the 550 was fitted with a six-speed manual gearbox which operated through the traditional Ferrari visible gate. However, from the 1998 season it became available with a Selespeed automatic box which dispensed with the conventional clutch pedal. Borrowing technology from Ferrari's Formula 1 cars, gear changes were effected by two paddles mounted just behind the steering wheel rim.

Cloaked in a magnificently proportioned but understated Pininfarina body, this uncompromising two-seater boasted Ferrari's traditional tubular steel chassis, all-independent suspension, and sophisticated ASR traction control.

After four years production, the coupé was joined in 2000 by the celebratory open-topped version. It was named the Barchetta in memory of Ferrari's first production car, the delectable Touring-bodied 166 open two-seater of 1948. Even more significantly it celebrated Pininfarina's foundation in 1930. First associated with Ferrari in 1952, and exclusively so since 1955, it is a partnership that continues to amaze and delight the motoring world.

No-frills barchetta concept

With a windshield reduced by 3.9in (100mm) in height, the open 550 remains true to the no-frills barchetta concept by dispensing with a top although a rudimentary cover is provided to protect the car's occupants in the event of sudden rain.

Twin roll-over bars feature at the rear with their contours echoed in the twin humped trunk lid. Inside there are new carbon-fiber leather trimmed seats, with lucky customers being able to specify their own exterior color and interior trim.

Although weighing about the same as the coupé (the lack of roof is offset by a reinforced body substructure), the Barchetta is slightly slower flat out than its stablemate, on account of the closed car's superior aerodynamics. It is thus capable of a mere 186mph (299km/)!

Below: Classic lines: by the nature of its body, the Barchetta's windshield is considerably shallower than that fitted to the 550M coupé.

Bottom left: Note that the retro-style twin fairings molded into the trunk cover echo the double roll-over hoops. The model comes complete with a rudimentary top.

Specification	Ferrari 550 Barchetta Pininfarina
Engine location	Front, in-line
Configuration	V12
Bore and stroke	88 x 75mm
Capacity	5474cc
Valve operation	Twin overhead camshafts per bank
Horsepower	485bhp @ 7000rpm
Transmission	Automatic
Drive	Rear
Chassis	Tubular steel
Suspension – front	Wishbones and coil spring
Suspension – rear	Wishbones and coil spring
Brakes	Ventilated disc
Top speed	186mph (299km/h)
Acceleration	0-60mph (0-96km/h): 4.6 seconds

Parradine 525S

**Top speed
204mph**
328km/h

*Right: The Parradine's
interior is both sumptuous
and ingenious with well-
upholstered leather-
trimmed Recaro seats and
a comprehensive array
of instruments.*

*Below: A real head-turner,
the 525S, as its name
suggests, is powered by a
supercharged Ford V8
engine. It attracted a
considerable amount of
attention at its launch at the
2000 British Motor Show.*

 The Parradine is a luxuriously equipped British roadster with a claimed top speed in excess of 200mph (322km/h). Described by its maker as what the AC Cobra should have become, production began in 2001.

John Parradine's first excursion into the specialist motor industry came in 1985 with his Rover SD1-powered Deltayn Proteus. In 1987 he began producing cars under his own name. The Pegasus V12 open two-seater used a space-frame chassis and Jaguar engine. A projected move to France failed to materialize but some 25 cars had been built by the time the project was discontinued in 1991. In 1998 the company, now based at Thealby, Yorkshire, revived the concept although production of the now supercharged Ford V8-engined Parradine V8S was limited to 50 cars.

A new model, the Parradine 525S, was launched at the 2000 British Motor Show with a $182,000 price tag. Based once again on a tubular space-frame chassis, its engine is a 4.6 liter alloy V8 that began life in the Ford Mustang. It has been modified to develop 525bhp, some 200bhp more than the standard unit. Final drive is via a close ratio speed gearbox and a Torsen differential.

The chassis is cloaked by an open two-seater carbon-fiber and glass-fiber body which is awash with retro influences. A distinctive feature is provided by hot air outlets introduced into each front fender. Although otherwise traditional in concept, the 21st century instrument panel features an analog rev counter and digital readout for speedometer, oil, water, and fuel levels.

High-tech image

The Parradine eschews conventional side mirrors; they have been replaced by a pair of miniature cameras and the images they produce are displayed on small screens mounted on either side of the instrument dials. The driver and co-passenger are accommodated in leather-clad Recaro seats, with each occupant protected by an individual roll-over bar. Carpeting is also appropriately opulent and is by Wilton.

A top speed of 204mph (328km/h) is claimed for the 525S with 60mph (96km/h) arriving in an exceedingly rapid 3.8 seconds. Such performance requires outstanding stopping power and the Parradine features massive 14.2in (362mm) front discs that are arrested by four-piston calipers. The rear discs measure a still impressive 11.4in (289mm).

Further planned variations on the theme are estate and coupé versions. With production scheduled to begin in 2002, the company's aim is to manufacture some 50 cars a year.

Above: The 525S's distinctive rear end complete with flared wheel arches, commodious trunk and no-nonsense twin exhaust system. The channelled sills convey cool air to the rear brakes. The snug hardtop (left) about to be fitted.

Specification	Parradine 525S
Engine location	Front, in-line
Configuration	Supercharged V8
Bore and stroke	90.2 x 90mm
Capacity	4601cc
Valve operation	Twin overhead camshafts per cylinder bank
Horsepower	525bhp @ 6400rpm
Transmission	Manual six-speed
Drive	Rear
Chassis	Space-frame
Suspension – front	Wishbones and coil spring
Suspension – rear	Wishbones and coil spring
Brakes	Ventilated disc
Top speed	204mph (328km/h)
Acceleration	0-60mph (96km/h): 3.8 seconds

2001 onwards
Bugatti Poised to Conquer

McLaren F1's reign as the world's fastest road car is now threatened by the Bugatti Veyron that is scheduled to enter production in 2003. Its projected top speed is in excess of 250mph (402km/h).

Owned since 1998 by Volkswagen, which also acquired Lamborghini in the same year (Lamborghini subsequently produced the acclaimed Murcielago), *and* Bentley, this German company now has a trio of top marques to challenge the long-time supremacy of its established Italian and home-grown rivals.

Add to this a resurgent Aston Martin's Vanquish, Porsche's projected Carrera GT, and Mercedes-Benz's much heralded SLR, and the world of the fast car has never looked more buoyant and mouth-watering!

Porsche GT2

**Top speed
196mph**
315km/h

*Right: The GT2's interior
is functional and devoid of
such weighty items as air
conditioning and electric
windows. The seats are
comfortable and the driving
position is excellent.*

*Below: The spoilered rear
reveals that this is a far
from ordinary 911 with a
large air intake for the 3.6
liter flat-six engine and rear
outlets for the heat
generated by the adjacent
ceramic discs.*

Capable of 196mph (315km/h), Porsche's
twin turbocharged GT2 is the fastest road
car in the company's history. Production
has been restricted to just 300 examples. Launched
at the 2001 Detroit Motor Show, it boasts a higher
flat-out speed than its four-wheel-drive Turbo
stablemate. Drawing on two variations on the 911
theme, its lightweight rear-wheel-drive chassis
came courtesy of Porsche's no-frills competition-
honed limited edition GT3 road car of 1999. The
power unit was the latest water-cooled 3.6 liter
version of the 911 Turbo engine which was boosted
by 36bhp.

At 3175lb (1440kg), the GT2 weighed a
significant 485lb (220kg) less than the current
Turbo. While the absence of four-wheel drive
accounted for some of this weight-saving, it also
reflected the lack of rear seats, the electric
activation of the front ones, and an air conditioning
system. This figure included a 35lb (16kg) saving
from an unexpected quarter because the GT2 is the
first production car to be fitted with race-bred
carbon ceramic brakes. They had the virtue of not
only improving the coupé's stopping power, but
also its steering.

Instantly identifiable

Outwardly the GT2 was modified to improve brake
cooling and engine ventilation. It is instantly
identifiable by the substantial air intakes incorporated
in the front spoiler to cool the 13.8in (350mm)
discs – the ducts mounted ahead of each rear wheel
arch perform the same function. Greater downforce
is provided by a fixed rear spoiler. It also sits 0.7in

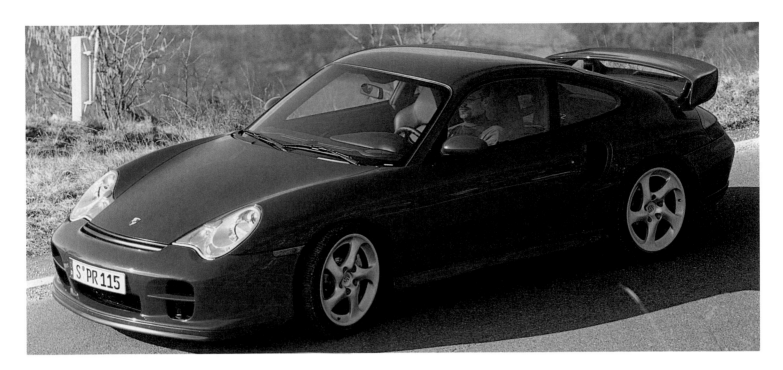

(20mm) lower than the standard cars and uses wider tires on larger 18in (457mm) alloy rims.

Although designed with competition in mind, the GT2 is a practical road car, although, as one overtakes you, any doubts about its identity will be banished by the presence of the name modestly adorning the back of the engine cover.

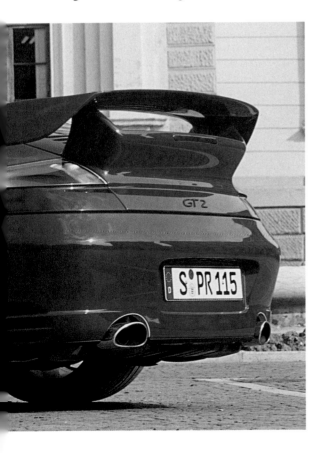

Power increase

Beneath it is the horizontally opposed six-cylinder GT3-based power unit with four valves per cylinder. It develops 456bhp rather than the Turbo's 420. This power increase was principally achieved by upping the boost pressure to the twin KKK K64 turbochargers. In addition, titanium connecting rods were fitted to permit the engine's revs to soar to an impressive 7900rpm.

However, while the GT2 can reach 62mph (100km/h) in an eye-blinking 4.1 seconds, the Turbo, on account of its four-wheel drive, is even more rapid and attains the same speed in four seconds. However, it forfeits 6mph (10km/h) flat-out speed to the lightweight Porsche, production of which ceased in 2001.

Above: The GT2 rides lower than the mainstream 911 with new wheels and tires added to cope with the great increase in power. Further weight has been saved by not retaining the Turbo 911's four-wheel drive; only the GT2's rear wheels are driven. Created with track use in mind, just 300 examples were completed during 2001.

Specification	Porsche 911 GT2
Engine location	Rear, in-line
Configuration	Twin turbocharged horizontally opposed six-cylinder
Bore and stroke	100 x 76mm
Capacity	3600cc
Valve operation	Twin overhead camshafts per bank
Horsepower	456bhp @ 5700rpm
Transmission	Manual six-speed
Drive	Rear
Chassis	Unitary
Suspension – front	McPherson strut and coil spring
Suspension – rear	Multi link and coil spring
Brakes	Ceramic disc
Top speed	196mph (315km/h)
Acceleration	0-60mph (0-96km/h): 4.1 seconds

Aston Martin Vanquish

**Top speed
196mph**
315km/h

*Right: The cockpit
perpetuates many of the
themes displayed in Project
Vantage. Gear changes are
effected by using racing-
style paddles behind the
steering wheel.*

*Below: Immensely
impressive, the Vanquish
represents a formidable
British challenger to
Ferrari. Handling has won
much praise.*

When, in 1997, stylist Ian Callum began
work on the design of what was to
become the Vanquish, he took a backward
look as well as casting his eyes forward. As a result
the company's new V12-engined coupé of 2001 is
visually related to the legendary DB4 GT Zagato of
1960 vintage.

Born of a desire by Ford's DB4-owning
president, Jac Nasser, to elevate Aston Martin,
which Ford has owned since 1987, to the status
Ferrari enjoys in Italy, this important corporate
project is also intended as a showcase for the
technological advances being made by the parent
company. There is no shortage of them!

Project Vantage concept car

As a first step Nasser sanctioned the Project
Vantage concept car which was launched at the
1998 Detroit Motor Show. And for all its retro
elements, beneath the coupé's gleaming green-
painted aluminum panels was a state-of-the-art
chassis. Receiving a rapturous reception from the
public, Ford accordingly gave the project the green
light and the result, some three years later, is the
beautifully built Vanquish.

Unveiled at the 2001 Geneva Motor Show, the
$220,000 model is outwardly almost identical to

the 1998 concept car although it is narrower by a mere 5.9in (151mm). The more obvious changes have taken place inside where detail alterations have been made to the dashboard, seats, and controls. And there isn't a trace of wood veneer to be seen, just burnished aluminum. Available in a choice of styles, the Vanquish comes as an uncompromising two-seater or as a rather cramped two-plus-two.

Under the hood is a 5.9 liter V12 engine, with twin overhead camshaft and four valves per cylinder. It first appeared in 420bhp guise in the DB7 Vantage of 1999. Beginning life as two Ford Montego V6's mounted on a common crankcase, further enhancement and revision by in-house Cosworth has produced a 460bhp unit with a glorious exhaust note that is able to propel the Vanquish to a top speed of 196mph (315km/h) and push it to 60mph (96km/h) in 4.8 seconds.

Power is transmitted by a six-speed gearbox, which also functions in wholly automatic mode with the latest Formula 1-style paddle shift although it retains a clutch pedal. The all-independent suspension is by wishbones with braking the province of beautifully hand-finished, cross-drilled ventilated discs.

At the Vanquish's heart is a central aluminum tub with a carbon-fiber transmission tunnel and windshield pillars made from the same material. The body structure is built up from aluminum extrusions that are bonded and riveted in place, while the outer panels are of the same material.

Aston Martin intends to produce 200 examples of its latest model in 2001 with numbers rising to 250/300 in 2002. Demand is likely to outstrip supply. Ferrari had better look to its laurels.

Above: One of the great appeals of the Vanquish is the exhaust note generated by the Cosworth-developed V12 engine. The 10J rear wheels possess excellent roadholding ability.

Left: The alloy V12 has been hailed as one of the outstanding aspects of the new Aston Martin Vanquish's specification. An underhood plate reveals the name of the individual who built this complex unit.

Specification	Aston Martin Vanquish
Engine location	Front, in-line
Configuration	V12
Bore and stroke	89 x 79mm
Capacity	5925cc
Valve operation	Twin overhead camshafts per bank
Horsepower	460bhp @ 6500rpm
Transmission	Manual six-speed
Drive	Rear
Chassis	Aluminum/carbon-fiber monocoque
Suspension – front	Wishbones and coil spring
Suspension – rear	Wishbones and coil spring
Brakes	Ventilated disc
Top speed	196mph (315km/h)
Acceleration	0-60mph (0-96km/h): 4.8 seconds

Right: The Vanquish, a model that manages to look right from whichever angle it is photographed. The lines of the 1998 Project Vantage concept car have only been subtly altered.

Below: The shape of the radiator grille relates to that of the Vanquish's DB7 contemporary, and also to the earlier DB series cars of the 1950s and 1960s.

Opposite top: The cabin from a passenger's viewpoint. The model was to be launched at the 2000 British show but was delayed for the 2001 Geneva event to improve the quality of the interior.

Opposite below: A soon-to-be-familiar view of the Vanquish as it overtakes you. Note the presence of a rear spoiler integrated with the bodywork.

Lamborghini Murcielago

Top speed 205mph*
330km/h
*Claimed by manufacturer

Right: Evolution rather than revolution – the visual relationship between the wedged-shaped Murcielago and its Diablo predecessor is very apparent.

Below: Scissor doors, a familiar Lamborghini feature that reach back to the Countach and were continued in the Diablo.

It has been hailed as the best designed and built Lamborghini for years, even if the Murcielago name is nothing like as memorable as Miura or Countach! Capable of 205mph (330km/h), this magnificent four-wheel-drive coupé for 2002 will, thanks to the investment of its Volkswagen owner, re-establish Lamborghini as a front-line supercar manufacturer.

In truth this Diablo replacement has been a long time a-coming, work on the project, coded L147, having begun in 1995 when Lamborghini was owned by the Indonesian consortium which had acquired it from Chrysler in 1993. In 1995 the long-running V12 engine had a capacity of 5.7 liters. The intention was to increase this to 6 liters to power the Diablo GT of 2000 before the powerplant was extended to the standard car and then to its successor.

The latter was to be called the Canto and in 1996 Lamborghini commissioned styling house Zagato to body four prototypes. The Milan company addressed the important matter of engine cooling by introducing two pronounced pod-like air scoops into the rear fenders.

Acquired by Volkswagen

Although corporate reservations regarding the design centered on fears that it would date too quickly, cash shortages meant that Lamborghini was stuck with it. That was until July of 1998 when the company was acquired by Volkswagen, which allocated the business to its Audi subsidiary – the performance arm of the VW empire.

Audi wasted little time in commissioning, in the early spring of 1999, a new design from Bertone which, in the person of its stylist Marcello Gandini, had been responsible for the celebrated lines of the Miura and Countach. Further initiatives were canvassed from Italian stylist IDEA and the French Heuliez concern.

With work underway on the body, Lamborghini's engineering director Massimo Ceccarani, now with greater funding available, recognized that the new model would be greatly enhanced by a more powerful engine. In mid 2000 the V12 was experimentally and reliably enlarged to 6.2 liters by lengthening the stroke from 84 to 86mm. The revised unit produced 571bhp at 7500rpm, an increase of 29bhp over the 6 liter.

But Volkswagen was still dissatisfied with the

appearance of the new car. It therefore turned to one of its own in-house stylists for his ideas regarding the design of what had to be one of the most prestigious cars in the motoring world. Belgian designer Luc Donckerwolke had previously been responsible for the exterior lines of the Audi 2 sedan and had also undertaken work for sister company Skoda.

Above: The Murcielago is extraordinarily wide, measuring 80.3in (2040mm), or 0.2in (5mm) more if the retractable exterior side mirrors are extended. The tires are Pirelli's new P-Zero Rosso covers.

Specification	Lamborghini Murcielago
Engine location	Mid, longitudinal
Configuration	V12
Bore and stroke	87 x 86mm
Capacity	6192cc
Valve operation	Twin overhead camshafts per cylinder bank
Horsepower	571bhp @ 7500rpm
Transmission	Manual six-speed
Drive	Rear
Chassis	Steel space-frame
Suspension – front	Wishbones and coil spring
Suspension – rear	Wishbones and coil spring
Brakes	Ventilated disc
Top speed	205mph (330km/h)*
Acceleration	0-60mph (96km/h): 3.8 seconds*

* Manufacturer's claim

Above: Open wide! The massive air intakes both at the front and ahead of the rear wheels proclaim performance and power.

Below: The superb cockpit is larger than the Diablo's and also more comfortable. The small Momo steering wheel is adjustable for both reach and height.

Initially he was asked to re-work Zagato's Canto concept although ultimately only its door apertures were retained. Otherwise his design was the product of the proverbial clean sheet of paper. In January 2001 it was assessed alongside the work of IDEA and Heuliez. Fortunately, in the light of future events, the Lamborghini board preferred Donckerwolke's version and the model's launch was scheduled for the Frankfurt Motor Show, some nine months later.

While the mechanicals essentially follow those of the Diablo, very few components are common to the two models. The new car has a wheelbase of 8ft 9in (2665mm), a mere 0.2in (5mm) more than the Diablo's, and it is also slightly wider and longer. The 6.2 liter V12 has been converted to dry sump lubrication which means that it has been possible to lower it by 2in (50mm) and in the process lower the new Lamborghini's center of gravity to the benefit of roadholding. A six-speed gearbox replaces the Diablo's five-speed unit.

While the coupé's lines essentially follow those of the Diablo, the new model's appearance is not only distinctive but it can clearly survive a respectable production run. Made entirely of carbon fiber, with the exception of the steel roof and the scissor-type doors, the Murcielago weighs 3638lb (1650kg), just 55lb (25kg) more than the Diablo.

Having dispensed with the Canto's bulbous rear pods, Donckerwolke overcame the problem of engine overheating by introducing movable flaps in the coupé's C-pillars above the cooling vents which automatically open when engine temperature exceeds 90°F (32°C). These are complemented by further visually impressive substantial air scoops introduced into the sills.

Not that this is the only movable aid. There is a rear spoiler that opens when the car passes the 80mph (130km/h) mark. The wing tilts at a 50 degree angle up until 137mph (220km/h); thereafter it exceeds 70 degrees. And should the driver encounter a speed bump within an urban context, he or she can also raise the front of the Murcielago by 1.8in (45mm) to prevent serious damage to the bodywork.

The interior is also the work of an Audi stylist, Ralph Luge. It is characteristically sober in presentation but is well executed and, above all, is more spacious than the Diablo's cabin. It is also easier to enter than its predecessor thanks to the lower sill lines.

Commentators have been greatly impressed by the new car's road manners and the consensus is that it is by far the easiest Lamborghini to drive. It goes without saying that the car offers huge reserves of power and excellent roadholding afforded by the well-proven four-wheel drive, and handling is both safe and predictable.

In short this new Lamborghini reflects well on the commitment and sureness of touch of the business's sixth owner. With a smaller model scheduled for 2003, perhaps Ferrari should take an unaccustomed glance over its shoulder…

But why Murcielago?

Like the Miura and a host of other Lamborghini model names, Murcielago, pronounced More-thea-lago, is a Spanish word in origin. Naturally it possesses the almost mandatory bullfighting

associations beloved of Lamborghini and it follows the naming precedent established by the marque's founder, Ferruccio Lamborghini, who was born under the Zodiac sign of Taurus the bull.

Murcielago was a fighting bull of such tenacity that, during a celebrated fight in 1879, he survived no less than 24 sword thrusts. His life was spared and he was acquired by Don Antonio Miura (sounds familiar?). Murcielago went on to sire a new generation of bulls for his proud owner…

Above: The movable flaps on the C-pillars allow cooling air to reach each of the V12's radiators.

Below: It looks great from whatever angle you view it. The Murcielago should re-establish Lamborghini as a top line supercar maker.

Porsche Carrera GT

**Top speed
205mph***
330km/h
*Claimed by
manufacturer

*Below: The mouth-watering
Carrera GT, publicly
launched at the 2000 Paris
Motor Show. Porsche was
heartened by the wholly
positive worldwide response
to the new car, although the
announcement to proceed
with the design was not
finally made until more
than a year later at the
2002 Detroit Motor Show.
Its launch is scheduled for
the second half of 2003.*

Scheduled for production in 2003, the race-bred Carrera GT is powered by a new V10 engine which develops no less than 558bhp. It makes it Porsche's fastest ever road car. Announced at the 2000 Paris Motor Show, the model will bristle with features that will act as a showcase for the company's formidable competence in the multifarious fields of automobile design and technology.

The starting point for this state-of-the-art Porsche is a racer that the company withdrew from the 2000 Le Mans race. Thereafter mothballed, its carbon-fiber monocoque hull will form the basis of the new car. Although the engine is located at the rear in 911 fashion, the Carrera GT bears no visual relationship to the current 911. Instead the company's California-based design studio, which essayed its impressive aerodynamically honed lines, drew on the body of Porsche's 718RS Spyder of 1961 vintage for inspiration.

Targa top

While the car unveiled at the model's Paris launch was a roadster, the production Carrera GT will have a more practical detachable Targa-style roof panel. And after over 50 years of producing horizontally opposed rear-mounted engines, the company is opting for a V10 to power the new car. Based on the unit developed for its aborted 2000 Le Mans sortie, this alloy 68 degree 5.5 liter engine is fitted with robust race-proven connecting rods so that it can rev to beyond 8000rpm. Attached directly to the monocoque hull, this compact engine drives the rear wheels courtesy of a racing-type three-plate clutch and six-speed gearbox.

Suspension has an impeccable pedigree, being also race-proven and is based on Porsche's GT1 that won Le Mans in 1998. It uses conventional wishbones at the front while rose-jointed wishbones are employed at the rear and they operate in conjunction with coil springs and pushrods.

Porsche optimistically prophesied that the Carrera GT would attain 60mph (96km/h) in less than 4 seconds and 120mph (193km/h) in under 10. Top speed is expected to be 205mph (330km/h).

Although this new car is based on a cocktail of sports racing components, the emphasis is on refinement and for this reason the cockpit displays a pleasing combination of fine leather and polished aluminum. A novel feature is a pop-up digital camera located between the seats that allows the driver to film him or herself while at the wheel!

Porsche plans to produce 1000 examples, having originally plannned 500, but hinted that it might increase numbers if demand for this $560,000 car exceeds supply. Production is to be based at the car company's new Leipzig factory which will also produce its new and luxurious Cayenne four-wheel-drive model.

Above: The mid-located V10 engine is a 68 degree unit and is a remarkably compact one, being only 22.4in (570mm) long.

Left: The utterly modern cabin with its multi-functional steering wheel and digital display.

Below left: The rear deck of the Carrera GT. The production version will probably have a Targa-type roof.

Specification	Porsche Carrera GT
Engine location	Mid, in-line
Configuration	V10
Bore and stroke	N/A
Capacity	5.5 liters
Valve operation	Twin overhead camshafts per cylinder bank
Horsepower	558bhp
Transmission	Manual six-speed
Drive	Rear
Chassis	Monocoque
Suspension – front	Wishbones and coil spring
Suspension – rear	Wishbones, coil spring and pushrod
Brakes	Ventilated disc
Top speed	205mph (330km/h)*
Acceleration	0-60mph (96 km/h): sub-4 seconds*

* Manufacturer's claim

Mercedes-Benz Vision SLR

**Top speed
197mph***

317km/h
*Claimed by
manufacturer

One of the most heavily trailed supercars of recent years, the SLR underpins an alliance forged in 1995 between Mercedes-Benz and British Formula 1 constructor McLaren. Not only this. The German company's flagship road car will, uniquely for Mercedes, be built in Britain.

Its forerunner, the SLR concept car, made its memorable debut at the 1999 Detroit Motor Show. With overall design responsibility vested in Gordon Murray, creator of the McLaren F1, the appropriately named Vision SLR was an alluring two-seater silver coupé and one of the undisputed stars of the event. And unlike many concepts, this vehicle was a runner which retained Mercedes-Benz's long-established and conventional front engine/rear drive configuration.

Based on the chassis of the impending SL convertible which appeared for the 2002 season, the Vision SLR's aluminum and carbon-fiber body was awesome, innovative, but indisputably Mercedes-Benz. Stylistically it was the work of Franz Lezher, who had previously been responsible for the lines of a diametrically opposed Mercedes concept: a quirky F300 three-wheeler that appeared at the 1997 Frankfurt Motor Show.

This SLR incorporates visual elements from the McLaren-Mercedes MP4/13 Formula 1 racer along with design cues from the SL coupé of 1954. The upward-opening doors are a distinctive feature although they are not of the gullwing type that featured on the legendary 300SL of the 1950s.

Above: The instrumentation is simple with the main dials consisting of an analog speedometer and rev counter. Unusually the steering wheel is oval-shaped. The cabin is finished in Alcantara and anodized aluminum. The consul also contains a color screen for navigation purposes.

Right: The Vision SLR gives only a hint of what the production version will look like – Mercedes-Benz has said it will differ outwardly from this concept car. The scissor doors evoke echoes of the gullwing units used on the 300 SL of the 1950s.

Twin-supercharged engine

Able to attain speeds nudging toward the 200mph (322km/h) mark, the SLR will be powered by a new twin-supercharged 557bhp 5.5 liter V8 engine, of which a detuned version may well appear in a version of the SL roadster.

Inside, the SLR concept was novel and ingenious with an oval steering wheel and a cabin finished in Alcanatra and anodized aluminum. Full length body-hugging carbon-fiber seats featured. And, unusually, the five-speed automatic gearbox was controlled by a control in the central console or from the steering column.

However, some design features of the upcoming SLR are still unknown. It is expected that the lower portion of the structural tub will be made from pre-impregnated carbon fiber which is similar to the material used in Formula 1 cars. The wishbones may be made of the same material.

Soon after journalists had an opportunity of driving the Vision in February 2000 came news that the production SLR would, in some respects, differ stylistically from it. These changes were dictated by the need to improve luggage space and also came in response to crash testing.

But whatever finally emerges, there can be no doubt that the Woking-built Mercedes-Benz, with its very special pedigree, should be a truly remarkable fast car.

Specification	Mercedes-Benz Vision SLR
Engine location	Front, in-line
Configuration	Twin-supercharged V8
Bore and stroke	97 x 92mm
Capacity	5496cc
Valve operation	Single overhead camshaft per cylinder bank
Horsepower	557bhp @ 6500rpm
Transmission	Semi-automatic five-speed
Drive	Rear
Chassis	Carbon-fiber monocoque
Suspension – front	Multi-link coil spring
Suspension – rear	Multi-link coil spring
Brakes	Ventilated disc
Top speed	197mph (317km/h)*
Acceleration	0-62mph (100km/h): 4.2 seconds*

* Manufacturer's claim

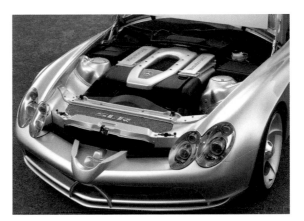

Left: The new 5.5 liter supercharged V8 engine develops 557bhp although it uses single- rather than the usual twin-overhead-camshafts.

Below: The Vision, Mercedes-Benz's flagship coupé, is awash with retro themes while also looking remarkably modern.

Bugatti Veyron

**Top speed
252mph***
405km/h
*Claimed by
manufacturer

*Below: Bugatti concepts
with the EB218 four-door
sedan of 1999 top left and
the 1998 EB118 coupé
alongside it. In the left
foreground is the Chiron of
1999, stylistically the work
of Ital Design with input
from VW design chief
Hartmut Warkuss who was
responsible for the Veyron's
stunning lines (right
foreground).*

This is the ultimate fast car! The fabulous Veyron coupé, which is intended to enter production in 2003, should decisively topple the 240mph (386km/h) McLaren F1 from its pole position as the world's fastest road car.

Performance figures are at the time of writing (2002) purely theoretical but the Bugatti's top speed is estimated at an incredible 252mph (405km/h) and it should be able to attain 60mph (96km/h) in just three seconds. That is not all. Its makers predict that it will be able to reach 300km/h (which is 186mph) in a mere 14 seconds…

This remarkable renaissance of the Bugatti marque is to the credit of Volkswagen and its charismatic chairman Ferdinand Piech. In September 1998 VW acquired the Bugatti name from Romano Artioli. It purchased Bentley and Lamborghini in the same year. Artioli, it will be recalled, had in 1993 produced the mid-engined four-wheel-drive EB110 coupé but his company had spectacularly collapsed in 1995.

Unveiled at Paris Motor Show

The new Volkswagen-initiated Bugatti has passed through a number of evolutionary phases. The first concept, coded EB118, appeared at the 1998 Paris Motor Show, only months after VW's purchase. It was based on an Ital Design-styled coupé version of a still-born front-engined EB112 four-door sedan that Artioli displayed at the 1993 Geneva event. Under the hood was a complex 6.3 liter W18 cylinder engine, consisting of three rows of six cylinders, that developed no less than 550bhp.

Next at the 1999 Geneva show came the massive EB218 four-door sedan version which evoked some echoes of Artiolo's EB112 of six years before and was also styled by Giugiaro's company. Recalling Ettore Bugatti's gargantuan

Left: Bugattis past and present: the Veyron with its 8 liter 16-cylinder engine exposed in company with a Type 51 Grand Prix Bugatti produced between 1931 and 1936. Note its classic horseshoe-shaped radiator which finds a modern interpretation on the Veyron. The famous Bugatti cast aluminum wheels first appeared in 1924 and survived well into the following decade.

Below left: The Veyron's magnificent 90 degree W16 engine, effectively two V8s mounted side by side. Two of the four sequential KKK turbochargers can be seen center left and the two intercoolers are mounted above the cylinder heads. The seven-speed gearbox was developed by British specialists Ricardo Engineering.

12.7 liter Royale of 1927, it was clearly targeted at Mercedes-Benz's revived Maybach and a new Rolls-Royce, the latter marque having been snatched from VW's grasp by rival BMW.

On reflection Piech decided that Ital Design's efforts were too derivative and lacked emotion. In short he wanted something more audacious and so looked in-house to his friend and VW design supremo Hartmut Warkuss. The resulting blue and black EB18.4 made its debut at the 1999 Tokyo Motor Show.

It represented nothing less than a root and branch re-think of the proposed Bugatti line. Out went the formal commodious sedan and in came a mid-engined sports coupé putting the new model foursquare in the performance category.

Named Veyron in memory of French racing driver Pierre Veyron, who co-drove a 57C Bugatti to victory at the 1939 Le Mans race, this in turn lead to the evolutionary EB16.4 that was finished in striking red and black, a color scheme reminiscent of Bugattis of the 1930s.

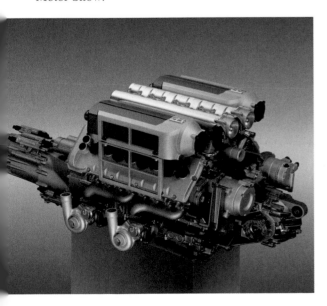

Specification	Bugatti Veyron
Engine location	Mid, in-line
Configuration	W16
Bore and stroke	86 x 86mm
Capacity	7993cc
Valve operation	Twin overhead camshafts per cylinder bank
Horsepower	987bhp @ 6000rpm
Transmission	Manual seven-speed
Drive	Four-wheel
Chassis	Unitary
Suspension – front	Wishbone and coil spring
Suspension – rear	Wishbone and coil spring
Brakes	Ventilated disc
Top speed	252mph (405km/h)*
Acceleration	0-60mph (96km/h): 3 seconds*

*Manufacturer's claim

Above: The Veyron's body is in the finest traditions of the marque, while the distinctive color combination featured on many Bugattis of the 1930s.

Below: A Veyron at rest with the retractable spoiler hidden within the tail. Note the different style of wheel.

For his inspiration Warkuss drew on the extravagant Type 57S Bugatti Atlantic coupé of 1936. Just three of these remarkable cars were built, and stylistically they were the work of Bugatti's talented son Jean. This influence is most apparent at the front of the car and is underlined by the presence of a discreet rib that runs down the center of the bodywork which is made from a combination of aluminum and carbon fiber.

A distinctive visual feature is the fact that the hood, roof, and foam-filled strengthening sills are finished in a contrasting color to the remainder of the body. This also applies to the rear of the car which encompasses the engine and rear suspension and sits proud of the nose and cockpit section to allow cooling air to reach the motor.

Aerodynamics have also played their part in refining the Veyron's appearance. A flat undertray runs the length of the car and a rear spoiler rises automatically to a height of 7.9in (200mm) to generate extra downforce. A nice touch is revealed when the driver turns off the ignition – the wing remains raised for a short period to allow hot air to escape from the engine compartment.

Distinctive styling

The EB118's 18-cylinder unit has been replaced in the Veyron with an 8 liter 16-cylinder engine that may be shared with in-house Bentley. This awesome engine, which incorporates four small KKK turbochargers and two intercoolers, develops no less than 987bhp. Daringly, the large aluminum induction pipes are partially exposed and sit proud of the bodywork to form a distinctive stylistic feature. And unorthodoxy again surfaces in the shape of the single exhaust pipe that is a square section outlet which emerges from the center of the tail.

With the engine mid-mounted and longitudinally positioned, power will pass through a seven-, yes seven-, speed gearbox and reach the four wheels courtesy of Volkswagen's Haldex system.

Suspension is by the customary all-round double wishbones although refinements could include electric damping and a variable ride height. Specially developed Michelin tires will be used and the brakes are the latest Brembo ceramic discs. They are race-proven and have the advantage of being considerably lighter than metal ones and they can operate at higher temperatures.

The Veyron's roomy interior also reflects Bugattis of the interwar years in that the cabin is leather-lined and instrumentation is impressive. It is dominated by an instrument binnacle that contains a tachometer and a large speedometer which read, respectively, to 8500rpm and 450km/h (that is the equivalent of 280mph). With the 8ft 10in (2700mm) wheelbase generous for a two-seater and the engine's dimension's compact, there is room in the reasonably sized trunk under the 'hood' for rather more than two suitcases.

Volkswagen is building a factory at Molsheim, Alsace, the French home town of the original Bugatti, to manufacture the car. Veyron production is expected to be a mere 50 cars a year. At the time of writing (2002), its price has yet to be decided but it is thought to be in the region of Euro 1 million which is the equivalent of some $900,000.

With production scheduled to begin in September 2003 and the new Bugatti destined for a four-year manufacturing life, the world of the supercar will never be quite the same again.

Above: The rear spoiler in the raised position. Daringly the peaks of the engine's aluminum induction system are exposed to view. The body structure is a mixture of carbon fiber and aluminum and an aerodynamically efficient undertray is fitted.

Left: There's plenty of room in the cockpit, thanks to the Veyron's long wheelbase. As with the exterior, old and new themes are juxtaposed with the cabin being leather-lined while the finish of the aluminum center console echoes 1920s Bugatti practice. The gearbox is operated by steering column-mounted racing-style paddles. The speedometer reads to 450km/h (280mph)!

Index